BERMUDA

1st Edition

Where to Stay and Eat
for All Budgets

Must-See Sights
and Local Secrets

Ratings You Can Trust

Excerpted from *Fodor's Bermuda*

Fodor's Travel Publications New York, Toronto, London, Sydney, Auckland

www.fodors.com

FODOR'S IN FOCUS BERMUDA

Series Editor: Douglas Stallings

Editor: Molly Moker

Editorial Production: Astrid deRidder

Editorial Contributors: Suzy Buckley, Michael de Zayas, Sirkka Huish, Dale Leatherman, Susan MacCallum-Whitcomb, Andrew Raine, Keisha Webb-Gibbs

Maps & Illustrations: David Lindroth, *cartographer*; Bob Blake and Rebecca Baer, *map editors*

Design: Fabrizio LaRocca, *creative director*; Guido Caroti, *art director*; Ann McBride, *designer*; Melanie Marin, *senior picture editor*

Cover Photo: Matt Gunther/Stone/Getty Images

Production/Manufacturing: Matthew Struble

COPYRIGHT

1st Edition

ISBN 978–1–4000–0710–3

ISSN 1940-8366

SPECIAL SALES

This book is available for special discounts for bulk purchases for sales promotions or premiums. Special editions, including personalized covers, excerpts of existing books, and corporate imprints, can be created in large quantities for special needs. For more information, write to Special Markets/Premium Sales, 1745 Broadway, MD 6-2, New York, New York, NY 10019, or e-mail specialmarkets@randomhouse.com.

AN IMPORTANT TIP & AN INVITATION

Although all prices, opening times, and other details in this book are based on information supplied to us at press time, changes occur all the time in the travel world, and Fodor's cannot accept responsibility for facts that become outdated or for inadvertent errors or omissions. **So always confirm information when it matters,** especially if you're making a detour to visit a specific place. Your experiences—positive and negative—matter to us. If we have missed or misstated something, **please write to us.** We follow up on all suggestions. Contact the Bermuda editor at editors@fodors.com or c/o Fodor's at 1745 Broadway, New York, NY 10019.

Be a Fodor's Correspondent

Your opinion matters. It matters to us. It matters to your fellow Fodor's travelers, too. And we'd like to hear it. In fact, we *need* to hear it. When you share your experiences and opinions, you become an active member of the Fodor's community. Here's how you can help improve Fodor's for all of us.

Tell us when we're right. We rely on local writers to give you an insider's perspective. But our writers and staff editors also depend on you. Your positive feedback is a vote to renew our recommendations for the next edition.

Tell us when we're wrong. We update most of our guides every year. But things change. If any of our descriptions are inaccurate or inadequate, we'll incorporate your changes in the next edition and will correct factual errors at fodors. com *immediately*.

Tell us what to include. You probably have had fantastic travel experiences that aren't yet in Fodor's. Why not share them with a community of like-minded travelers? Share your discoveries and experiences with everyone directly at fodors.com. Your input may lead us to add a new listing or a higher recommendation.

Give us your opinion instantly at our feedback center at www.fodors.com/feedback. You may also e-mail editors@ fodors.com with the subject line "Bermuda Editor." Or send your nominations, comments, and complaints by mail to Bermuda Editor, Fodor's, 1745 Broadway, New York, NY 10019.

Happy Traveling!

Tim Jarrell, Publisher

CONTENTS

ABOUT THIS BOOK

Our Ratings

We wouldn't recommend a place that wasn't worth your time, but sometimes a place is so experiential that superlatives don't do it justice: you just have to be there to know. These sights, properties, and experiences get our highest rating, **Fodor's Choice** indicated by orange stars throughout this book. Black stars highlight sights and properties we deem **Highly Recommended** places that our writers, editors, and readers praise again and again.

Credit Cards

Want to pay with plastic? **AE, D, DC, MC, V** following restaurant and hotel listings indicate whether American Express, Discover, Diners Club, MasterCard, and Visa are accepted.

Restaurants

Unless we state otherwise, restaurants serve both lunch and dinner daily. We mention dress only when there's a specific requirement and reservations only when they're essential or not accepted—it's always best to book ahead.

Hotels

Unless we tell you otherwise, you can assume that the hotels have private bath, phone, TV, and air-conditioning. We always list facilities but not whether you'll be charged an extra fee to use them, so when pricing accommodations, find out what's included.

Many Listings
- ★ Fodor's Choice
- ★ Highly recommended
- ⊠ Physical address
- ♦ Directions
- ⌂ Mailing address
- ☎ Telephone
- 🖷 Fax
- ⊕ On the Web
- ✉ E-mail
- 🎟 Admission fee
- ☉ Open/closed times
- Ⓜ Metro stations
- ⊟ Credit cards

Hotels & Restaurants
- 🏨 Hotel
- ↪ Number of rooms
- ♿ Facilities
- ¶◎¶ Meal plans
- ✕ Restaurant
- 🍴 Reservations
- ⌐ Smoking
- ☖ BYOB
- ✕🏨 Hotel with restaurant that warrants a visit

Outdoors
- ⅄ Golf
- ⊿ Camping

Other
- ☺ Family-friendly
- ⇨ See also
- ⊠ Branch address
- ☞ Take note

Bermuda

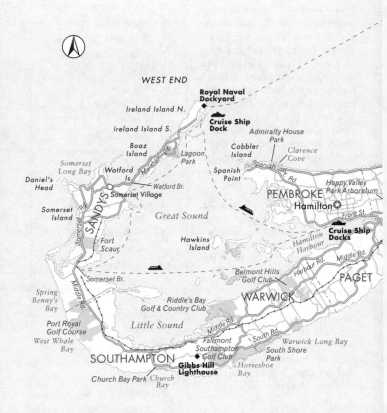

WEST END

Royal Naval Dockyard

Ireland Island N.

Cruise Ship Dock

Ireland Island S.

Admiralty House Park

Cobbler Island

Clarence Cove

Boaz Island

Lagoon Park

Spanish Point

Somerset Long Bay

Watford Is.

Spanish Pt. Rd.

Happy Valley Park Arboretum

Daniel's Head

Somerset Village

Watford Br.

PEMBROKE

Hamilton

Somerset Island

Great Sound

Front St.

Cruise Ship Docks

Fort Scaur

Hawkins Island

Hamilton Harbour

Somerset Br.

Belmont Hills Golf Club

Harbour Rd.

Middle Rd.

PAGET

Spring Benny's Bay

Riddle's Bay Golf & Country Club

WARWICK

Port Royal Golf Course

Little Sound

Middle Rd.

West Whale Bay

Fairmont Southampton Golf Club

South Rd.

Warwick Long Bay

South Shore Park

SOUTHAMPTON

Gibbs Hill Lighthouse

Horseshoe Bay

Church Bay Park

Church Bay

SANDYS

Somerset Rd.

Middle Rd.

Malabar Rd.

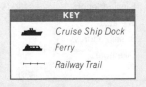

KEY	
⛴	Cruise Ship Dock
🚢	Ferry
+—+	Railway Trail

0   2 miles

0   3 km

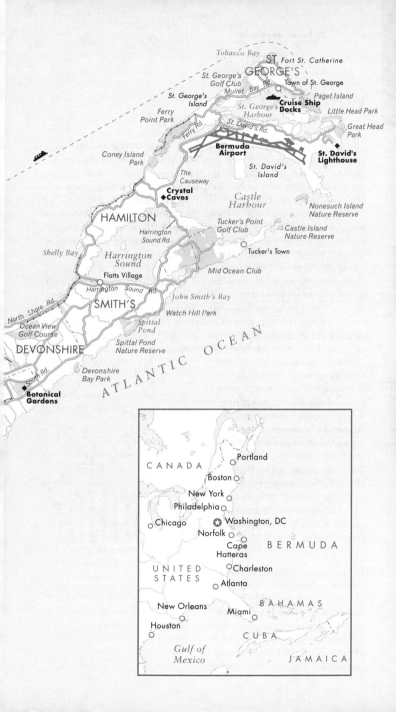

WHEN TO GO

The important thing to remember when planning your trip is that subtropical Bermuda is in the Atlantic—*not* the Caribbean. High season here is April through October, when the sun shines brightest and the warm waters beckon. During the summer months particularly, the island teems with activity. Off-season—November through March—the weather is often perfect for golf or tennis, and on sunny days you can take advantage of uncrowded beaches. Nevertheless, the pace is considerably slower. A few restaurants and shops close, some excursion boats are dry-docked, and typically only taxis operate tours of the island. Most hotels remain open, but with rates slashed by as much as 40%. As an added incentive for off-peak travelers, the Department of Tourism sponsors the Bermuda Heart & Soul program: a series of daily activities (the majority of which are free) that include guided walks, high teas, and golf tournaments.

Climate

Bermuda has a remarkably mild climate that seldom sees extremes of either heat or cold. In winter (December through March), temperatures range from around 55°F at night to 70°F in early afternoon. High, blustery winds can make the air feel cooler, however, as can Bermuda's high humidity. The hottest times are between May and mid-October, when temperatures generally range from 75°F to 85°F. It's not uncommon for the mercury to reach 90°F in July and August, but it often feels hotter due to humidity levels. Although summer is somewhat drier, rainfall is spread fairly evenly throughout the year. In August and September, hurricanes moving north from the Caribbean occasionally hit the island, causing storm damage and flight delays.

Forecasts Bermuda Weather Service (☎441/297–7977 *for a recorded update* ⊕ *www.weather. bm*). **Weather Channel** (⊕ *www. weather.com*).

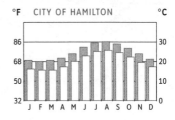

°F CITY OF HAMILTON °C

Exploring Bermuda

WORD OF MOUTH

"I was not expecting such beauty. Bermuda is unlike any other island we have visited. I think it's the combination of great views, friendly people, really good restaurants, variety of things to do, and efficient transportation that makes Bermuda so special, in my opinion."

—mnag

By Susan
MacCallum-
Whitcomb

BERMUDA IS JUSTIFIABLY FAMOUS for pink-sand beaches, impossibly blue water, and kelly-green golf courses. But that's only the beginning. Thanks to its colorful past, this small sliver of land also has a surprising number of historic sites. In addition to countless quaint old cottages, it's said to have the oldest continually inhabited town of English origin in the Western Hemisphere and—because of its strategic Atlantic location—more forts per square mile than any other place on earth.

Bermuda has a distinctive culture, too: one that combines a reverence for British traditions dating back to colonial days with a more relaxed attitude befitting a subtropical island. In court, for instance, local lawyers may still wear formal flowing robes—yet there's a good chance that they're sporting Bermuda shorts beneath them. So while you're here, take time to look beyond the obvious and savor *all* that Bermuda has to offer.

There is certainly no shortage of things to see. The town of St. George's, at the island's East End, is the original 1600s settlement and a UNESCO World Heritage Site. The city of Hamilton (not to be confused with the parish of the same name farther northeast) is home to Bermuda's principal harbor and most of its shops. It's also the main departure point for sightseeing boats, ferries, and the pink-and-blue buses that ramble all over the island. The Royal Naval Dockyard, at the West End, is a former British shipyard that has been transformed into a stunning tourist attraction.

All three of these destinations can be explored easily on foot. The rest of the island, however, is best discovered by taxi, motor scooter, or bicycle—but only if you're fit, because Bermuda is hilly! The main roads connecting the parishes are North Shore Road, Middle Road, South Road (also known as South Shore Road), and Harbour Road. Their names make it easy for you to get your bearings and almost all the traffic traversing the island's 21-mi length is concentrated on them, although some 1,200 smaller roads also crisscross it.

To make the most of your money, as well as your time, consider buying a $25 Heritage Passport if you plan on visiting several of the following sites: the Bermuda National Gallery; Bermuda Underwater Exploration Institute; Bermuda Maritime Museum; Fort St. Catherine; Bermuda National Trust Museum in the Globe Hotel; Verdmont; Tucker House; and the Bermuda Aquarium, Museum

BERMUDA TOP 5

■ Lose yourself (and the crowds) on the winding side streets and mazelike back alleys of 400-year-old St. George's.

■ Head to the Dockyard's Maritime Museum for a crash course in island history and up-close animal encounters.

■ Kick back with the kids at the engaging—often interactive—Bermuda Aquarium, Museum & Zoo.

■ Glimpse a surreal subterranean world filled with stalactites and stalagmites at the Crystal Caves.

■ Hike through Paget Marsh: an unspoiled 25-acre nature preserve minutes from bustling Hamilton.

& Zoo. The passport allows unlimited admission to all eight sites for seven consecutive days. You can purchase it online at ⊕*www.bermudatourism.com* or in person at individual attractions. Passports are also available at the island's visitor information centers. Return travelers should note that these replaced the former visitor service bureaus in the spring of 2007. Along with a new name (and new hours) they also have new locations. If you want pamphlets and brochures—not quizzical looks—be sure to check our maps first to see where the new locations are.

ST. GEORGE'S

The settlement of Bermuda began in what is now the town of St. George's when the *Sea Venture*—flagship of an English fleet carrying supplies to Jamestown, Virginia—was wrecked on Bermuda's treacherous reefs in 1609. Today, nearly 400 years later, no visit to the island would be complete without a stop in this picturesque and remarkably preserved example of an early New World outpost.

Although St. George's is a living community—not a living-history museum—it retains the patina of authenticity. In fact, in 2000 it was named a UNESCO World Heritage Site. That designation puts it on a par with spots like the Great Wall of China and the Taj Mahal in India. But don't expect awe-inspiring edifices here. On the contrary, St. George's chief charm lies in tiny walled cottages, simple colonial churches, and labyrinthine alleys that beg to be explored.

Numbers in the text correspond to numbers in the margin and on the Town of St. George's and Hamilton maps.

A GOOD WALK

Start your tour in **King's Square ❶**, then stroll out onto **Ordnance Island ❷** to see a replica of *Deliverance II*: the ship built as a replacement for the *Sea Venture*. Behind you, just up the street is the **Bermuda National Trust Museum at the Globe Hotel ❸**, and across the square is the town hall.

Walk up Princess Street to Duke of York Street and turn right, following the sidewalk to the **Bermudian Heritage Museum ❹**. Across Duke of York Street, you can find **Somers Garden ❺**, where Sir George Somers's heart is reportedly buried. After walking through the garden, climb the steps to Blockade Alley for a view of the **Unfinished Church ❻** on a hill ahead. To your left are Duke of Kent Street, Featherbed Alley, and the **St. George's Historical Society Museum, Printery & Garden ❼**. Next, cross Clarence Street to Church Lane and turn right on Broad Alley to reach the **Old Rectory ❽**. Straight ahead (or as straight as you can go among these twisted streets) is Printer's Alley, which in turn links to **Nea's Alley ❾** where a whiff of 19th-century scandal still lingers.

Return to Church Lane and enter the yard of **St. Peter's Church ❿**, a centuries-old sanctuary that, until the building of the Old State House, did double duty as the colony's only public meeting place. (The main entrance is on Duke of York Street.) From the church, continue down Duke of York Street until you reach Queen Street on your right. A short walk up it brings you to the **Bermuda Perfumery & Gardens ⓫** at Stewart Hall, which will be on the left. Turn around and walk back to Duke of York Street and go right until you get to Barber's Alley, turning left to reach **Tucker House ⓬**, which has been transformed from a prominent merchant's home into a museum. From there continue along Water Street, veering left again on Penno's Drive to visit the new **World Heritage Centre ⓭** at Penno's Wharf.

TIMING

Given its small size, St. George's has a disproportionately large number of historical buildings, plus pleasant gardens and enticing shops. They say you can't get lost here—but

St. George's

Bermuda National
Trust Museum at
the Globe Hotel, **3**

Bermuda Perfumery
& Gardens, **11**

Bermudian Heritage
Museum, **4**

King's Square, **1**

Nea's Alley, **9**

Old Rectory, **8**

Ordnance Island, **2**

Somers Garden, **5**

St. George's
Historical Society
Museum, Printery
& Garden, **7**

St. Peter's Church, **10**

Tucker House, **12**

Unfinished Church, **6**

World Heritage
Centre, **13**

you can certainly lose track of time. So give yourself a day
to explore its nooks and crannies.

WHAT TO SEE

★ ❸ **Bermuda National Trust Museum at the Globe Hotel.** Erected as
a governor's mansion around 1700, this building became
a hotbed of activity during the American Civil War. From
here, Confederate Major Norman Walker coordinated the
surreptitious flow of guns, ammunition, and war supplies
from England, through Union blockades, into American
ports. It saw service as the Globe Hotel during the mid-19th
century and became a National Trust property in 1951. A
short video, *Bermuda, Centre of the Atlantic,* recounts the
history of Bermuda, and a memorabilia-filled exhibit enti-
tled "Rogues & Runners: Bermuda and the American Civil
War" describes St. George's when it was a port for Confederate blockade runners. ⊠*32 Duke of York St.* ☎*441/297–
1423* ⊕*www.bnt.bm* ☞*$5; $10 combination ticket includes
admission to Tucker House and Verdmont* ⊘*Nov.–Mar.,
Wed.–Sat. 10–4; Apr.–Oct., Mon.–Sat. 10–4.*

★ ⓫ **Bermuda Perfumery & Gardens.** In 2005 the perfumery moved
from Bailey's Bay in Smith's Parish, where it had been based

since 1928, to historic Stewart Hall. Although the location is new, the techniques it uses are not: the perfumery still extracts natural fragrances from island flowers, and manufactures and bottles all products on-site. Frangipani, jasmine, orchids, oleander, and passion flowers are only a few of the ingredients used in making the sweet-smelling Bermudian scents. Guides are available to explain the entire process, and there's a small museum that outlines the company's history. You can also wander around the gardens and stock up on your favorite fragrances in the showroom. ⊠ *5 Queen St.* ☎ *441/293–0627* ⊕ *www.bermuda-perfumery. com* ☜ *Free* ⊙ *Mon.–Sat. 9–5.*

❹ Bermudian Heritage Museum. The history, trials, and accomplishments of black Bermudians are highlighted in this converted 1840s warehouse. Photographs of early black residents including slaves, freedom fighters, and professionals line the walls, and the works of black artisans are proudly exhibited. Look, in particular, for the display about the *Enterprise*, a slave ship that was blown off course to Bermuda while sailing from Virginia to South Carolina in 1835. Since slavery had already been abolished on the island, the 78 slaves on board were technically free—and the Local Friendly Societies (grassroots organizations devoted to liberating and supporting slaves) worked to keep it that way. Society members obtained an injunction to bring the slaves' case into court and escorted the "human cargo" to their hearing in Hamilton, where many spoke in their own defense. All except one woman and her four children accepted the offer of freedom. Today, countless Bermudians trace their ancestry back to those who arrived on the *Enterprise*. Appropriately enough, the museum building was once home to one of the Friendly Societies. It's now a Bermuda National Trust property. ⊠ *Water and Duke of York sts.* ☎ *441/297–4126* ☜ *$4* ⊙ *Tues.–Sat. 10–3.*

❶ King's Square. In a town where age is relative, King's Square is comparatively new. The square was created in the 19th century after a marshy part of the harbor was filled in. Today it still looks rather inauspicious, more a patch of pavement than a leafy common, yet the square is St. George's undisputed center. Locals frequently congregate here for civic celebrations. Visitors, meanwhile, come to see the replica stocks and pillory. Formerly used to punish petty crimes, these grisly gizmos—together with a replica "ducking stool"—are now popular props for photo ops. Reenactments of historical incidents, overseen by a

1

town crier in full colonial costume, are staged in the square November through March on Wednesday and Saturday at noon, and April through October on Monday, Wednesday, Thursday, and Saturday at noon. In high season, King's Square also hosts St. George's Market Nights, a weekly street festival with craft vendors, Gombey dancers, and more reenactments from 6:30 to 9:30 on Tuesday nights, May through September.

❾ While roaming the back streets, look for **Nea's Alley.** Nineteenth-century Irish poet Thomas Moore, who lived in St. George's during his tenure as registrar of the admiralty court, waxed poetic about both this "lime-covered alley" and a lovely woman he first encountered here: his boss's teenaged bride, "Nea" Tucker. Though arguably the most amorous, Moore wasn't the only writer to be inspired by Bermuda. Mark Twain wrote about it in *The Innocents Abroad,* and his exclamation "you go to heaven if you want to; I'd druther stay in Bermuda" remains something of a motto in these parts. Two 20th-century playwrights, Eugene O'Neill and Noel Coward, also wintered—and worked—on the island. Bermuda resident Peter Benchley took the idea for his novel *The Deep* from the ships lost off shore. ✉ *Between Printer's Alley and Old Maid's La.*

❽ The Old Rectory. Built around 1699 by part-time privateer George Dew, this charming limestone cottage takes its name from a later resident, Alexander Richardson (the rector of St. Peter's Church), who lived here between 1763 and 1805. In addition to handsome gardens, the house with its cedar beams, multiple chimneys, and "welcoming arms" entrance is a lovely example of traditional Bermudian architecture. Want more than a quick look inside? The Old Rectory currently operates as a bed-and-breakfast. Rates for the two guest rooms run between $100 and $150 per night, based on double occupancy, with a minimum three-night booking. ✉ *1 Broad Alley, behind St. Peter's Church* ☎ *441/297–4261* ⊕ *www.bnt.bm for tours, www.bermudagetaway.com for overnight stays* ✉ *Donations accepted* ⊙ *Sightseeing visits Nov.–Mar., Wed. only 1–5.*

★ ❷ Ordnance Island. Ordnance Island, directly across from King's Square, is dominated by a splendid bronze statue of Sir George Somers, commander of the *Sea Venture.* Somers looks surprised that he made it safely to shore—and you may be surprised that he ever chose to set sail again when you spy the nearby *Deliverance II.* It's a full-scale replica of one of two ships—the other was the *Patience*—built under Somers's supervision to carry survivors from the 1609 wreck onward to Jamestown. But considering her size (just 57 feet from bow to stern) *Deliverance II* hardly seems ocean-worthy by modern standards. You can scramble on board for a small fee; however, it's easy enough to imagine the cramped conditions by simply comparing the small vessel to the contemporary cruise ships that moor behind her. ⊠*Across from King's Sq.* ☎*441/297–1459* ⊠*$3* ⊘*Apr.–Oct., weekdays 9:30–5.*

❺ Somers Garden. After sailing to Jamestown and back in 1610, Sir George Somers—the British admiral charged with developing the Bermudian colony—fell ill and died. According to local lore, Somers instructed his nephew Matthew Somers to bury his heart in Bermuda, where it belonged. Matthew sailed for England soon afterward, sneaking Somers's body aboard in a cedar chest so as not to attract attention from superstitious sailors, and eventually burying it near his birthplace in Dorset. Although it can't be proven that Matthew actually carried out his uncle's wishes, it's generally believed that Admiral Somers's heart was indeed left behind in a modest tomb at the southwest corner of the park. When the tomb was opened many years later, only a few bones, a pebble, and some bottle fragments were found. Nonetheless, ceremonies were held at the empty grave in 1920, when the Prince of Wales christened this pleasant, tree-shrouded park Somers Garden. ⊠*Bordered by Shinbone and Blockade alleys, Duke of Kent and Duke of York sts.* ⊠*Free* ⊘*Daily 8–4.*

❼ St. George's Historical Society Museum, Printery & Garden. Furnished to resemble its former incarnation as a private home, this typical Bermudian building reveals what life was like in the early 1700s. Along with period furnishings, it has assorted documents and artifacts (like ax heads and whale-blubber cutters) pertaining to the colonial days. But it's the re-created kitchen—complete with palmetto baskets and calabash "dipping" gourds—that really takes the cake. Downstairs the printery (accessible from Featherbed Alley) features a working replica of a Gutenberg-style press, as well as early editions of island newspapers. The beautiful cottage gardens behind the museum are also worth a visit. ⊠*Duke of Kent St. and Featherbed Alley* ☎*441/297–0423* ⊠*$5* ⊘*Apr.–Nov., weekdays 10–4; Jan.–Mar., Wed. 11–4.*

★ Fodor'sChoice **St. Peter's Church.** Because parts of this white-
❿ washed stone church date back to 1620, it holds the distinc-
tion of being the oldest continuously operating Anglican
church in the Western Hemisphere. It was not, however,
the first house of worship to stand on this site. It replaced a
1612 structure made of wooden posts and palmetto leaves
that was destroyed in a storm. The present church was
extended in 1713 (the oldest part is the area around the
triple-tier pulpit), with the tower and wings being added in
the 19th century. Befitting its age, St. Peter's has many trea-
sures. The red cedar altar, carved in 1615 under the supervision of Richard Moore (a shipwright and the colony's
first governor) is the oldest piece of woodwork in Bermuda.
The baptismal font, brought to the island by early settlers,
is about 500 years old; and the late 18th-century bishop's
throne is believed to have been salvaged from a shipwreck.
There's also a fine collection of communion silver from the
1600s in the vestry. Nevertheless, it's the building itself that
leaves the most lasting impression. With rough-hewn pil-
lars, exposed cedar beams and candlelit chandeliers, the
church is stunning in its simplicity. After viewing the interior, walk into the churchyard to see where prominent Bermudians, including Governor Sir Richard Sharples who was
assassinated in 1973, are buried. A separate graveyard for
slaves (to the west of the church, behind the wall) is a poi-
gnant reminder of Bermuda's segregated past. ⊠ *33 Duke
of York St.* ☎ *441/297–2459* ⊕ *www.anglican.bm* ⊠ *Donations accepted* ⊗ *Mon.–Sat. 10–4, Sun. service at 11:15.*

★ ⓬ **Tucker House.** Tucker House is maintained, owned, and
lovingly preserved as a museum by the Bermuda National
Trust. It was built in the 1750s for a merchant who stored
his wares in the cellar (a space that now holds an archaeo-
logical exhibit). But it's been associated with the illustri-
ous Tucker family ever since Henry Tucker, president of
the Governor's Council and a key participant in the Bermuda Gunpowder Plot, purchased it in 1775. His descen-
dents lived here until 1809 and much of the fine silver and
heirloom furniture—which dates primarily from the mid-
18th and early-19th centuries—was donated by them. As
a result, the house is essentially a tribute to this well-con-
nected clan whose members included a Bermudian governor, a U.S. treasurer, a Confederate navy captain, and an
Episcopal bishop.

The kitchen, however, is dedicated to another notable—
Joseph Haine Rainey—who is thought to have oper-

ated a barber's shop in it during the Civil War. (Barber's Alley, around the corner, is also named in his honor.) As a freed slave from South Carolina, Rainey fled to Bermuda at the outbreak of the war. Afterward he returned to the United States and, in 1870, became the first black man to be elected to the House of Representatives. A short flight of stairs leads down to the kitchen, originally a separate building, and to an enclosed kitchen garden. ⌧5 *Water St.* ☎441/297–0545 ⊕*www.bnt.bm* ⌧*$5; $10 combination ticket includes admission to National Trust Museum in Globe Hotel and Verdmont* ⊙*Nov.–Mar., Wed.–Sat.; Apr.–Oct., Mon.–Sat. 10–4.*

❻ Unfinished Church. Work began on this intended replacement for St. Peter's Church in 1874. But, just as it neared completion, construction was halted by storm damage and disagreements within the church community. Hence the massive Gothic-revival pile sat—unfinished and crumbling—until the Bermuda National Trust stepped in to stabilize the structure in 1992. With soaring stone walls, a grassy floor and only the sky for a roof, it's the sort of atmospheric ruin that poets and painters so admire. ⌧*Duke of Kent St.* ☎441/236–6483 ⊕*www.bnt.bm* ⌧*Free* ⊙*Daily dawn–dusk.*

⓭ World Heritage Centre. Housed in an 1860 customs warehouse next to the Penno's Wharf Cruise Ship Terminal, the center is still a work-in-progress. However, Phase One of this multiyear, multimillion-dollar project opened in the summer of 2006. You can now visit the ground-floor Orientation Exhibits Gallery showcasing several hundred years of civic history, and view a brief film (*A Stroll through St. George's*). Developed under the auspices of the St. George's Foundation, the World Heritage Centre is set to include further exhibition space, a library, theater, and retail outlets when completed. ⌧*19 Penno's Wharf* ☎441/297–5791 ⊕*www.stgeorgesfoundation.com* ⌧*Free* ⊙*Tues.–Sat. 10–4.*

HAMILTON

St. George's and Hamilton are about 10 mi and 200 years apart. The latter wasn't even incorporated as a town until 1792; and by the time Hamilton became capital in 1815, St. George's had already celebrated its bicentennial. The age difference is apparent. The charmingly gnarled lanes of the island's first town straighten out here into proper streets, and topsy-turvy colonial cottages give way to more formal Victorian facades. As Bermuda's economic and social hub, Hamilton has a different vibe, too.

With a permanent resident population of 1,500 households, this city in Pembroke Parish still doesn't qualify as a major metropolis. Yet it has enough stores, restaurants, and offices to amp up the energy level. Moreover, it has a thriving international business community (centered on financial and investment services, insurance, telecommunications, global management of intellectual property, shipping, and aircraft and ship registration), which lends it a degree of sophistication seldom found in so small a center.

A GOOD WALK

Any tour of Hamilton should begin on **Front Street ❶**, a tidy thoroughfare lined with ice-cream–color buildings, many with cheery awnings and ornate balconies. The **Visitor Information Centre** in the No. 1 Passenger Terminal (the most westerly of Hamilton's two cruise ship facilities) is a good starting point. Stroll toward the intersection of Front and Queen streets where you can see the Birdcage, a much-photographed traffic box named for its designer, Michael "Dickey" Bird; then continue west and swing down Point Pleasant Road to **Albuoy's Point ❷** for a splendid view of Hamilton Harbour. Afterward, retrace your steps, passing the Ferry Terminal Building where passengers board boats for sightseeing excursions. (You can also depart from here on more affordable round-trip rides to the Dockyard via the Sea Express ferry.)

Back at the Birdcage, turn up Queen Street to see the 19th-century Perot Post Office. Just beyond it is the **Museum of the Bermuda Historical Society/Bermuda Public Library ❸**. Follow Queen Street away from the harbor to Church Street to reach the **City Hall & Arts Centre ❹**, which houses the Bermuda National Gallery, the Bermuda Society of Arts Gallery, and a performing arts center. Saturday mornings from November to June, you can continue on to the **City Market ❺**, which sets up about five minutes north on Canal Road.

Returning to the City Hall steps, turn east on Church Street and pass the Hamilton Bus Terminal. One block farther, the imposing **Cathedral of the Most Holy Trinity ❻** looms up before you. Next, past the cathedral near the corner of Church and Parliament streets, you'll come to **Sessions**

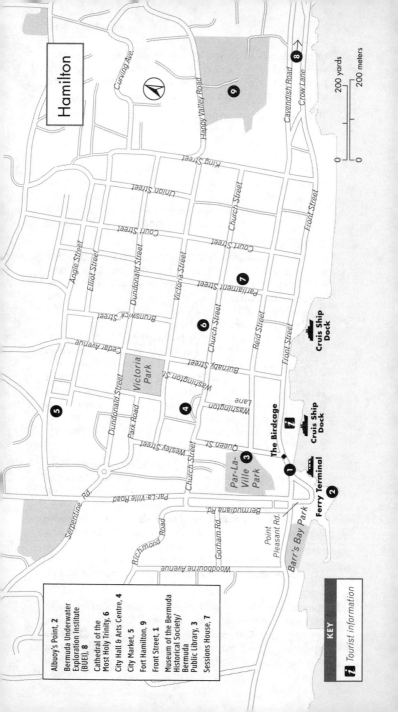

Hamilton

KEY

🛈 Tourist Information

Albuoy's Point, **2**

Bermuda Underwater Exploration Institute (BUEI), **8**

Cathedral of the Most Holy Trinity, **6**

City Hall & Arts Centre, **4**

City Market, **5**

Fort Hamilton, **9**

Front Street, **1**

Museum of the Bermuda Historical Society/Bermuda Public Library, **3**

Sessions House, **7**

0   200 yards
0   200 meters

1

House **7**. Keep going down Parliament to Front Street for a look at the Cabinet Building and, in front of it, the Cenotaph for fallen Bermudian soldiers. From here, you might head back to Front Street for a leisurely stroll past (or into!) the shops, then linger over lunch in one of the many cafés overlooking the harbor.

If you're up for a longer walk (about 15 minutes east from the Cenotaph) or are traveling by scooter or taxi, head to the **Bermuda Underwater Exploration Institute (BUEI) 8. Fort Hamilton 9** is another worthwhile destination, though the road to it—north on King Street, then a sharp right on Happy Valley Road—is a bit too steep for casual walkers. The moated fort has gorgeous grounds, underground passageways, and great views of Hamilton and its harbor.

Timing Although it's possible to buzz through Hamilton in a few hours, you should plan to give it a day if you're going to take in some of the museums, Fort Hamilton, and the Bermuda Underwater Exploration Institute. Serious shoppers should set aside another half day to browse around the shops.

WHAT TO SEE

2 **Albuoy's Point.** It's always a pleasure to watch sailboats and passenger ferries zigzag around the many islands that dot Hamilton Harbour. For a ringside seat to the show, grab a bench beneath the trees at Albuoy's Point, a small waterside park. Nearby is the **Royal Bermuda Yacht Club**, founded in 1844 and granted the use of the word "Royal" by Prince Albert in 1845. Today luminaries from the international sailing scene hobnob with local yachtsmen and business executives at the club's 1930s headquarters. If you're around between April and November, you might catch one of the many club-sponsored racing events, such as the Newport–Bermuda Race in June or the King Edward VII Gold Cup Match Race Tournament in October. ✉*Off Front St.*

★ **8** **Bermuda Underwater Exploration Institute (BUEI).** The 40,000-square-foot Ocean Discovery Centre showcases local contributions to oceanographic research and undersea discovery. Guests can ogle the world-class shell collection amassed by resident Jack Lightbourne (three of the 1,000 species were identified by and named for Lightbourne himself); or visit a gallery honoring native-born archaeologist Teddy Tucker to see booty retrieved from Bermudian shipwrecks. The types of gizmos that made such discoveries possible are also displayed: including a replica of the bathysphere William Beebe and Otis Barton used in their record-smashing 1934 dive. (Forget the Bermuda Triangle: the real mystery is how they descended ½ a mile in a metal ball less than 5 feet in diameter!) A more modern "submersible," Nautilus-X2, lets wannabe explorers take a simulated seven-minute trip to the ocean floor. Special events, like lectures and whale-watching trips, are available, too, for an added fee. If all that activity makes you hungry, Harbourfront Restaurant (which replaced La Coquille as the on-site eatery in May 2007) is a lovely choice for lunch. Pedestrians may access the BUEI by following the sidewalk on the water side of Front Street. Motorists must drive out of town on Front Street, round the traffic circle, and exit at the lane signposted for the BUEI because it's only accessible to in-bound vehicles. ✉*40 Crow Lane, off E. Broadway* ☎*441/292–7219* ⊕*www.buei.org* ✇*$12.50* ☉*Weekdays 9–5, weekends 10–5, last admission at 4.*

★ ❻ **Cathedral of the Most Holy Trinity.** After the original Anglican sanctuary on this site was torched by an arsonist in 1884, Scottish architect William Hay was enlisted to design a replacement. True to his training, he set out to erect a Gothic-style structure in the grand European tradition. Mission accomplished. Inside, the clerestory in the nave is supported by piers of polished Scottish granite; soaring archways are trimmed in stone imported from France; and the choir stalls and bishop's throne are carved out of English oak. The pulpit, meanwhile, is modeled on the one in Hay's hometown cathedral (St. Giles in Edinburgh), and the whole thing is crowned by a copper roof that stands out among Bermuda's typical white-topped buildings. Yet for all the European flourishes, Bermuda Cathedral still has a subtropical flair. After all, the limestone building blocks came from the Par-la-Ville quarry and one of its loveliest stained-glass windows—the Angel Window on the east wall of the north transept—was created by local artist Vivienne Gilmore Gardner. After sauntering around the interior, you can climb the 155 steps of the church tower for a heavenly view of Hamilton and its harbor. ✉*Church St.* ☎*441/292–4033* ⊕*www.anglican.bm* ✇*Cathedral free; tower $3* ☉*Church daily 7:30–5 and for Sun. services, tower weekdays 10–4.*

★ ❹ **City Hall & Arts Centre.** Set back from the street behind a
☺ fountain and lily pond, City Hall contains Hamilton's administrative offices as well as two art galleries and a per-

formance hall. Instead of a clock, its tower is topped with a bronze wind vane—a prudent choice in a land where the weather is as important as the time. The statues of children playing in the fountain are by local sculptor Desmond Fountain, whose lifelike characters you may encounter elsewhere on the island. The building itself was designed in 1960 by Bermudian architect Wilfred Onions, a champion of balanced simplicity. Massive cedar doors open onto an impressive lobby notable for its beautiful chandeliers and portraits of mayors past and present. To the left is City Hall Theatre, a major venue for concerts, plays, and dance performances. To the right are the civic offices where you can find the Benbow Stamp Collection and an exhibit of Bermudian antiques. A handsome cedar staircase leads upstairs to two second-floor art galleries. (An elevator gets you there, too.)

On the first landing, in the East Exhibition Room, is the **Bermuda National Gallery** (☎441/295–9428 ⊕*www.bng.bm* ✉*Free*), home to Bermuda's national art collection. The permanent exhibits include paintings by island artists as well as European masters like Gainsborough and Reynolds; African masks and sculpture; and photographs by internationally known artists, such as Bermudian Richard Saunders (1922–87). The fine and decorative art pieces in the Bermuda Collection reflect the country's multicultural heritage. Temporary exhibits are also a major part of the museum's program, and on any given day you can see a selection of local work along with a traveling exhibit from another museum. For a comprehensive look at the collections, join one of the free docent-led tours offered Thursday at 10:30 or sign on for the $8 Cultural Art Tour that begins each Tuesday at 11 (reservations required). Lectures and other special events are listed in the gallery's online calendar. Farther up the stairs, in the West Wing, the **Bermuda Society of Arts Gallery** (☎441/292–3824 ⊕*www.bsoa. bm* ✉*Donations accepted*) displays work by its members. Its frequently changing juried shows attract talented local painters, sculptors, and photographers. Art collectors will be pleased to learn that many pieces may also be purchased. ✉*17 Church St.* ☎*441/292–1234* ⊙*City Hall weekdays 9–5; National Gallery and Society of the Arts Mon.–Sat. 10–4.*

❺ One of the best places to mingle with Onions and, yes, buy a few edible ones is the **City Market** held every Saturday, 8 to 1, from November to June. It features up to 50 vendors who sell only Bermuda-grown, -caught or -made products. Along with organic produce, fresh fish, and assorted home-baked items, goodies like handcrafted soaps and honey derived from the pollen of island wild flowers are up for sale. The market, at the Bull's Head Car Park on Canal Road, is about a five-minute walk north of City Hall. ☎441/517–4101.

★ ❾ **Fort Hamilton.** This imposing moat-ringed fortress has
☺ underground passageways that were cut through solid rock by Royal Engineers in the 1860s. Built to defend the West End's Royal Naval Dockyard from land attacks, it was outdated even before its completion but remains a fine example of a polygonal Victorian fort. Even if you're not a big fan of military history, the hilltop site's stellar views and stunning gardens make the trip worthwhile. On Monday at noon, from November to March, bagpipes echo through the grounds as the kilt-clad members of the Bermuda Islands Pipe Band perform a traditional skirling ceremony. Due to one-way streets, getting to the fort by scooter can be a bit challenging. From downtown Hamilton head north on Queen Street, turn right on Church Street, then turn left to go up the hill on King Street. Make a sharp right turn (270-degree) onto Happy Valley Road and follow the signs. Pedestrians may walk along Front Street to King Street. ⊠*Happy Valley Rd.* ☎*441/292–1234* ⊜*Free* ☉*Daily 9:30–5.*

❶ **Front Street.** Running along the harbor, Hamilton's main thoroughfare bustles with small cars, motor scooters, bicycles, buses, pedestrians, and the occasional horse-drawn carriage. When cruise ships are in port, it also bustles with tourists who tend to cram into the street's high-class low-rise shops. Return visitors will notice that Triminghams Department Store (a Bermuda institution since 1842) has closed; however, there are still plenty of places on Front Street offering retail therapy. Don't overlook small offshoots and alleyways, like Chancery Lane, Bermuda House Lane, and the Walkway, where you'll stumble upon hidden-away boutiques. The **Visitor Information Centre** (☎441/734–3233) is a good place to strike out from when you're ready to explore the rest of Hamilton. Open weekdays 9–4 and Saturday 10–4, it's the place to go for pamphlets, maps, or transit passes. It's also the departure point for a free city walking tour that leaves Monday mornings, November to March, at 10. In case you can't make it, the bureau has brochures for a self-guided walk as well.

★ ❸ **Museum of the Bermuda Historical Society/Bermuda Public Library.** Mark Twain admired the giant rubber tree that stands on Queen Street in the front yard of this Georgian house, formerly owned by William Bennet Perot and his family. Though charmed by the tree, which had been imported from what is now Guyana in the mid-19th century, Twain lamented that it didn't bear rubbery fruit in the form of overshoes and hot-water bottles. The library, about which he made no comment, was established in 1839 and its reference section has virtually every book ever written about Bermuda, as well as a microfilm collection of Bermudian newspapers dating back to 1784.

The museum is to the left of the library entrance. Established in 1955, it chronicles Bermuda's past through interesting—and in some cases downright quirky—artifacts. One display, for instance, is full of tools and trinkets made by Boer War prisoners who were exiled to Bermuda in 1901 and 1902. Another features an unusual 18th-century sedan chair. Check out the portraits of Sir George Somers and his wife, painted around 1605, and of Postmaster Perot and his wife that hang in the entrance hall. Time permitting, also ask to see a copy of the letter George Washington wrote in 1775: addressed TO THE INHABITANTS OF BERMUDA, it requests gunpowder for use in the American Revolution. ⊠ *13 Queen St.* ☎ *441/295–2905 library, 441/295–2487 museum* ⊕ *www.bermudanationallibrary.bm* ⊠ *Donations accepted* ☉ *Library Mon.–Thurs. 8:30–7, Fri. 10–5, Sat. 9–5, Sun. 1–5; closed Sun. in July and Aug.; museum Mon.–Sat. 9:30–3:30* ☞ *Tours by appointment.*

❼ **Sessions House & Jubilee Clock Tower.** This eye-catching Italianate edifice, erected in 1819, is where the House of Assembly (the lower house of Parliament) and the Supreme Court convene. The Florentine towers and colonnade, decorated with red terra-cotta, were added to the building in 1887 to commemorate Queen Victoria's Golden Jubilee. The Victoria Jubilee Clock Tower made its striking debut—albeit a few years late—at midnight on December 31, 1893. Bermuda's Westminster-style Parliament meets on the second floor, where the speaker rules the roost in a powdered wig and robe. (The island has approximately 14 times as many politicians per capita as Europe or North America, so maintaining order is no small feat!) Sartorial splendor is equally evident downstairs in the Supreme Court where wigs and robes (red for judges, black for barristers) are again the order of the day. You're welcome to watch the colorful proceedings: bear in mind, though, that visitors, too, are required to wear appropriate attire. Call first to find out when parliamentary sessions and court cases are scheduled. ⊠*21 Parliament St.* ☎*441/292–7408 Parliament, 441/292–1350 Supreme Court* ⊕*www.gov.bm* ▧*Free* ☉ *Weekdays 9–12:30 and 2–5.*

THE WEST END & DOCKYARD

Bermuda is denser than you might imagine. But in contrast to Hamilton and St. George's, the island's West End seems positively pastoral. Many of the top sites here are natural ones: namely the wildlife reserves, wooded areas, and beautiful waterways of Sandys Parish. The notable exception is Bermuda's single largest tourist attraction—the Royal Naval Dockyard.

Its story begins in the aftermath of the American Revolution, when Britain suddenly found itself with neither an anchorage nor a major ship-repair yard in the western Atlantic. Around 1809, just as Napoleon was surfacing as a serious threat and the empire's ships were becoming increasingly vulnerable to pirate attack, Britain decided to construct a stronghold in Bermuda. Dubbed the "Gibraltar of the West," the Dockyard operated as a shipyard for nearly 150 years. The facility was closed in 1951, although the Royal Navy maintained a small presence here until 1976 and held title to the land until 1995.

The Bermudian government and development groups began to plan for civilian use of the Dockyard in 1980. Since then, $21 million in public funds and $42 million in private money has been spent to make the area blossom. Now trees and shrubs grow where there used to be vast stretches of concrete. Private yachts calmly float where naval vessels once anchored, and cruise ships dock at the terminal. Historic structures—like the Clocktower and Cooperage buildings—house restaurants, galleries, shops, even a movie theater. A strip of beach now serves as a snorkel park. And, at the center of it all, are the Maritime Museum & Dolphin Quest: two popular facilities that share a fortified 6-acre site. You can reach the Dockyard from Hamilton in 45 minutes by bus or a half hour by fast ferry.

The Bermuda Railway

1

The history of the Bermuda Railway—which operated on the island from 1931 to 1948—is as brief as the track is short. Bermuda's Public Works Department considered proposals for a railroad as early as 1899, and Parliament finally granted permission, in 1922, for a line to run from Somerset to St. George's. But laying tracks was a formidable undertaking, requiring the costly and time-consuming construction of long tunnels and swing bridges. By the time it was finished, the railway had cost investors $1 million, making it, per mile, the most expensive railway ever built.

"Old Rattle and Shake," as it was nicknamed, began to decline during World War II. Soldiers put the train to hard use, and it proved impossible to obtain the necessary maintenance equipment. At the end of the war the government acquired the distressed railway for $115,000. Automobiles arrived in Bermuda in 1946, and train service ended in 1948 when the railway was sold in its entirety to British Guiana (now Guyana). Then, in the 1980s, the government gave new life to the ground it had covered by converting the tracks into trails.

Today the secluded 18-mi recreational Bermuda Railway Trail runs the length of the island, offering fabulous coastal views along the way. Restricted to pedestrians, horseback riders, bicyclists, and scooter drivers, the trail is a delightful way to see the island away from the traffic and noise of main roads. You might want to rent a bike or scooter if you plan to cover the entire trail, as many enthusiastic travelers do. Do note, though, that many portions of the trail are isolated—so you should avoid setting out alone after dark. Regardless of when you go, it's wise to first pick up a free copy of the Bermuda Railway Trail Guide available at visitor information centers.

–revised by
Susan MacCallum-Whitcomb

A GOOD TOUR

To make the most of your visit to the West End, plan to combine sea and land transportation. If you've bought a bus pass (rather than tickets), it will work on both ferries and buses, allowing you to hop on and off wherever you please. If you have a bicycle or scooter, you can bring it on the ferry; however, you'll be charged an extra adult fare to take the scooter, and space is sometimes limited. Once you arrive, you can see the Dockyard itself can be covered easily on foot. But other sights are rather far apart. So plan to take a taxi, bus, or ferry if you're continuing on to Somerset or elsewhere.

The logical place to begin a tour is the Royal Naval Dockyard. Start your day by visiting the **Bermuda Maritime Museum & Dolphin Quest**, which are housed together in a stone fortress. Next to the entrance is the **Snorkel Park**, a small protected reef with underwater "trails" where you can get up close to marine life. Across from the museum entrance, the tempting art gallery and permanent art-and-crafts market in the **Old Cooperage** also warrant a visit. To the west are a pottery shop, glassblowing center and other businesses that occupy attractive old military warehouses; just south is the **Clocktower Mall & Clocktower Parade,** where you can find still more shops plus the new **Visitor Information Centre.** Finish your tour here, or continue via ferry to Somerset Island.

For an interesting change of pace, opt for the slow boat (not the one heading directly to Hamilton) out of the Dockyard. You'll pass by Boaz and Watford islands on your way to Somerset Island, fringed on both sides with beautiful secluded coves, inlets, and bays. Getting off the ferry at Watford Bridge, you can make a quick jaunt into **Somerset Village,** which consistently ranks among Bermuda's prettiest communities.

The next sights, reached via Somerset Road, are best visited by bus or scooter. About 2 mi east of Somerset Village, opposite the Willowbank Hotel, is the entrance to the **Heydon Trust Property,** which boasts both wide-open spaces and a tiny 1616 chapel. Around the bend on your left is **Fort Scaur,** a serene spot with sweeping views of the Great Sound. Linking Somerset Island with the rest of Bermuda is **Somerset Bridge.** Near it is the Somerset ferry landing, where you can catch a boat back to Hamilton. Across the bridge, Somerset Road becomes Middle Road, which leads into Southampton Parish.

TIMING Allow a full day for exploring this area. Before setting out, you should check bus and ferry schedules carefully because, by water, the trip can take from 30 minutes to more than an hour depending on which ferry you choose. There are, however, worse ways to spend your time than boating on Bermuda's Great Sound. Buses 7 and 8 depart from Hamilton about every 15 minutes, taking either South Road or Middle Road to the West End.

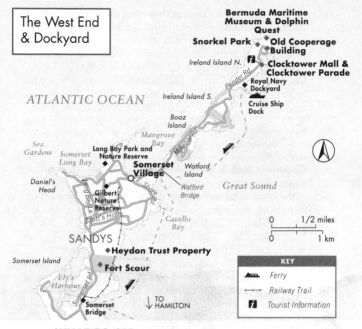

The West End & Dockyard

Bermuda Maritime Museum & Dolphin Quest

Snorkel Park

Old Cooperage Building

Ireland Island N.

Clocktower Mall & Clocktower Parade

Royal Navy Dockyard

Ireland Island S.

Cruise Ship Dock

ATLANTIC OCEAN

Boaz Island

Mangrove Bay

Sea Gardens

Somerset Long Bay

Long Bay Park and Nature Reserve

Somerset Village

Watford Island

Great Sound

Daniel's Head

Gilbert Nature Reserve

Watford Bridge

Scott's Hill

Cavello Bay

SANDYS

Heydon Trust Property

Somerset Island

Fort Scaur

Ely's Harbour

↓ TO HAMILTON

Somerset Bridge

0   1/2 miles
0   1 km

KEY
🛳 Ferry
←→ Railway Trail
🛈 Tourist Information

WHAT TO SEE

★ **Fodor's**Choice **Bermuda Maritime Museum & Dolphin Quest.** The Maritime Museum, ensconced in Bermuda's largest fort, displays its collections in a series of old munitions warehouses that surround the parade grounds and Keep Pond. Insulated from the rest of the Dockyard by a moat and massive stone ramparts, you'll enter by way of a drawbridge. At the Shifting House, right inside the entrance, you can wander through rooms filled with relics from some of the 350-odd ships wrecked on the island's reefs. Other buildings are devoted to seafaring pursuits such as whaling, shipbuilding, and yacht racing. More displays are in the 19th-century **Commissioner's House,** on the museum's upper grounds. Built as both home and headquarters for the Dockyard commissioner, the house later served as a barracks during World War I and was used for military intelligence during World War II. Today, after an award-winning restoration, it contains exhibits on Bermuda's social and military history.

After immersing yourself in maritime history, you can immerse yourself—literally—in the wonderful world of dolphins. **Dolphin Quest** (☎441/234–4464 ⊕*www.dolphin-*

quest.org) offers a range of in-water programs that allow adults and children ages five or older to pet, play with, and swim alongside Atlantic bottlenose dolphins in the historic Keep Pond. There are even specially designed sessions, conducted from a submersible bench, for younger kids. Since entry to the Dolphin Quest area is free with museum admission, anyone can watch the action. Participation in the actual programs, however, costs $150 to $285 and advance booking is recommended. ⊠*Maritime Museum, Dockyard* ☎*441/234–1418* ⊕*www.bmm.bm* ☎*$10* ⊙*Daily 9:30–5, last admission 4.*

Clocktower Mall & Clocktower Parade. A pair of 100-foot towers make it impossible to miss the Clocktower Mall. (Observant folks will note that one of them features a standard clock, the other a tide indicator!) Inside this 19th-century building, the Royal Navy's administrative offices have been replaced by distinctly Bermudian boutiques—including specialty shops and branches of Front Street favorites. These are particularly popular on Sunday because most stores outside the Dockyard area are closed. Just in front of the mall is the former military parade ground, which now hosts special events (like the Beat Retreat Ceremony) and is the site of a new **Visitor Information Centre** (☎*441/799-4842*). If you need pamphlets, bus and ferry tickets, or a phone card, the latter is open daily from 9 to 5. ⊠*Dockyard* ☎*441/234–1709* ☎*Free* ⊙*Mid Apr.–Sept., Mon.–Sat. 9:30–6, Tues. 9:30–10, Sun. 10–5; Oct–mid-Apr., Mon.–Sat. 10–5, Sun. 11–5.*

Fort Scaur. The British chose the highest hill in Somerset for the site of this fort, built in the late 1860s and early 1870s to defend the flank of the Dockyard from possible American attacks. British troops were garrisoned here until World War I; and American forces were, ironically, stationed at the fort during World War II. Today its stone walls are surrounded by 22 acres of pretty gardens and the view of the Great Sound from the parapet is unsurpassed. Be sure to check out the early-Bermuda Weather Stone, which is billed as a "perfect weather indicator." A sign posted nearby solemnly explains all. ⊠*Somerset Rd., Ely's Harbour* ☎*441/234–0908* ☎*Free* ⊙*Daily 8–4.*

Heydon Trust property. A reminder of what the island was like in its early days, this blissfully peaceful 43-acre preserve remains an unspoiled open space, except for a few citrus groves and flower gardens. Pathways with well-

1

positioned park benches wind through it, affording some wonderful water views. If you persevere along the main path, you'll reach rustic **Heydon Chapel**. Built in the early 1600s, it's Bermuda's smallest church. Nondenominational services featuring stirring Gregorian chants are still held in the single-room sanctuary Monday through Saturday at 3. ⊠ *16 Heydon Dr., off Somerset Rd.* ☎ *441/234–1831* 🖷 *Free* ☉ *Daily dawn–dusk.*

Old Cooperage Building. Ready to do some shopping? Inside this former barrel-making factory, you can find the **Bermuda Craft Market** and the **Bermuda Arts Centre**. The former—arguably the island's largest and best-priced craft outlet—showcases the wares of more than 60 craftspeople, including quilters, candle makers, and wood carvers. The latter is a member-run art gallery that displays innovative high-end work. Exhibits change every six weeks and may include watercolors, oils, sculpture, and photography— much of which is for sale. Half-a-dozen artists also maintain studios on the premises, so leave some time to watch them at work. ⊠ *Dockyard* ☎ *441/234–3208 Craft Market, 441/234–2809 Arts Centre* ⊕ *www.artbermuda.bm* 🖷 *Free* ☉ *Craft Market: Apr.–Oct., daily 9:30–5; Nov.–Mar., daily 10–5. Arts Centre: daily 10–5.*

★ ☺ **Snorkel Park.** Evidence of the Dockyard's naval legacy can also be viewed at this protected inlet, accessed through a stone tunnel adjacent to the Maritime Museum. Beneath the water's surface lie cast-iron cannons dating from 1550 to 1800, plus an antique anchor and gun-carriage wheel. The true attractions, however, are colorful fish (you might see more than 50 varieties) and other sea creatures including anemones, sea cucumbers, and assorted species of coral. Thanks to amenities like marked reef trails and floating rest stations, snorkeling could hardly be easier. But if you'd rather not swim you can always rent an underwater scooter—a battery-operated, fan-propelled gadget that would make James Bond proud. Kayaks, paddleboats, and paddle-bikes are also available for rent. ⊠ *Dockyard* ☎ *441/234–6989* 🖷 *Admission free, equipment rental extra, available Mon.–Sat. 10:30–6* ☉ *Apr.–Nov., daily 9–6.*

Somerset Village. Its position on Mangrove Bay once made it a popular hideout for pirates. But judging by Somerset Village's bucolic appearance, you'd never guess that now. The shady past has been erased by shady trees, quiet streets, and charming cottages. As far as actual attractions go, this quaint one-road retreat has only a few eateries and shops—most of them offshoots of Hamilton stores. However, it provides easy access to the Gilbert Nature Reserve: a 5-acre woodland with paths that connect to some of the most scenic portions of Bermuda's Railway Trail.

ELSEWHERE IN THE PARISHES

Bermuda's other points of interest—and there are many—are scattered throughout the nine parishes. This section, covering the length and breadth of the island, focuses on the major ones. Yet half the fun of exploring Bermuda is wandering down forgotten lanes or discovering little-known coves and beaches. A motor scooter, or bicycle if you don't mind hills, is ideal for this kind of travel. You can also take public transportation. Pick up ferry and bus maps and schedules at any visitor information center. A guided taxi tour (about $90 for three hours) is the quickest way to see the sights in all the parishes, and it's safer than biking. Many taxi-tour drivers are experienced, knowledgeable guides who will lead you along the roads less traveled for a look at real Bermudian life.

TIMING

With roads as narrow and winding as Bermuda's, it takes longer to traverse the island than you'd think. So it's smarter to stick with a couple of close-by sights rather than trying to cover them all in a single day. The parishes *are* less congested than the towns, but the area to the east of Hamilton—especially the traffic circle where Crow Lane intersects with the Lane and Trimingham Road—is very busy during morning (7:30–9) and afternoon (4–5:30) rush hours.

THREE GOOD TOURS

St. George's Parish Starting in the town of St. George's, walk north about 25 minutes on Duke of Kent Street, following the signs to **Fort St. Catherine**. (Those who would rather not hoof it can check at the visitor information centre to see if the minibus is operating from King's Square.) From here, fort aficionados may continue on to **Alexandra Battery** and **Gates Fort**. If you have a Wednesday morning free, you might also consider a guided tour of the **Bermuda Institute of Ocean Sciences (BIOS)**. To reach it, take a bus or taxi across the Ferry Reach to St. David's Road. Afterward, head east to explore quiet **St. David's Island**.

Hamilton & Smith's Parishes Hamilton and Smith's Parishes encircle Harrington Sound. Starting on the northeastern end of the sound, take a bus, taxi, or scooter onto Wilkinson Avenue to access the millennium-old limestone formations in **Crystal Caves**. North Shore Road leads to Flatts Village, site of the **Bermuda Aquarium, Museum & Zoo**. Before leaving Flatts, stand on the bridge to watch the power of the water as it rushes through the narrows. Your next stop should be **Verdmont**, a historic home in Smith's Parish. If you have energy to spare at the end of the day, head down Collector's Hill to South Road, turn left, and in less than a mile you'll be at **Spittal Pond Nature Reserve**.

Devonshire, Paget, Warwick & Southampton Parishes If you're interested in botany, begin by nosing around the varied plant collections at the **Botanical Gardens**. Exiting through the north gate puts you on Berry Hill Road. From here you can take a bus, taxi, or scooter to Waterville, a harbourside house that serves as headquarters for the Bermuda National Trust. Next, walk or ride along the lane, turning right at the traffic circle onto Harbour Road, then left onto Lover's Lane, which will take you to **Paget Marsh**, where you can see what Bermuda was like before settlement. Leaving the marsh, round the corner to Middle Road and catch the bus to **Gibb's Hill Lighthouse** in Southampton for breathtaking views.

WHAT TO SEE

★ Fodor'sChoice **Bermuda Aquarium, Museum & Zoo.** The BAMZ, established in 1926, has always been a pleasant diversion. But following an ambitious decade-long expansion program, it now rates as one of Bermuda's premier attractions. In the aquarium, the big draw is the Northrock Exhibit: a 140,000-gallon tank that gives you a diver's-eye view of the area's living coral reefs and the colorful marine life it sustains. The museum section has multimedia and interactive displays focusing on native habitats and the impact humans have had on them. The island-theme zoo, meanwhile, displays more than 300 birds, reptiles, and mammals. Don't miss the "Islands of Australasia" exhibit with its lemurs, wallabies, and tree kangaroos or "Islands of the Caribbean," a huge walk-through cage that gets you within arm's-length of ibises and iguanas. Other popular areas include an outdoor seal pool and cool kid-friendly Discovery Room. ⊠ *40 N. Shore Rd., Flatts Village, Hamilton Parish* ☎ *441/293–2727* ⊕ *www.bamz.org* ⊠ *$10* ⊙ *Daily*

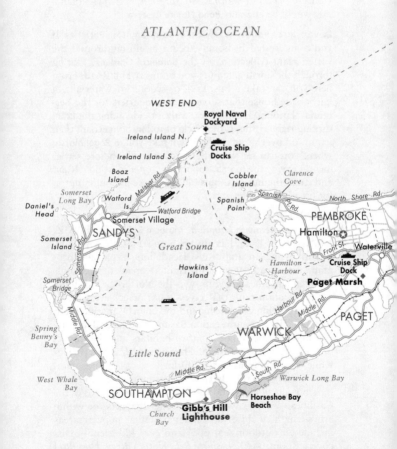

Elsewhere in the Parishes

ATLANTIC OCEAN

WEST END

Royal Naval Dockyard

Ireland Island N.

Cruise Ship Docks

Ireland Island S.

Boaz Island

Cobbler Island

Clarence Cove

Somerset Long Bay

Watford Is.

Malabar Rd.

Spanish Point

Spanish Pt. Rd.

North Shore Rd.

Daniel's Head

Watford Bridge

Somerset Village

SANDYS

PEMBROKE

Hamilton

Waterville

Front St.

Somerset Island

Somerset Rd.

Great Sound

Hawkins Island

Hamilton Harbour

Cruise Ship Dock

Paget Marsh

Somerset Bridge

Harbour Rd.

Middle Rd.

PAGET

Spring Benny's Bay

Middle Rd.

Little Sound

WARWICK

West Whale Bay

Middle Rd.

South Rd.

Warwick Long Bay

SOUTHAMPTON

Church Bay

Gibb's Hill Lighthouse

Horseshoe Bay Beach

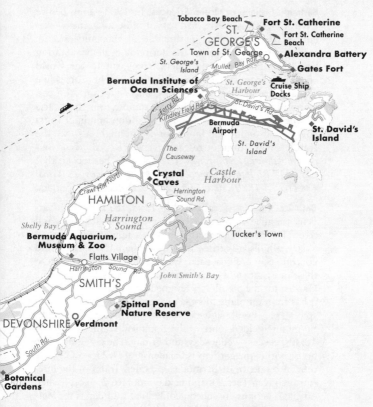

Tobacco Bay Beach
ST. GEORGE'S
Fort St. Catherine
Fort St. Catherine Beach
Town of St. George
St. George's Island
Mullet Bay Rd.
Alexandra Battery
Gates Fort
Bermuda Institute of Ocean Sciences
St. George's Harbour
Cruise Ship Docks
Ferry Rd.
Kindley Field Rd.
St. David's Rd.
Bermuda Airport
St. David's Island
St. David's Island
The Causeway
Castle Harbour
Crystal Caves
Harrington Sound Rd.
HAMILTON
Crawl Hill North
Harrington Sound
Shelly Bay
Bermuda Aquarium, Museum & Zoo
Flatts Village
Harrington Sound Rd.
Tucker's Town
John Smith's Bay
SMITH'S
DEVONSHIRE **Verdmont**
Spittal Pond Nature Reserve
South Rd.
Botanical Gardens

ATLANTIC OCEAN

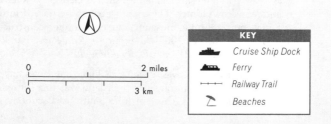

0 — 2 miles
0 — 3 km

KEY	
Cruise Ship Dock	
Ferry	
Railway Trail	
Beaches	

9–5, last admission at 4; North Rock dive talk and seal feeding 1:10 daily Apr.–Sept.; Oct.–Mar., weekends only.

Bermuda Institute of Ocean Sciences. In 1903—long before environmental issues earned top-of-mind awareness—scientists began studying marine life at this mid-Atlantic facility formerly known as the Bermuda Biological Station for Research. Now researchers from around the world come here to work on projects dealing with hot topics like global warming, marine ecology, and acid rain. You can learn all about them on a free 90-minute tour that starts Wednesday morning at 10 in the reception building. Tours cover the grounds and laboratory. You might also see the station's new 168-foot research vessel, *R/V Bank of Bermuda Atlantic Explorer*, if it happens to be docked that day. ✉*17 Biological Lane, Ferry Reach, St. George's Parish* ☎*441/297–1880* ⊕*www.bios.edu* ✆*Donations accepted.*

Botanical Gardens. Established in 1898, the Botanical Gardens are filled with exotic subtropical plants, flowers, and trees. The 36-acre property features a miniature forest, an aviary, a hibiscus garden with more than 150 species, and collections of orchids, cacti, fruits, and ferns. In addition to these must-see sights is an intriguing "must-smell" one: the Garden for the Sightless. Designed primarily for the blind, it has fragrant plants (like geranium, lemon, lavender, and spices), plus Braille signage. Weather permitting, free 60- to 90-minute guided tours of the Botanical Gardens begin at 10:30 Tuesday, Wednesday, and Friday. The gracious white house within the gardens is **Camden** (☎*441/236–5732*), the official residence of Bermuda's premier. Tours of the interior are given Tuesday and Friday noon to 2, except when official functions are scheduled. Behind Camden is the **Masterworks Arts Centre** (☎*441/236–2950* ⊕*www.bermudamasterworks.com* ✆*Free*), open weekdays from 10 to 4 and on Saturday by appointment. The theme of this not-for-profit foundation is "Bermuda through the Eyes of Artists," and it counts among its collection works by native-born painters as well as international figures such as Georgia O'Keeffe and Winslow Homer. These are slated to be moved into a new purpose-built museum (currently under construction nearby) late in 2007. ✉*169 South Rd., Paget Parish* ☎*441/236–4201* ✆*Free* ⊘*Daily dawn–dusk.*

★ **Fodor's**Choice **Crystal Caves.** Bermuda's limestone caves have
☾ been attracting attention since the island was first settled. As far back as 1623, Captain John Smith (of Pocahontas

fame) commented on these "vary strange, darke, and cumbersome" caverns. Nevertheless, it came as a surprise when two boys, attempting to retrieve a lost ball, discovered Crystal Cave in 1907. The hole through which the boys descended is still visible. But, thankfully, you can now view their find without having to make such a dramatic entrance. Inside, tour guides will lead you across a pontoon bridge that spans a 55-foot-deep subterranean lake. Look up to see stalactites dripping from the ceiling or down through the perfectly clear water to see stalagmites rising from the cave floor. Amateur spelunkers can also journey through geologic time at Crystal's smaller sister cave, Fantasy. After being closed to the public for decades, it reopened in 2001. Set aside 30 minutes to see one cave; 75 minutes if you plan to take in both. ⊠8 Crystal Caves Rd., off Wilkinson Ave., Bailey's Bay, Hamilton Parish ☎441/293–0640 ⊕www. bermudacaves.com ☜One cave $16; combination ticket $23 ⊙Daily 9:30–4:30, last combination tour at 4.

★ ☺ **Fort St. Catherine.** This restored hilltop fort is arguably the most impressive one on the island. Surrounded by a dry moat and accessed by a drawbridge, it has enough tunnels, towers, redoubts, and ramparts to satisfy even the most avid military historian—or adrenaline-fueled child. The original fort was built around 1614, but it was remodeled and enlarged at least five times. In fact, work continued on it until late in the 19th century. On site you can find detailed dioramas depicting island history, an audiovisual presentation about Bermuda's fortifications, and replicas of Britain's Crown Jewels. A collection of antique weapons is also on display. Standing out among the pistols and muskets is an 18-ton muzzle-loading cannon, which was capable of firing 400-pound shells a full half mile. ⊠15 Coot Pond Rd., St. George's Parish ☎441/297–1920 ☜$5 ⊙Daily 10–4.

★ ☺ **Gibb's Hill Lighthouse.** The second cast-iron lighthouse ever built soars above Southampton Parish. Designed in London and opened in 1846, the tower stands 117 feet high and 362 feet above the sea. The light was originally produced by a concentrated burner of four large, circular wicks. Today the beam from the 1,000-watt bulb can be seen by ships 40 mi out to sea and by planes 120 mi away at 10,000 feet. The haul up the 185 spiral stairs is an arduous one—particularly if you dislike heights or tight spaces. But en route to the top you can stop to catch your breath on eight landings, where photographs and drawings of the lighthouse help divert attention from your aching appendages. Once on the balcony, you'll be rewarded by panoramic island views. ✉ *68 St. Anne's Rd., Southampton Parish* ☎ *441/238–8069* ⊕ *www.bermudalighthouse. com* ✎ *$2.50* ☉ *Daily 9–4:30* ☉ *Closed Jan.*

★ **Fodor'sChoice Paget Marsh.** Take a walk on the wild side at Paget Marsh: a 25-acre tract of land that's remained virtually untouched since presettlement times. Along with some of the last remaining stands of native Bermuda palmetto and cedar, this reserve—jointly owned and preserved by the Bermuda National Trust and the Bermuda Audubon Society—contains a mangrove forest and grassy savanna. These unspoiled habitats can be explored via a boardwalk that features interpretive signs describing the endemic flora and fauna. When listening to the cries of the native and migratory birds that frequent this natural wetland, you can quickly forget that bustling Hamilton is just minutes away. ✉ *Lover's La., Paget Parish* ☎ *441/236–6483* ⊕ *www.bnt. bm* ✎ *Free* ☉ *Daily dawn–dusk.*

★ **Spittal Pond Nature Reserve.** This Bermuda National Trust park has 64 acres for roaming, though you're asked to keep to the well-marked walkways that loop through the woods and along the spectacular shoreline. More than 30 species of waterfowl—including herons, egrets, and white-eyed vireos—winter here between November and May, making the reserve a top spot for birders. Get your timing right and you may be able to spy migrating whales as well! History buffs may be more interested in climbing the high bluff to Spanish Rock. Early settlers found this rock crudely carved with the date 1543 along with other markings that are believed to be the initials "RP" (for *Rex Portugaline*, King of Portugal) and a cross representing the Portuguese Order of Christ. The theory goes that a Portuguese ship was wrecked on the island and that her sailors marked the occasion before departing on a newly built ship. The rock was removed to prevent further damage by erosion, and a bronze cast of the original stands in its place. A plaster-of-paris version is also on display at the Museum of the Bermuda Historical Society in Hamilton. Guided 90-minute tours are offered Tuesday afternoons, starting at 1:30 from Waterville. Tours cost $50 per person with transportation included. ✉ *South Rd., Smith's Parish* ☎ *441/236–6483* ⊕ *www.bnt.bm* ✎ *Free* ☉ *Daily dawn–dusk.*

CLOSE UP

Slavery in Bermuda

1

Within a few years of the colony's founding, slavery had become a fact of life in Bermuda. As early as 1616, slaves—most of whom were "imported" as household servants and tradespeople rather than field workers—began arriving, first from Africa and then from the Caribbean. In the mid-1600s, they were joined by Native American captives (among them, the wife of a Pequod chief). The practice flourished to such an extent that by the time British legislation finally abolished it in 1834, slaves made up more than half of the island's population.

The date the abolition decree was issued, August 1, continues to be marked island-wide. Known as Emancipation Day, it's a time for cricket matches, concerts, and, of course, Gombey dancing: a colorful form of self-expression, rooted in African tradition, that slave owners had banned. If you can't time your trip to coincide with the festivities, you can still bone up on the backstory by following the African Diaspora Heritage Trail. Affiliated with UNESCO's international Slave Route Project, it highlights sites related to the Bermudian slave trade.

Some of the trail's 11 stops are already tourist staples. For instance, in St. George's, the slave graveyard at St. Peter's Church is a designated site; as is Tucker House, where Joseph Rainey (the first black man to be elected to the U.S. House of Representatives) sat out the Civil War. Also on the list is the Commissioner's House at the Royal Naval Dockyard, which has an exhibit that vividly evokes the age of slavery through artifacts like iron shackles and glass trade beads.

Other sites are obscure, but nonetheless illuminating. Take Cobb's Hill Methodist Church in Warwick Parish. Dedicated in 1827, seven years before Emancipation, it was the first sanctuary in Bermuda built by and for blacks. Because they struggled to complete it in their rare off-hours (often working by candlelight!), the church is both a religious monument and a symbol of human resilience. For further details on the African Diaspora Heritage Trail, click on ⊕ *www.adht.net* or pick up a brochure at any visitor information center.

–Susan MacCallum-Whitcomb

St. David's Island. In a place famous for manicured lawns and well-tended gardens, St. David's Island feels comparatively wild. The island was long populated by fishermen, so it seems appropriate that one of the top attractions here is the **Black Horse Tavern** (⊠ *101 St. David's Rd.* ☎441/297–

1991), which specializes in seafood concoctions like shark hash and curried conch stew. However, the real highlight is—quite literally—**St. David's Lighthouse.** Built in 1879 of Bermuda stone and occupying the tallest point on the East End, this red-and-white striped lighthouse rises 208 feet above the sea, providing jaw-dropping views of St. George's, Castle Harbour, and the reef-rimmed south shore. Since operating hours at the lighthouse are subject to change, it's advisable to check with the **Park Ranger's Office** (☎*441/236–5902*) before visiting. ✉*St. George's Parish* 🎫*Free* ☉*Apr.–Oct., weekdays 8:30–5.*

★ ☺ **Verdmont.** Even if you think you've had your fill of old houses, Verdmont deserves a look. The National Trust property, which opened as a museum in 1956, is notable for its Georgian architecture. Yet what really sets this place apart is its pristine condition. Though used as a residence until the mid-20th century, virtually no structural changes were made to Verdmont since it was erected around 1710. Former owners never even added electricity or plumbing (so the "powder room" was strictly used for powdering wigs!). The house is also known for its enviable collection of antiques. Some pieces—such as the early-19th-century piano—were imported from England. However, most are 18th-century cedar, crafted by Bermudian cabinetmakers. A china coffee service, said to have been a gift from Napoléon to U.S. President James Madison, is also on display. The president never received it, since the ship bearing it across the Atlantic was seized by a privateer and brought to Bermuda. ✉*6 Verdmont La., off Collector's Hill, Smith's Parish* ☎*441/236–7369* ⊕*www.bnt.bm* 🎫*$5; $10 combination ticket with Bermuda National Trust Museum in Globe Hotel and Tucker House* ☉*Nov.–Mar., Wed.–Sat. 10–4; Apr.–Oct., Tues.–Sat. 10–4.*

Where to Eat

WORD OF MOUTH

"We have had dinner at Fourways, Waterlot, and Aqua. I would choose Aqua. You can request a table outside, and have a beautiful view—practically right on the water. Even if you want to be inside, you will still have a beautiful view. The food is wonderful!"

—1scs1

"The Speciality Inn on the Southshore has great breakfast and very cheap! Their banana pancakes are to die for!"

—Tanya

www.fodors.com/forums

Updated
by Sirkka
Huish

**WHAT'S INCREDIBLE ABOUT THE BERMUDA RESTAU-
RANT SCENE** isn't so much the number or high quality of
restaurants, but the sheer variety of ingredients and cuisines represented on the menus, especially considering that
Bermuda is such a tiny, secluded place. The island is host
to a medley of global cuisines—British, French, Italian,
Portuguese, American, Caribbean, Indian, Chinese, Japanese, and Thai—palatable reminders of Bermuda's history
of colonization. Many superior, well-funded independent
and resort restaurants attract a constant and steady stream
of internationally acclaimed chefs, assuring that the latest
techniques and trends are menu regulars. At the same time,
virtually all restaurant menus list traditional Bermudian
dishes and drinks, so you have the opportunity to taste
local specialties at almost any meal.

As you might expect, methods are not all that's imported.
Roughly 80% of Bermuda's food is flown or shipped in,
most of it from the United States. This explains why restaurant prices are often higher here than on the mainland. Nevertheless, there are a number of delicious local ingredients
that you should look for. At the top of the list is extraordinary seafood, like lobster (September through March),
crab, oysters, mussels, clams, red snapper, rockfish, tuna,
and wahoo. Additionally, many chefs work with local
growers to serve fresh, seasonal fruits and vegetables, such
as potatoes, carrots, leeks, tomatoes, corn, broccoli, and
Bermuda onions (one of the island's earliest exports); and
in the dessert department, strawberries, cherries, bananas,
and loquats (small yellow fruit used for preserves). Imports
notwithstanding, Bermudian cuisine really begins and ends
with local ingredients and traditional preparations, and
therein lies the island's culinary identity.

WHAT IT COSTS IN U.S. DOLLARS				
RESTAURANTS				
¢	$	$$	$$$	$$$$
under $10	$10–$20	$21–$30	$31–$40	over $40

KNOW-HOW

RESERVATIONS

Reservations are always a good idea. We mention them only when they're essential or not accepted. Book as far ahead as you can and reconfirm when you arrive, especially in high season. Many restaurants close—or curtail hours, or days of service—in the off-season, so call ahead before setting out for lunch or dinner.

DRESS

Bermuda has had a reputation for strict sartorial standards, but most of the mid-price restaurants are much more casual these days. In many of the pubs and bars in town you would not be out of place in shorts and a T-shirt. It's a different story in more upscale restaurants, often attached to the hotels. Even when not required, a jacket for men is rarely out of place. In our restaurant reviews, we mention dress only when men are required to wear either a jacket or a jacket and tie.

PRICES

Much harder to swallow than the delicious Bermuda fish chowder are the prices of dining out. Bermuda has never sought a reputation for affordability, and restaurants are no exception. A few greasy spoons serve standard North American fare (and a few local favorites) at a decent price, but by and large you should prepare for a bit of sticker shock. Don't be surprised if dinner for two with wine at one of the very top places—the Newport Room, for example—puts a $200–$300 dent in your pocket. A 15% service charge is almost always added to the bill "for your convenience."

HAMILTON & ENVIRONS

AFRICAN

$$–$$$ ✕**Café Cairo.** Experience the cuisine and ambience of North Africa at this relaxed restaurant. Boasting a menu of exotic flavors, this popular eatery shows Bermuda's culinary adventurous streak at its best, satisfying the well-traveled palates of both islanders and tourists. Specialties include Egyptian and Moroccan dishes; don't miss the hummus, kofta lamb and couscous, or the shish kebab. After your meal, settle in on the low-seated sofas and enjoy a pipe of sheesha (fruit tobacco) or Turkish coffee as belly dancers sashay around you. It's one of the few Front Street restaurants to serve food until the early hours of the morning,

and the place becomes a lively nightspot after 10. ✉*93 Front St., Hamilton* ☎*441/295–5155* ▱*AE, MC, V.*

AMERICAN

$$–$$$ ✕**Greg's Steakhouse.** A must for meat-lovers, Greg's is Bermuda's only steak house where you can tuck into certified Angus beef. Prepared to your liking, choose from filet mignon, T-bone, rib eye, or New York strip. The menu also offers plenty of international flair with fish, pasta, and vegetarian dishes. Watch the chefs prepare your food in the exhibition open-flame kitchen. The restaurant's bright and modern decor also features a bar and a more casual dining area on the first floor. Try the champagne Sunday brunch buffet for something different, and for those sweet tooths out there, the dessert menu is to die for! ✉*39 Church St., Hamilton* ☎*441/297–2333* ▱*AE, MC, V.*

ASIAN

$$–$$$ ✕**L'Oriental.** Located above its sister restaurant, Little Venice, this Asian hot spot is a favorite among locals for its fresh sushi bar. Take the footbridge—over an indoor stream—to the raised seating at the lively teppanyaki table where trained chefs stylishly slice, stir, and season your steak and veggies onto your plate. Home to several "Best of Bermuda Gold Awards," the menu includes traditional Asian soups and entrées and a variety of Indonesian and Thai dishes (don't miss the curries!), as well as nightly specials. Choose from a selection of wines, sakes, and Japanese beers to wash it all down. The backdrop of colorful dragons and a handcrafted pagoda add to the Asian flavor. L'Oriental's Take Out Express location is on the corner of Church and Par-La-Ville Road. ✉*32 Bermudiana Rd., Hamilton* ☎*441/296–4477* ▱*AE, MC, V* ⊘*No lunch weekends.*

BERMUDIAN

$$–$$$ ✕**Harley's.** Serene water views and gracious service com-
★ bine with top-notch Continental and Bermudian cuisine to make Harley's one of the best restaurants in Hamilton. Dry-aged beef is always cooked to perfection. Try slow-cooked prime rib or grilled porterhouse, along with Harley's Mash—potatoes with caramelized onion, butternut squash, and black trumpet mushrooms. As for fish, Harley's chefs prepare a wonderful Bermudian specialty: almond-crusted and banana-glazed baked rockfish, which might be accompanied by a pumpkin risotto and sweet-pepper sauce. If you prefer something vegetarian, try

hand-rolled cannelloni filled with ricotta cheese and grilled vegetables with a blackened-tomato coulis. The restaurant is bright and airy, and in summer, has the added bonus of a large outside canopy. ⊠*Fairmont Hamilton Princess Hotel, 76 Pitts Bay Rd., Hamilton* ☎*441/295–3000* ⊟*AE, DC, MC, V.*

2

$–$$ ✕**Bouchée.** Formerly known as Monty's, this once greasy spoon café has reinvented itself into a shiny new restaurant. It's worth the walk west out of Hamilton to see why this charming spot is a firm favorite with locals and tourists alike. The atmosphere is casual and the prices affordable. Recommended starters are crab cakes or fish chowder with sherry pepper sauce. For dinner, make the most of the local fish, cooked to your liking. What's more, you'll never go hungry as it's open all day, every day, serving breakfast, lunch, and dinner. The portions are a healthy size and the knowledgeable staff will keep you entertained. An easy-listening live duo also performs at dinner on Friday nights. ⊠*75 Pitts Bay Rd., near Woodburne Ave., Hamilton* ☎*441/295–5759* ⊟*AE, DC, MC, V.*

☺ $–$$ ✕**The Pickled Onion.** This former whiskey warehouse is now a lively restaurant serving creative, contemporary Bermudian cuisine, as well as a handful of Latin- and Asian-flavored dishes. Try the flame-seared tuna, dressed with avocado, tomato, and cilantro salsa. If it's beef you're after, they grill it to perfection here. For those lazy weekends, they also do a great all-day Sunday brunch. For dessert, go straight for Melanie's Bermuda banana bread with brûléed bananas. Then sample a martini or two on the veranda overlooking Front Street and the harbor. A live band playing Tuesday to Saturday, from April to December, and a great cocktail list makes this a fabulous spot to hang out after dinner, too. The pub has recently undergone a complete renovation and now has a New York City wine bar feel. ⊠*53 Front St., Hamilton* ☎*441/295–2263* ⊟*AE, MC, V.*

★ Fodor'sChoice ✕**Aggie's Garden & Waterside Café.** The charm
$ of this tiny restaurant is its location beside the water, just a few hundred yards from Hamilton. A brick stairway through fern-covered walls takes you to a harborside garden planted with herbs and flowers. The open kitchen—where cooking classes are taught at night—is on the harbor level of an old Bermuda home. The seating is mostly in the garden, with former church pews and umbrellas over the tables. The house and garden are quite an escape from

the surrounding office blocks, and businesspeople often come here for lunch. Some patrons even moor their boats along the dock and skip the stairs altogether. The creative, seasonal menu lists soups, sandwiches, and salads made with locally grown produce, as well as grilled local fish, free-range chicken, and homemade pizza with organic toppings. Daily sweets, such as ginger or oatmeal-nut cookies, and fresh-fruit tarts are perfect with a cup of fair-trade tea or coffee. ⊠*Falconer House, 108 Pitts Bay Rd., Hamilton* ☎*441/296–7346* ⊟*No credit cards* ⊘*No dinner.*

BRITISH

$–$$ ✕**Hog Penny Pub.** Veterans of London pub crawls may feel nostalgic at this dark, wood-filled watering hole off Front Street. Those die-hard aficionados of old-style British comfort food will adore the Yorkshire pudding, shepherd's pie, steak-and-kidney pie, fish-and-chips, and bangers and mash. You can work up an appetite just deciding from the impressive burger selection, and the British ale on tap will wash the food down nicely. This is Hamilton's oldest licensed establishment, opened in 1957. There's live, toe-tapping music most nights in summer and less frequently in winter. ⊠*5 Burnaby Hill, Hamilton* ☎*441/292–2534* ⊟*AE, DC, MC, V* ⊘*No lunch Sun.*

CARIBBEAN

$–$$ ✕**Spring Garden Restaurant & Bar.** If you've never had Barbadian, or as Barbados natives like to call it, "Bajan" food, come sit under the indoor palm tree and try panfried flying fish—a delicacy in Barbados. Another good choice is the broiled mahimahi served in creole sauce, with peas and rice. During lobster season, an additional menu appears, featuring steamed, broiled, or curried lobster ($35 for the complete dinner). For dessert, try coconut cream pie or raspberry-mango cheesecake. ⊠*19 Washington Lane, off Reid St., Hamilton* ☎*441/295–7416* ⊟*AE, MC, V* ⊘*Closed Sun. Nov.–Apr. No lunch Sun. May–Oct.*

CHINESE

☾ $–$$ ✕**Chopsticks.** The menu here is a mix of Szechuan, Hunan, Cantonese, and Thai favorites. Top Chinese choices include beef with vegetables in ginger sauce, sweet-and-spicy chicken, and sweet-and-sour fish. For Thai tastes, try beef with onion, scallions, and basil in hot chili sauce, or shrimp *panang* (in coconut-curry sauce). The food is good, but you won't get U.S. prices or portions. ⊠*88 Reid St., Hamilton* ☎*441/292–0791* ⊟*AE, MC, V.*

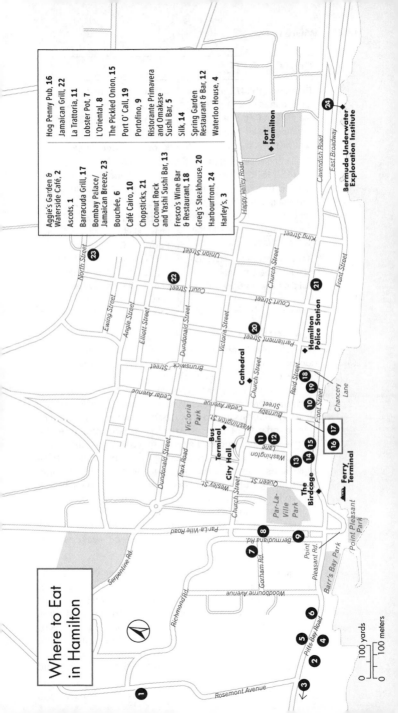

Where to Eat in Hamilton

Aggie's Garden & Waterside Café, **2**
Ascots, **1**
Barracuda Grill, **17**
Bombay Palace/Jamaican Breeze, **23**
Bouchée, **6**
Café Cairo, **10**
Chopsticks, **21**
Coconut Rock and Yashi Sushi Bar, **13**
Fresco's Wine Bar & Restaurant, **18**
Greg's Steakhouse, **20**
Harbourfront, **24**
Harley's, **3**

Hog Penny Pub, **16**
Jamaican Grill, **22**
La Trattoria, **11**
Lobster Pot, **7**
L'Oriental, **8**
The Pickled Onion, **15**
Port O' Call, **19**
Portofino, **9**
Ristorante Primavera and Omakase Sushi Bar, **5**
Silk, **14**
Spring Garden Restaurant & Bar, **12**
Waterloo House, **4**

QUICK BITES

Delicious (☎441/295–5890), located inside the Washington Mall on Reid Street, offers a—you guessed it—delicious sandwich.

Cheap and cheerful **H20** (☎441/295–4903), inside the Hamilton Pharmacy on Parliament Street, is a good spot for a good burger. There are sandwiches, too, and the service is fast.

Kathy's Kaffee (☎441/295–5203), in the Emporium Building next to Bank of

Butterfield on Front Street, serves robust breakfasts and satisfying lunches at reasonable prices.

Kentucky Fried Chicken (☎441/296–4532) on Queen Street between Front and Reid is always busy. Bring cash: they don't take plastic.

Watch your waistline with a tasty salad or sandwich from **Paradiso Café** (☎441/295–3263) on Reid Street. But be warned, this place is popular, and you'll probably have to wait for a table.

CONTINENTAL

★ Fodor's Choice ✕**Ascots.** In an elegant former mansion just out-
$$$–$$$$ side downtown Hamilton, Ascots gives you a wonderful excuse for leaving the city. When weather permits, meals are served on the covered terrace, with its stone fountain, or on the front veranda, as well as indoors. You can assemble at the handsome cedar bar before and after meals. The high standards of owners Angelo Armano and Edmund Smith—the chef and manager, respectively—result in creative and seasonal menu offerings that incorporate fresh ingredients from local farmers and fishermen. You might find grilled grouper on panfried potatoes with spinach-and-crab rolls, or pan-seared lamb chops with vegetable risotto. An extensive wine list is available to complement your meal. ⊠ *Royal Palms Hotel, 24 Rosemont Ave., Pembroke Parish* ☎441/295–9644 ⊟*AE, MC, V* ☉*No lunch weekends.*

ECLECTIC

$ ✕**Coconut Rock and Yashi Sushi Bar.** Whether you're in the mood for shrimp tempura and sashimi served in a quiet room with black lacquer tables and paper lanterns, or you would rather have chicken chimichanga, fried tiger shrimp, or grilled sirloin steak surrounded by loud music videos on multiple screens at a popular nighttime venue—or if you want a little of both—these adjoining restaurants can satisfy. The underground restaurant is dark and dingy and remains well hidden beneath Hamilton's main shopping street. But it's an old favorite with locals, and the fusion of different flavors and good-size portions make it worth the wait for a table. ✉ *Williams House, downstairs, 20 Reid St., Hamilton* ☎ *441/292–1043* ▤ *AE, MC, V.*

FRENCH

$$$–$$$$ ✕ **Waterloo House.** This restaurant and small hotel in a for-
★ mer private house on Hamilton Harbour serves traditional Continental specialties, such as lamb and veal, plus a number of Bermudian dishes, including just-off-the-boat fish. The menu changes every day, and you can't go wrong with any choice. Fish can be grilled or panfried upon request. Anton Mosimann of Horizons is the restaurant's consultant chef. You can dine either on the waterside patio (in good weather) or in the more formal dining room, with its deep-raspberry walls, rich chintzes, and attractive lighting. Fodors.com users are full of praise for the menu, but have criticized the slow service. ✉ *100 Pitts Bay Rd., Hamilton* ☎ *441/295–4480 Jacket and tie after 6 pm* ▤ *AE, MC, V.*

INDIAN

$ ✕ **Bombay Palace/Jamaican Breeze.** This small eatery features two restaurants in one. Chef Nanak Chand of Bombay Palace whips up northern Indian cuisine and items cooked in the tandoor oven, whereas Jamaican Breeze offers traditional Jamaican food and natural juices. On a sunny day you may find Jamaican Chef Huntley Septimus—who is also a locally renowned musician—working up some tasty jerk chicken on the outdoor barbecue. He won't bite, so be sure to ask for a sample. Then grab a table in the relaxed dining room, or if the weather permits, sit on the outside patio. A delicious lunch buffet featuring favorites from both cuisines is offered every day for $12.95. Takeout is also available. ✉ *60 North St., Hamilton* ☎ *441/296–4094* ▤ *AE, MC, V* ⊘ *Closed Sun.*

ITALIAN

$$–$$$ ✕ **Ristorante Primavera and Omakase Sushi Bar.** High-backed, elegant banquettes and crisp, white tablecloths set the scene for delicious Italian meals delivered with superlative service. Those hankering for authentic Italian classics will love the beef carpaccio with Parmesan and pesto over arugula, and the *vongole al vino bianco* (baby clams sautéed with white wine, garlic, and parsley). Other excellent pastas here include the *penne al gorgonzola e noci* (penne sautéed with Gorgonzola and walnuts) and the *ravioli neri*

(black ravioli) filled with lobster meat and served in a light, pink sauce. The sushi bar, Omakase, is upstairs, but you may order from downstairs as well. Delicacies include the Bermuda maki roll stuffed with crabmeat, avocado, and cucumber. Several vegetarian rolls, stuffed with asparagus or shiitake, are also on the menu. Worth every mouthful is the all-you-can-eat sushi bar special on Tuesday evenings. ✉ *69 Pitts Bay Rd., Hamilton* ☎ *441/295–2167* ⊟ *AE, MC, V* ⊘ *No lunch weekends.*

$–$$ ✕ **La Trattoria.** Tucked away in a Hamilton alley, you can't go wrong with this no-nonsense trattoria, which is pleasant and unpretentious. Any of the pastas, such as lasagna, manicotti, and spaghetti with mixed seafood, can be served in smaller portions as appetizers. Fish fillets are generally panfried with olive oil, garlic, and herbs. La Trattoria's pizzas are cooked in Bermuda's only brick wood-burning pizza oven. About 20 inventive topping combinations (such as arugula and prosciutto) are on the menu, but the chef will mix and match whatever you like. ✉ *22 Washington Lane, Hamilton* ☎ *441/295–1877* ⊟ *AE, MC, V* ⊘ *No lunch Sun.*

☾ **$–$$** ✕ **Portofino.** Bermuda's scaled down version of Ocean Avenue in South Beach, this is the place to see and be seen on a hot summer night. The outside dining area is bustling most evenings, especially Friday, so arrive early. Inside, you'll be transported to Italy with little shuttered windows and traditional brick walls covered in pictures from the family album. Start with calamari or garlic bread, the two starters the restaurant is renowned for. The pizzas are the best, and we especially favor the pepperoni and artichoke variety. The Bistecca and the fettuccine Alfredo pasta are delicious. Prices and portions are good, too. A separate take-out section with its own entrance means you can get the good food while avoiding people-watchers. If it's busy, be prepared to wait. ✉ *20 Bermudiana Rd., off Front St., Hamilton* ☎ *441/292–2375 or 441/295–6090* ⊟ *AE, MC, V* ⊘ *No lunch weekends.*

JAMAICAN

$–$$ ✕ **Jamaican Grill.** Journey outside the familiar city limits to Court Street and you'll find Jamaican food at its best. The owners are proud of their Jamaican heritage and want everyone to taste the Caribbean flavors with them. Classics like jerk and curry chicken, escovitched fish, hot wings, rice and beans, dumplings, and meat and veggie patties adorn

THE DISH ON LOCAL DISHES

Shark hash made of minced shark meat sautéed with spices may not sound too appetizing but it's a popular Bermudian appetizer, usually served on toast.

Bermudians love codfish cakes—made of salted cod mashed with cooked potatoes and fresh thyme and parsley, then shaped into a patty and panfried. They taste great topped with a zesty fruit salsa and a side of mesclun salad.

The island's traditional weekend brunch is a huge plate of boiled or steamed salt cod with boiled potatoes, onions, and sliced bananas, all topped with a hard-boiled egg or tomato sauce, and, sometimes, avocado slices.

Cassava pie—a savory blend of cassava, eggs, sugar, and either pork or chicken—is a rich, flavorful dish (formerly reserved for Christmas dinner) often offered as a special side. More common is mussel pie, made of shelled mussels, potatoes, and onions, baked and seasoned with thyme, parsley, and curry.

As for Bermudian desserts, bananas baked in rum and brown sugar are to die for and loquat or banana crumble is sweet and rich.

the menu. Be sure to order Jamaica's own Ting grapefruit drink to wash down the tasty homemade cakes and cookies. It's no-frills food, but the prices are good and the takeout service makes for a great beach picnic. ⊠*32 Court St., Hamilton* ☎*441/296–6577* ⊟*MC, V* ⊘*Closed Sun.*

MEDITERRANEAN

$$–$$$ ✕**Fresco's Wine Bar & Restaurant.** This cozy restaurant
★ is tucked away, but well worth discovering for the way it mixes Mediterranean cuisine with a hint of Bermuda. Fresco's is known for its homemade pasta, seafood, and vegetarian specialties; consider the *tarte Provençal* (roasted vegetables and caramelized onions in a freshly baked pastry crust), panfried yellowtail snapper with zucchini-lime couscous and sweet red-pepper reduction, or lobster medallions roasted with vanilla. At lunch, ask for a table in the courtyard. With the fountain, palms, and flowers it's just like being in Europe. Before or after dinner, you can swirl a glass of *rosso* (red wine) beneath the vaulted ceiling of the wine bar, which boasts Bermuda's largest selection of wines by the glass. ⊠*Chancery Lane, off Front St., Hamilton* ☎*441/295–5058* ⌁*Reservations essential* ⊟*AE, MC, V* ⊘*No lunch weekends.*

$$-$$$ ✕ **Harbourfront.** When you dine at a table beside the enor-
★ mous open windows at Harbourfront, you might feel as
though you were floating on the harbor yourself. Nearly
every seat in the house has beautiful views of the quiet
waters. Few Bermuda restaurants have menus as long
and wide-ranging as this busy spot, where sushi is served
alongside Continental and Mediterranean specialties. For
lunch, you might have a good burger, a salad, or a couple
of sushi rolls. For dinner, start with calamari or carpaccio,
followed by lobster, buffalo steak, rack of lamb, or any of
the excellent pastas. Sushi devotees can order miso soup,
tempura, and sushi platters. Businesspeople and BUEI
(Bermuda Underwater Exploration Institute) visitors alike
partake of the delicious seafood. ⊠*Bermuda Underwater
Exploration Institute (BUEI), East Broadway, Hamilton*
☎*441/292–6122* ⊟*AE, MC, V* ⊘*Closed Sun.*

SEAFOOD

$$$-$$$$ ✕ **Barracuda Grill.** The tastefully decorated contemporary
dining room—mahogany-framed chairs and banquettes,
soft-gold lights over the tables—is reminiscent of sophis-
ticated big-city restaurants, and the food that comes to the
table is created by a culinary team dedicated to excellence.
The island-style fish chowder and the steak-and-tomato
salad with blue cheese and roasted garlic in balsamic vin-
aigrette are two good ways to start your meal. Moving on
to entrées, you might try roasted salmon with caramelized
onion, smoked bacon, and white-bean cassoulet; classically
prepared rack of Australian lamb; or rigatoni Bolognese.
If you save room for dessert, opt for the chocolate-banana
bread pudding or perhaps the chocolate fondue for two.
There's also a great cocktail bar to sit at while you wait
for your table. And if you're looking for a romantic dinner,
reserve the "snug corner," which is a table for two, tucked
away out of sight of other diners. ⊠*5 Burnaby Hill, Hamil-
ton* ☎*441/292–1609* ⊟*AE, MC, V* ⊘*No lunch weekends.*

★ **Fodor'sChoice** ✕ **Port O' Call.** Resembling the interior of a yacht,
$$-$$$ Port O' Call is a popular little restaurant. It's one of the few
ground-level dining spots on Front Street, with an outdoor
dining area reminiscent of a European sidewalk café. Fresh
local fish—such as wahoo, tuna, grouper, and snapper—is
cooked perfectly, and the preparations are creative. Con-
sider the pan-roasted snapper, the seafood stir-fry, or the
sesame-crusted tuna. ⊠*87 Front St., Hamilton* ☎*441/295–
5373* ⊟*AE, DC, MC, V* ⊘*No lunch weekends.*

2

☺ **\$\$** ✕**Lobster Pot.** Bermudians swear by this spot, where the maritime-theme dining room is filled with brass nautical gear, lobster traps, and sun-bleached rope. The fresh local lobster, available September through March, is most requested next to yellowtail or rockfish with bananas and almonds, all local favorites. The "Cup Match Special" is everything locals love about fried seafood dinners: crispy fish strips on a bun with a decent helping of coleslaw and fries. If you're looking for a good deal, there's also a limited-availability three-course set meal for about \$20. ✉6 *Bermudiana Rd., Hamilton* ☎*441/292–6898* ▭*AE, MC, V* ⊘*No lunch weekends.*

THAI

\$\$ ✕**Silk.** This culinary and aesthetic gem offers a unique Thai experience with a picturesque harbor view. One step inside the restaurant transports you into an authentically Asian environment. The colorful, trendy hangout is Bermuda's only Thai restaurant. The team of chefs from the Shangri-La restaurant in Bangkok concentrate more on taste than presentation. Menu options include plenty of Thai curries and noodle dishes. Don't miss the *Yam Ped Yang* (duck and mango salad) or *Ba-Miii Thalay* (fried noodles). Weather permitting you should dine on the covered patio for a superb view of Front Street and Hamilton Harbor. ✉*Masters Bldg., 55 Front St., Hamilton* ☎*441/295–0449* ▭*AE, MC, V* ⊘*Closed Sun. No lunch Sat.*

ST. GEORGE'S

BRITISH

\$\$–\$\$\$ ✕**Carriage House.** Hearty British fare is the daily bread at the Carriage House, an attractive slice of the restored Somers Wharf area. Try to secure a table outside on the patio or inside by a window so you can watch the action on the harbor. This is the place to tuck into roast prime rib, cut to order tableside, or roast leg of lamb with rosemary. But don't overlook the fresh Bermuda fish, like panfried wahoo in lemon-butter sauce. Sunday the Carriage House lays out a generous brunch buffet that includes champagne, while a pianist plays background music. Afternoon tea with all the trimmings is served daily except Sunday. On Friday and Saturday nights, a jazz combo entertains. ✉*Somers Wharf, Water St.* ☎*441/297–1270 or 441/297–1730* ▭*AE, DC, MC, V.*

ITALIAN

○ $-$$ ✕**Cafe Gió.** This is waterside dining at its best with great views of St. George's Harbor. It's not unusual to see hungry boaters pull up and tie their vessels alongside the restaurant's sundeck. The popular spot offers tasty Italian cuisine, with the addition of a few Asian dishes, in a pleasant, romantic setting. The fettuccine is good and the Caesar salad is great. ✉*36 Water St.* ☎*441/297–1307* ▭*MC, V.*

ELSEWHERE IN THE PARISHES

THE CENTRAL PARISHES

AMERICAN

$$-$$$ ✕**Blu Bar & Grill.** This is a great spot for lunch or dinner with impressive views across the golf course and out to the sea. There's standard American cuisine, including steaks and ribs, but the eclectic chefs like to add bold flavors with lots of exotic herbs and spices. The wide variety of fresh seafood is your best bet. Follow up your fish chowder with lobster, yellowfin tuna, rockfish, snapper, or wahoo. ✉*Belmont Hill Golf Course, 97 Middle Rd., Warwick Parish* ☎*441/232–2323* ▭*AE, MC, V.*

BERMUDIAN

★ **Fodor's**Choice ✕**Horizons.** The dining room at Horizons cot-
$$$$ tage colony is one of Bermuda's most elegant, and reservations can be difficult to secure even weeks in advance. Chef Anton Mosimann's delicate, healthful, fusion cuisine brings the world's rich, famous, and trim to his table. Dinner is a five-course, prix-fixe (around $45) affair with a menu that changes nightly but may include vegetable terrine with basil oil and tomato coulis, and roasted snapper over sun-dried tomato polenta. The staff is, naturally, impeccably trained, swift, and discreet. You can linger over coffee on the terrace and listen to the sounds of the local tree frogs. ✉*Horizons & Cottages, 33 S. Shore Rd., Paget Parish* ☎*441/236–0048* ⌂*Reservations essential. Jacket and tie* ▭*AE, MC, V.*

$$$-$$$$ ✕**Aqua.** Everything about Aqua is wonderfully romantic.
★ Set on the island's southern coast, it has spectacular views overlooking a lovely beach and the endless Atlantic Ocean. Enjoy an unforgettable alfresco dining experience at one of the many tables on the large, covered deck, right next to the waves, or savor the view from the warmth of the dining

2

room. The colors inside emulate the turquoise and deep-blue hues of the ocean. Blue glassware complements the white tablecloths, the white-wood beams, and slate flooring of the porch. The varied and ever-changing menu takes you on a journey through Europe, the Far East, and the Caribbean. For starters, the sugar-cured beef carpaccio on roasted peppers with cashews and parsnip chips is beyond compare. Seafood addicts should go for the panfried scallops on arugula. The choices of delectable entrées make a decision difficult: tandoori-spiced rack of lamb with citrus yogurt on cumin flat bread is a winner, as is panfried snapper on soba noodles with pickled-ginger sauce. Aqua is sometimes closed for lunch in winter. ⊠*Ariel Sands Hotel, 34 S. Shore Rd., Devonshire Parish* ☎*441/236–2332* ▭*AE, DC, MC, V.*

★ $$$ ✕**Seahorse Grill.** A chic, enduring restaurant with minimalist Bermuda stone walls and wood-beam interiors, Seahorse is a perennial favorite of local hipsters and professionals. The ever-changing menu showcases locally grown produce and fresh Bermuda fish prepared in a light, contemporary style with a nod to island tastes. On the menu, ingredients are described in detail, with even their geographic origins named. If it's listed, try the baked Caesar salad and anchovy tempura for an appetizer, and the seafood paella for a main course. The service can be island-time, so come prepared to linger between courses. Sunday brunch is divine. ⊠*Elbow Beach Hotel, 60 S. Shore Rd., Paget Parish* ☎*441/239–6885 or 441/236–3535* ▭*AE, MC, V.*

$$–$$$ ✕**Palms.** A low-key and romantic hideaway, this is the per-
★ fect place to escape the world. Dining can be outside by the pool overlooking the ocean or in the plant-filled garden dining room, with its wall of French doors that open to the outside. The menu is not extensive, but the dishes listed are all creative and flavorful. Popular appetizers include goat cheese, leek, and apple tart with saffron sauce, and fresh-vegetable-and-shrimp spring roll with savory Asian-style sauce. When it's available, go for the signature rockfish entrée, cooked in a sumptuous blend of coconut curry and served with stir-fried vegetables. Another good entrée is the classic duck à l'orange. Desserts are worth every calorie—two of the best are the rum cake with rum-and-raisin ice cream and the crème brûlée of the day. ⊠*Surf Side Beach Club, 90 S. Shore Rd., Paget Parish* ☎*441/236–7100* ▭*AE, MC, V* ⊗*Closed Jan. and Feb.*

CONTINENTAL

$$$–$$$$ ✕ **Fourways Inn.** Fourways has risen to preeminence as much
★ for its lovely 17th-century surroundings as for its reliable
cuisine. The elegant yet charming interior, with mahogany
banisters, burgundy carpeting, impressionist prints, and
silver-and-crystal table settings, evokes the image of a fine
French manor. Traditional Continental dishes, such as veal
scaloppine and roast duck, are beautifully presented and
delicious. A pianist adds to the leisurely dining style. Be
sure to visit the on-site "Peg Leg" bar for a step back in
time. And definitely don't forget to stop in the on-site pas-
try shop, the chocolate-dipped strawberries are a must. ⊠ *1
Middle Rd., Paget Parish* ☎ *441/236–6517 Jacket required*
▤ *AE, MC, V.*

ITALIAN

$$–$$$ ✕ **Lido Restaurant.** On the beachfront terrace at the Elbow
★ Beach Hotel, with waves breaking just below, Café Lido
is often invoked as one of the island's most romantic set-
tings. You could easily just stare out the window all eve-
ning. Food and service are top notch to give you a truly
memorable dining experience. Items to try: the Angus rib-
eye steak, Bermuda lobster, and the succulent roasted lamb.
Dance off the desserts at the Elbow Beach complex disco,
the Deep. It's best to reserve a table, but regardless, the
place gets crowded and sometimes feels like you're on top
of the other diners. ⊠ *Elbow Beach Hotel, 60 S. Shore Rd.,
Paget Parish* ☎ *441/236–9884* ⚑ *Reservations essential*
▤ *AE, MC, V* ⊘ *No lunch.*

THE WESTERN PARISHES

AMERICAN

$$–$$$ ✕ **Wickets Brasserie.** Simple but satisfying Italian and Ameri-
can fare and prompt service make this cricket-theme restau-
rant a great spot for families. You can find all the classics:
salads, burgers, sandwiches, pastas, and pizza as well as
good fish-and-chips, chicken cacciatore, and grilled steak.
End your meal on a sweet note with delicious tiramisu and
chocolate-crunch cheesecake. The casual restaurant offers
all-day dining with great pool and ocean views. ⊠ *Fairmont
Southampton Resort, 101 S. Shore Rd., Southampton Par-
ish* ☎ *441/239–6969* ▤ *AE, DC, MC, V* ⊘ *Closed Jan.*

BERMUDIAN

$$$$ ✕**Coconuts.** Nuzzled between high cliff rocks and a pristine private beach on the southern coast, this outdoor restaurant is one of the best places to nab that table overlooking the ocean. The view is made even more dramatic at night by floodlights. The menu changes often, but you can always be sure of fresh, local produce, and fish prepared with a mix of contemporary Bermudian and international culinary styles. A fixed price of about $65 (including 15% gratuity) includes four courses at dinner. A simpler, less-expensive lunch menu includes daily specials, burgers, sandwiches, and salads. ✉*The Reefs, 56 S. Shore Rd., Southampton Parish* ☎*441/238–0222* ⚄*Reservations essential* ▭*AE, MC, V* ⊘*Closed Nov.–Apr.*

★ **Fodor'sChoice** ✕**Waterlot Inn.** This graceful, two-story manor
$$$$ house, which dates from 1670 and once functioned as a bed-and-breakfast, now holds one of Bermuda's most elegant and elaborate restaurants. The service is impeccable, with waiters that have just enough island exuberance to take the edge off their European-style training. Nestled in Jew's Bay, the restaurant also offers breathtaking sunset views. The Bermudian–Continental menu changes every season, but always offers an excellent fish chowder. Seafood ravioli is another stellar appetizer choice. Grilled fish-of-the-day over a plate of local, colorful vegetables makes a perfect main course. Decadent desserts, like profiteroles in sweet vanilla cream, round off an extremely satisfying meal. The restaurant is also known for its fine wine list and its cigar selection. ✉*Fairmont Southampton Hotel, 101 S. Shore Rd., Southampton Parish* ☎*441/239–6967 Jacket required* ▭*AE, DC, MC, V* ⊘*Closed Jan.–mid-Mar. No lunch.*

$–$$ ✕**Traditions.** Eat like a local. Fresh caught fish with crispy french fries, creamy homemade mac and cheese, or mushy peas and rice are just a few of the hearty home-cooked local favorites waiting for you here on the West End of the island. You can also find the typical hamburgers, sandwiches, etc., but that would be depriving your taste buds of some good home cooking. ✉*2 Middle Rd., Sandys* ☎*441/234–3770* ▭*AE, MC, V* ⊘*Closed Sun.*

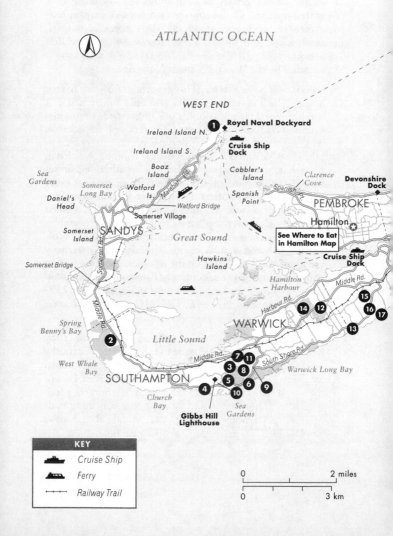

Where to Eat in the Parishes

ATLANTIC OCEAN

WEST END

Ireland Island N.

Royal Naval Dockyard ❶

Cruise Ship Dock

Ireland Island S.

Sea Gardens

Boaz Island

Cobbler's Island

Clarence Cove

Devonshire Dock

Daniel's Head

Somerset Long Bay

Watford Is.

Watford Bridge

Spanish Point

Malabar Rd.

PEMBROKE

Hamilton ✈

See Where to Eat in Hamilton Map

Somerset Village

Somerset Island

SANDYS

Great Sound

Hawkins Island

Cruise Ship Dock

Somerset Bridge

Spring Benny's Bay ❷

Little Sound

Hamilton Harbour

Harbour Rd.

Middle Rd.

WARWICK

❶⓭ ❶⓬

⓯

⓰ ⓱

⓭

West Whale Bay

Middle Rd.

❼ ⓫

❸ ❽

❺ ❻ ❾

South Shore Rd.

Warwick Long Bay

SOUTHAMPTON

❹ ❺ ❿

Church Bay

Gibbs Hill Lighthouse

Sea Gardens

KEY	
🚢	*Cruise Ship*
⛴	*Ferry*
┼─┼	*Railway Trail*

0		2 miles
0		3 km

Aqua, **18**	Henry VIII, **5**	Seahorse Grill, **17**
Bacci, **3**	Horizons, **15**	The Specialty Inn, **20**
Black Horse Tavern, **23**	Lido Restaurant, **16**	Swizzle Inn, **21**
Blu Bar and Grill, **12**	Lighthouse Tea Room, **10**	Tio Pepe, **9**
Café Gio, **25**	Newport Room, **8**	Tom Moore's Tavern, **22**
Carriage House, **24**	North Rock Brewing Company, **19**	Traditions, **2**
Coconuts, **4**	Palms, **13**	Waterlot Inn, **7**
Fourways Inn, **14**		Whaler Inn, **6**
Frog & Onion Pub, **1**		Wickets Brasserie, **11**

CLOSE UP

Picnic Perfect

Ditch your proper place settings for a little sea breeze with that sandwich.

With verdant open spaces sprinkled with shady poinciana trees, the **Botanical Gardens**, on Middle Road in Paget, make a peaceful inland setting for a picnic. The gardens have a few picnic tables and plenty of benches, plus spacious lawns where you can spread a blanket. Bring your own supplies as there's no on-site café.

Clearwater Beach in St. David's is one of Bermuda's nicest picnic spots, with tables near to and on the beach. You can pick up picnic supplies at the grocery store about ¼-mi away or order lunch to go from one of St. David's casual eateries.

Just west of popular Warwick Long Bay, tiny, tranquil **Jobson** **Cove** beach is backed by the dramatic cliffs and greenery of South Shore Park. There are no tables and no snack bars, and often no people—perfect for a private picnic on the sand.

If you want a tried-and-tested picnic spot, head to **John Smith's Bay** in Smith's Parish. The wooden picnic tables beneath the trees make it a popular spot for locals. Get there early if you want a good spot overlooking the beach.

Adjacent to a Bermuda Audubon Society nature reserve, **Somerset Long Bay Park** in Sandys has a semicircular beach, fluffy spruce trees, and shallow water. It's also a terrific place for birding: it borders on an Audubon Society sanctuary. You can find tables under the trees near the beach, and a grocery store less than ½-mi away.

BRITISH

$$–$$$ ✕**Henry VIII.** As popular with locals as it is with vacationers from nearby Southampton resorts, the lively Henry VIII sports an Old English charm that stops just short of "wench" waitresses and Tudor styling. It's a bit pricey for what you get, but you can find a mix of English and Bermudian menu favorites, including steak-and-kidney pie, rack of lamb, and fish chowder. Save room for the sticky toffee pudding. Sometimes a strolling singer serenades diners. After dinner you can move along to the bar for a round of calypso. The outdoor tables have compelling views of the southern coast. There's live entertainment nightly from DJs and singers in season, and Sundays (when there's also a weekly brunch) are always popular with locals. ✉69 S.

Shore Rd., Southampton Parish ☎441/238–1977 ☰AE, MC, V.

C $-$$ ✕**Frog & Onion Pub.** This is a pub lover's dream with everything on the menu named after old English pubs. The food is good, as is the ale and the atmosphere. With its vaulted limestone ceilings and thick walls, the former Royal Naval Dockyard warehouse is a fitting place for this nautically decorated pub and its large poolroom. The food caters to every palate, from hearty English pub fare and light European dishes to a selection of fresh local fish plates. Fodors.com users love the bangers and mash, the Argus Bank fish sandwich, panfried local rockfish or tuna, and the Frog & Onion burger. There's a children's game room and a gift shop where you can purchase hot toddy mix. ✉*The Cooperage, Dockyard* ☎441/234–2900 ☰AE, MC, V.

c ✕**Lighthouse Tea Room.** At the base of Gibbs Hill Lighthouse, in the old home of the former lighthouse keeper, this adorable little teahouse is the perfect place to rest after the climb up and down the tower's 185 spiraling steps. You can find expertly blended black teas and unusual herbal teas, such as dandelion and juniper berry, served iced as well as hot. A lunch menu lists homemade soups and sandwiches, smoked trout and pork pie with chutney, and a range of refreshing fruit smoothies. For dessert, try the fresh banana cake or gingerbread with lemon sauce. Dinner on Friday and Saturday, which is by reservation only, boasts a weekly changing menu, and breakfast is served daily. This is also a popular spot to enjoy romantic sunsets. ✉*68 St. Anne's Rd., Southampton Parish* ☎441/238–8679 ☰AE, MC, V ⊗*No dinner Dec.–Apr.*

FRENCH

★ **Fodor'sChoice** ✕**Newport Room.** Glistening teak and models of $$$$ victorious America's Cup yachts give this fine restaurant a nautical theme. Each dish is beautifully presented, matching the clientele, which is made up of Bermuda's elite. The menu changes every season and the chef works with as much local produce as possible. Appetizers of Scottish smoked salmon, carved tableside, or Hudson Valley foie gras with a port sauce will send the taste buds soaring. But it's the entrées that really shine. You might have pan-seared Arctic char and bay scallops in a lobster-vanilla sauce, or black angus beef tenderloin with tomato tart, foie-gras mousse, and Madeira jus. For dessert, try the soufflé of the day or the ginger-and-lime crème brûlée with pineapple spears and red-currant frozen yogurt. ⊠*Fairmont Southampton Resort, 101 S. Shore Rd., Southampton Parish* ☎*441/239–6964 Jacket and tie* ⊟*AE, DC, MC, V* ⊗*Closed Jan. No lunch.*

ITALIAN

$$–$$$ ✕**Bacci.** A winning combination of authentic Italian cuisine with fine dining is what you can find at Bacci. On the upper floor of the gold clubhouse, the restaurant is decorated in bright and bold colors with impressive golf course views. Bacci celebrates all that is great about Italy and the chefs are not afraid to experiment with the latest cooking trends. The menu combines traditional and modern Italian recipes with many dishes low in fat and carbohydrates. Make sure you leave room for dessert—there's a selection of more than 10 different gelatos and sorbets. It's a great place for families during the day, but at night the lights are dimmed and candles are lighted to create a more romantic atmosphere. ⊠*Fairmont Southampton Resort, 101 S. Shore Rd., Southampton Parish* ☎*441/238–2555* ⚭*Reservations essential* ⊟*AE, MC, V* ⊗*No lunch.*

☾ $–$$ ✕**Tio Pepe.** You don't have to spend much money for healthy portions of home-style cooking at this Italian restaurant with a Mexican name. The easygoing atmosphere makes it an ideal stop for bathers returning from a day at nearby Horseshoe Bay Beach—just grab a seat at one of the plastic tables on the porch and get ready to chow down. The pizzas are worth every bite (they're freshly made with superb sauces) and there's an extensive list of comforting, classic Italian dishes, including lasagna and spaghetti. ⊠*117 S. Shore Rd., Southampton Parish* ☎*441/238–1897 or 441/238–0572* ⊟*AE, MC, V.*

SEAFOOD

★ Fodor's Choice ✕**Whaler Inn.** From your table overlooking the
$$$–$$$$ crashing surf, you can sometimes see fishing boats offshore, catching the seafood for this restaurant's next meals. The Whaler Inn is one of the top seafood restaurants on the island, serving only the freshest of fish delivered daily by local fishermen. The grilled Bermuda seafood triangle of tuna and swordfish fillets, and shrimp on sugarcane brochette, each with a different sauce, gives the palate plenty to savor. If you prefer landside fare, go for the grilled pork chop with pumpkin-and-potato mash, or chicken breast stuffed with goat cheese and sun-dried tomatoes accompanied with corn risotto and spiced pineapple coulis. Des-

Where to Take Tea

When afternoon arrives, Bermuda, like Britain, pauses for tea. Usually, tea is served between 3 and 5, but teatime can mean anything from an urn or thermos and cookies sitting on a sideboard, to the more formal stiff-pinkie-presentation of brewed-to-order tea in a porcelain or silver teapot, served with cream and sugar on a tray, and accompanied by finger sandwiches and scones with clotted cream and jam.

Elbow Beach Hotel (✉Paget Parish ☎441/236–3535) takes tea in the lobby. The $20 charge includes everything from cucumber and egg-and-tomato sandwiches to pound cake and French pastries.

Fairmont Hamilton Princess (✉Hamilton ☎441/295–3000 or 800/441–1414) serves a posh afternoon tea in its Heritage Court, adjacent to the lobby and Japanese Koi pond. Fine Eastern teas are brought to your Italian linen–covered table in shining

silver teapots and poured into delicate Belgian china. The cost is $11 for tea, miniature sandwiches, and cakes.

Lighthouse Tea Room (✉Southampton Parish ☎441/238–8679) has imported and special tea blends served with panoramic views at the hilltop. A pot of tea costs $8.

Waterloo House (✉Hamilton ☎441/295–4480) serves a very proper English high tea. In summer, tea-takers sip from their cups in the coolness of the ocean breeze on the harborside terrace. A pot of tea costs $7 for nonhotel guests.

The **Willowbank** (✉Sandys Parish ☎441/234–1616) tearoom features a slightly ersatz collection of Victorian memorabilia. High tea arrives on a triple-tiered china tray and at $13.50 for nonguests, it's one of the better tea deals on the island.

serts, such as the coconut-and-chocolate-brownie sundae, are unforgettable. The restaurant closes for one month in winter, usually January. ✉*Fairmont Southampton Resort, 101 S. Shore Rd., Southampton Parish* ☎*441/239–6968* ▤*AE, DC, MC, V* ⊘*No lunch Nov.–Mar.*

THE EASTERN PARISHES

BERMUDIAN

★ Fodor'sChoice ✕**Tom Moore's Tavern.** In a house that dates
$$$$ from 1652, Tom Moore's Tavern has a colorful past,
thanks to the Irish poet for whom it's named. Tom Moore
visited friends here frequently in 1804 and caused a scandal by writing odes to a local woman who was already
married. Today, fireplaces, casement windows, and ship-
builders' cedar joinery capture a sense of history that in no
way interferes with the fresh, light, and innovative cuisine.
Broiled scampi, Bermuda lobster (in season), and sautéed-
then-broiled Bermuda fish with pine nuts stand out. Souf-
flés are always excellent, as is the chef's pastry. Both change
daily. Eat in one of five cozy rooms; by special arrangement, groups may dine alfresco on a terrace that overlooks
Walsingham Bay. ✉ *Walsingham La., Bailey's Bay, Hamil-*
ton Parish ☎*441/293–8020 Jacket and tie* ▭*AE, MC, V*
☺*Closed Jan.–mid-Feb. No lunch.*

$$–$$$ ✕**North Rock Brewing Company.** The copper and mahogany
tones of the handcrafted beers and ales are reflected in the
warm interior of this bar and restaurant, Bermuda's only
brewpub. Seating surrounds the glass-enclosed brewery
where David Littlejohn, who runs North Rock with his
wife, Heather, tinkers with the gleaming copper kettles.
Sit in the dining room or outside on the breezy patio for
fish-and-chips, codfish cakes, or prime rib. ✉ *10 South Rd.,*
Smith's Parish ☎*441/236–6633* ▭*AE, MC, V.*

★ Fodor'sChoice✕**Black Horse Tavern.** Way off the main tourist
$–$$ trail in a remote corner of St. David's, the Black Horse is a
dark horse, or at least a well-kept local secret. Its beer garden overlooks a picturesque bay dotted with fishing boats
and tiny islands. This is a great place for island originals:
fish chowder and curried conch stew with rice are favorites, as are the straightforward renderings of amberjack,
rockfish, shark, tuna, wahoo, and Bermuda lobster. Just
about everything is deep-fried, so if that doesn't suit, then
request it be cooked the way you like. ✉ *101 St. David's*
Rd., St. George's Parish ☎*441/297–1991* ▭*AE, MC, V*
☺*Closed Mon.*

★ **$–$$** ✕**Swizzle Inn.** No trip to Bermuda is complete without stop-
☺ ping off at the Swizzle. In fact, Swizzle Inn created one
of Bermuda's most hallowed (and lethal) drinks—the rum
swizzle (amber and black rum, triple sec, orange and pineapple juices, and bitters). This place is a Bermuda land-

mark with a warm and welcoming atmosphere, friendly staff, and plenty of affordable pub fare. Try a "Swizzle-burger" (a bacon cheeseburger), or a huge plate of nachos and chili, which will challenge even the biggest of appetites. The Friday and Saturday barbecues with ribs, steaks, and seafood are a mouthwatering feast capable of satisfying any carnivore. With so many jugs of the island's national drink being consumed day and night, there's never a dull moment. It's also customary to leave your business card or scribble your name on the pub's colorful walls. A sister restaurant, Swizzle Inn South Shore, is now open in Warwick. ⊠*Blue Hole Hill, Bailey's Bay, Hamilton Parish* ☎*441/293–1854* ☐*AE, MC, V.*

ITALIAN

☼ $ ✕**Speciality Inn.** You may have to wait a few minutes for a table, but it's worth it. A favorite of locals and families, this south shore restaurant is cheerful and clean, with low prices, and always packed come dinnertime. The no-frills food is Bermudian with Italian and Portuguese accents. There's something for every diner with a sushi bar, tasty soups, and pizza. Carnivores should try the meaty Bermudian pizza. ⊠*Collectors Hill, 4 S. Shore Rd., Smith's Parish* ☎*441/236–3133* ☐*MC, V.*

Where to Stay

WORD OF MOUTH

"For a true Bermuda experience you may want to go for a cottage colony. My husband and I stay at the Pink Beach Club in quiet Tucker's Town. No TVs, but splurge for oceanfront, leave your French doors open, and fall asleep to the waves. Ahh . . ."

—thereadbaron

"The most central location is the Elbow Beach hotel or its neighbor, the Coco Reef. Elbow Beach, frankly, is the best beach on the island. "

—fernlover

Updated by Michael de Zayas

Few places in the world can boast the charm of Bermuda's curvaceous, colorful waterfront. It's a boon, then, that the lagoons, coves, coasts, as well as its inland sanctuaries are filled with equally colorful, alluring places to stay.

The quintessential accommodation on the island is a pink cottage—a cute, clean, unpretentious one-story house amid manicured gardens and coral stone pathways. Terraced whitewashed roofs (designed to capture rainwater) sit atop walls of pinks, peaches, and pastels, looking like cakes of ice cream in pink wafer sand. Add a waterfront setting, and voilà—the lure of Bermuda.

If you find yourself craving a beachfront resort, and you can afford it, several places in this chapter offer quality right-on-the-sand stays; another handful are a stone's throw away from the beach. If you find yourself craving a beachfront resort, and you *can't* afford it, don't despair. The island is blessed with clean, well-maintained public beaches. These are easily reached by bus, and aren't far from any point on the island.

The capital city has many sophisticated choices, but vacationers who are looking for beachfront relaxation will be disappointed in beachless Hamilton. With only a couple exceptions, beachfront lodging choices are along a 7-mi stretch of coast that runs along the central to western tail of the island, west from Paget to Warwick, Southampton, and Sandys. Lodging choices on the north coast of the island often are on glittering Hamilton Harbour or have deepwater access to the Atlantic, but not beaches.

Except for the older Fairmont Southampton, and the tall but unobtrusive larger main building at Elbow Beach, there are no high-rises in Bermuda—and nowhere do neon signs sully the landscape. Indeed, many of Bermuda's lodging properties are guesthouses, identifiable only by small, inconspicuous signs or plaques. Those who prefer bed-and-

WHAT IT COSTS IN U.S. DOLLARS

FOR TWO PEOPLE

¢	$	$$	$$$	$$$$
under $110	$110–$200	$200–$300	$300–$400	over $400

breakfasts will have no problem finding quaint retreats with local attention.

RESORTS & HOTELS

$$$$ ☒ **Coco Reef Hotel.** Coco Reef is at one end of highly desirable Elbow Beach. Staying here, then, you get to enjoy the restaurants and explore the large grounds of the immediate neighbor, Elbow Beach resort. This would make it a bargain, except that Coco Reef, a much simpler hotel, still charges nearly as much as Elbow Beach. No matter, the views are dazzling: few rooms on the island are as closely set to the beach. A few steps beyond the multimirrored lobby is a pool terrace providing another dramatic vista. Two peach two-story buildings—one beachfront, the other slightly up hill—have tiled rooms with wicker furniture, colorful aqua-and-peach floral quilts, and plastic furniture on the outdoor patios and balconies. So what, the rooms aren't stylish, but the beach is, stretching almost a mile to Coral Beach Tennis Club. This is also the closest beach resort to Hamilton town. **PROS:** close to the beach, nice pool, steps from Elbow Beach's restaurants. **CONS:** limited restaurants on-site, expensive for what you get. ☒ *8 College Dr., Paget Parish PG04* ☎*441/236–5416* ⊕*www.cocoreef-bermuda.com* ⤙*64 rooms* ⌂*In-room: safe, refrigerator. In-hotel: restaurant, bar, tennis courts, pool, beachfront, no elevator, laundry service* ☐*AE, MC, V* ⊙*BP.*

★ **$$$$** ☒ **Elbow Beach.** Some Mandarin Oriental properties are exercises in orchestrated perfection. This one trails far behind any such level of finesse, yet many highly appealing components still make Elbow Beach worth a stay. Foremost is its proximity to the beach, even if that means crossing a long series of lawns. In fact, these forced cross-campus walks give the property a breezier feel than the Fairmont Southampton, the island's other outsize upscale resort. Elbow's four restaurants have something for everyone, and there's poolfront service and a nightclub. Oddly enough the dining highlight may be breakfast at the Sea Horse Grill, where the service is impeccable. The spa is the most superlative in Bermuda because of its pervasive sense of tranquillity—it's here that the Mandarin touch is fully realized. Rooms off the main five-story building are all freshly furnished and have private sunning gardens—these are a breed apart. Some rooms in the main building are also renovated, with soothing blond- or dark-wood notes, luxurious marble floors

KNOW-HOW

Bermuda is a land of cottage colonies, cliff-top apartments, and beachfront resort hotels. Hidden along small parish roads, however, you can also find family-run, flower-filled guesthouses and simple, inexpensive efficiencies. The lodgings we list are the cream of the crop in each price category.

FACILITIES & SERVICES

Considering Bermuda hotel rates, it might come as a surprise that perks like 24-hour room service and same-day laundry service are rare. Fortunately, however, personalized attention, exceptionally comfortable rooms, and trim, scenic surroundings are not. The number and quality of facilities vary greatly according to the size and rates of the property. Resort hotels are the best equipped, with restaurants, pools, beach clubs, gyms, and (in the case of Fairmont Southampton) a golf course. Cottage colonies also typically have a clubhouse with a restaurant and bar, plus a pool or private beach, and perhaps a golf course. Each cottage has a kitchen, so you can cook your own meals, and housekeeping services are provided. Small hotels usually have a pool, and some have a restaurant or guest-only dining room, but few have fitness facilities or in-room extras like minibars. Efficiencies or housekeeping apartments almost always come with a kitchen or kitchenette. Some properties have pools, but you may have to take the bus or a scooter to get to the beach. Even the smallest property can arrange sailing, snorkeling, scuba, and deep-sea fishing excursions, as well as sightseeing.

All lodgings listed are equipped with private bathrooms and air-conditioning. In each review, we list the facilities that are available, but we don't specify whether they cost extra; when pricing accommodations, always ask what's included and what entails an additional charge. Most lodgings offer a choice of meal plans, several with "dine-around" privileges at other island restaurants. Under a Full American Plan (FAP), breakfast, lunch, and dinner are included in the hotel rate. A Modified American Plan (MAP) covers breakfast and dinner. A Breakfast Plan (BP) includes a full, cooked-to-order breakfast, and a Continental Plan (CP) means pastries, juice, and coffee. Unless otherwise noted, the rates quoted below are based on the European Plan (EP), which includes no meals at all.

and baths, and Caribbean hues. **PROS:** great beach, kids' activities, many restaurants to entertain. **CONS:** Somewhat generic, very expensive, huge property can mean a lot of walking. ✉ *60 S. Shore Rd., Paget Parish PG 04* ☎ *Box HM 455, Hamilton HM BX* ☎ *441/236–3535, 800/223–7434 in U.S. and Canada* ⊕ *www.elbowbeach.com* ➫ *169 rooms, 75 suites, 2 cottages* ☖ *In-room: safe, refrigerator, Ethernet, Wi-Fi. In-hotel: 4 restaurants, room service, bars, tennis courts, pool, gym, spa, beachfront, children's programs (ages 4–11), concierge* ▭ *AE, DC, MC, V* ☖ *BP, EP, MAP.*

★ **Fodor'sChoice** ▦ **The Fairmont Southampton.** This is the island's
☀ **$$$$** most inclusive resort, with the best restaurants, the best kids' club, the biggest spa, the best hotel golf course, lobby, shops—and so on. If the lodgings, based in an older ¼-mi-long hotel, sat on a fine beach, and were a little less of a clunky high-rise, the Southampton would be the unchallenged island favorite. It does have a private beach—one of the very best in Bermuda—but it takes a quick shuttle or a five-minute walk to reach it from the vast grounds that stretch the entire width of the island. Still, there's much to recommend this hotel, as the island's most complete full-service resort, for those who like big hotels. The Willow Stream Spa has 15 treatment rooms, three lounges, two hot tubs overlooking the ocean, and an indoor heated pool with waterfalls. Ask to see a room before checking in—views vary—and avoid ones on the first three floors of the west and north wings, as they overlook a rooftop. **PROS:** all-year kids' camp with arcade, full-service resort with golf course, great restaurants, private beach. **CONS:** hotel building itself is unattractive and older, slightly long walk to beach. ✉ *101 S. Shore Rd., Southampton Parish SN02* ☎ *Box HM 1379, Hamilton HM FX* ☎ *441/238–8000 or 800/441–1414* ⊕ *www.fairmont.com* ➫ *594 rooms, 24 suites* ☖ *In-room: safe, kitchen (some), refrigerator, Ethernet. In-hotel: 7 restaurants, room service, bars, golf course, tennis courts, pools, gym, spa, beachfront, diving, water sports, children's programs (ages 4–16), laundry service, concierge, executive floor, public Internet, public Wi-Fi, some pets allowed* ▭ *AE, DC, MC, V.*

☀ **$$$$** ▦ **Pompano Beach Club.** Pompano, which is passionately run by an American family, understands its customers—and those customers return year after year for the casual atmosphere and wonderful small beach. A new dining room with two-story glass windows seems to hover high over

72 <

Where to Stay in
the East & West Ends

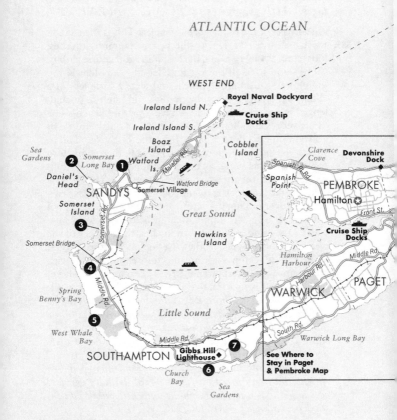

See Where to
Stay in Paget
& Pembroke Map

KEY

⛴	Cruise Ship
⛴	Ferry
┝━━┥	Railway Trail

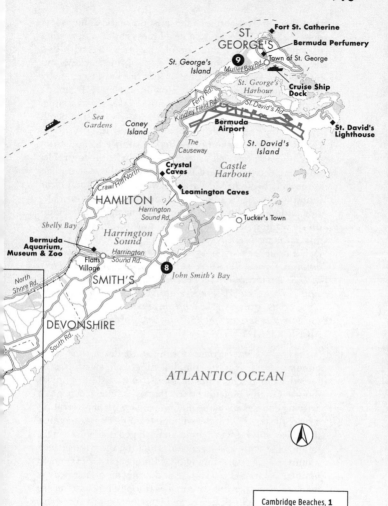

St. George's Island

ST. GEORGE'S

Fort St. Catherine

Bermuda Perfumery

Town of St. George

9 Mullet Bay Rd.

St. George's Harbour

Cruise Ship Dock

St. George's Island

Ferry Rd.
Kindley Field Rd.
St. David's Rd.

Bermuda Airport

St. David's Lighthouse

Sea Gardens

Coney Island

The Causeway

St. David's Island

Castle Harbour

Crystal Caves

Crawl Hill North

HAMILTON

Harrington Sound Rd.

Leamington Caves

Tucker's Town

Shelly Bay

Harrington Sound

Harrington Sound Rd.

Bermuda Aquarium, Museum & Zoo

Flatts Village

8

John Smith's Bay

North Shore Rd.

SMITH'S

DEVONSHIRE

South Rd.

ATLANTIC OCEAN

Cambridge Beaches, **1**

The Fairmont Southampton, **7**

Garden House, **4**

9 Beaches, **2**

Pink Beach Club & Cottages, **8**

Pompano Beach Club, **5**

The Reefs, **6**

The St. George's Club, **9**

Willowbank, **3**

the ocean, making it one of the most dramatic dining spots on the island. There's also a new fitness room, a new wing of waterfront suites, and notably a game room with two PlayStation video game consoles, pool, air hockey, and ping-pong. (Games for adults or kids are hard to come by in Bermuda.) If you didn't come all the way to Bermuda to play video games, glass-bottom kayaks are available. Of three hot tubs, two enjoy a privileged cliff-side perch overlooking the beach. Pompano abuts the Port Royal Golf Course, and the hotel offers a shuttle to and from the clubhouse (as well as to the ferry). Most memorable, however, the water here is clear and shallow—you can wade out through 250 yards of waist-high, crystal clear liquid to one of two floating platforms. A spacious cliff-side patio high above the ocean has a heated pool, a children's wading pool, pool bar, and hot tub. **PROS:** private and intimate small resort, three hot tubs. **CONS:** rooms lack a designer's style. ⊠ *36 Pompano Beach Rd., Southampton Parish SB 03* ☎*441/234–0222, 800/343–4155 in U.S.* ⊕*www.pompanobeachclub.com* ⤳*58 rooms, 16 suites* ⌂*In-room: safe, refrigerator. In-hotel: 2 restaurants, bars, pools, gym, spa, beachfront, water sports, no elevator, laundry service, public Internet, public Wi-Fi* ▭*AE, MC, V* ⑩*MAP.*

★ $$$$ ▣ **The Reefs.** What accounts for the accolades at this wildly popular resort? Is it the complimentary rum swizzles, self-served from pitchers in the lobby, that sustain a jovial mood? Or the bulletin board that welcomes each day's arriving couples by name and home city, perhaps creating a sense of spirit? Well, the winning formula goes something like this: pink buildings intimately ringed around a small, fabulous beach + restaurants overlooking the water + nice infinity-edged pool + intangible winning spirit = extremely popular resort. As a wedding and honeymoon getaway it manages to be private; for families (though most guests are couples) it remains carefree and large enough to entertain, though formal enough in its restaurant to create balance. All rooms have ocean views and balconies, but not all are created equal: suites near the beach and overlooking the ocean each have a Jacuzzi tub, large walk-in shower for two, and complete entertainment system; for seclusion and tranquillity, the cliff-side rooms perched above wave-washed boulders at the far end of the resort are impeccable. **PROS:** intimate resort that caters to North American couples, cute beach. **CONS:** a small property like the Reefs can get repetitive. ⊠ *56 South Rd., Southampton Parish SN*

Spaaaah Resorts

Befitting their lovely island location, the best of Bermuda's hotel spas are spectacular in appearance, with white columns, marble floors, flowing linens, and burbling fountains. Bermuda has three full-service spas, located at the Fairmont Southampton, Elbow Beach, and Cambridge Beaches. Day spas are available at Ariel Sands, Pompano Beach, and the Fairmont Princess.

A favorite among Bermuda's society ladies, the day spa at the former **Ariel Sands** offers head-to-toe pampering in a lovely beachside-retreat setting. Although the cottage colony is currently closed, the spa is still open for blisstime.

Sunlight dapples the indoor swimming pools at the **Cambridge Beaches Ocean Spa,** inside a traditional, two-story Bermudian cottage with pink-stucco walls and a ridged roof. The glass dome that covers the pools is opened in warm weather, allowing salt-tinged ocean breezes to drift into the villa. The treatments offered here are hard to find outside Europe. Both full-day and half-day packages include lunch on a bayside terrace.

The Fairmont Southampton's Willow Stream Spa is the island's largest facility. Besides a complete health club, including personal trainers, there's a garden-enclosed indoor pool, a sundeck overlooking the ocean, two Jacuzzis, three lounges, steam rooms, inhalation rooms, and 15 treatment rooms. Specially designed lengthy treatments combine baths, wraps, and massage conducted with the utmost skill.

The serene **Spa at Elbow Beach** offers personal and couples spa suites overlooking the Atlantic. The suites include personal showers, vanity area, and granite bath. Treatments are based on ayurvedic principles, and use ESPA products. This is the most lavish, personal, private, and relaxing spa on the island.

Serenity Spa at Pompano Beach Club offers a full range of individual and couple treatments from its four treatment rooms facing the ocean.

02 ☎441/238–0222, 800/742–2008 in U.S. and Canada ⊕www.thereefs.com ⇆45 rooms, 4 suites, 8 junior suites, 8 cottage suites ♿In-room: safe, DVD, VCR, dial-up. In-hotel: 3 restaurants, room service, bars, tennis courts, pool, gym, spa, beachfront, laundry service, public Internet, public Wi-Fi ➡AE, MC, V ⋈MAP.

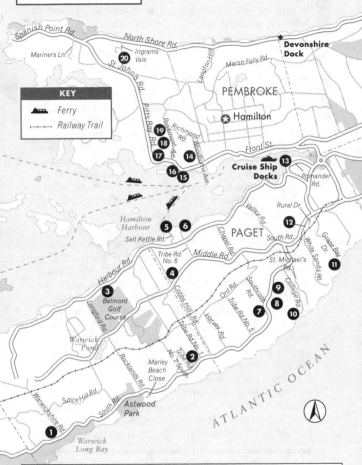

0   1/2 mile

0   1/2 km

KEY

⛴ Ferry

---- Railway Trail

Spanish Point Rd.

North Shore Rd.

Devonshire Dock

Mariners Ln.

Ingrams Vale

St. John's Rd.

Langton Hill

Marsh Folly Rd.

PEMBROKE

⭐ Hamilton

Pitts Bay Rd.

Rosemont Ave.

Richmond Rd.

Woodbourne Ave.

Front St.

⑲

⑱

⑰

⑭

⑬

Cruise Ship Docks

Pomander Rd.

⑯ **⑮**

Hamilton Harbour

Valley Rd.

Rural Dr.

⑫

PAGET

⑤ **⑥**

Salt Kettle Rd.

Chapel Rd.

South Rd.

St. Michael's Rd.

White Sands Rd.

Grape Bay Dr.

⑪

Tribe Rd. No. 6

Middle Rd.

④

Harbour Rd.

Cobbs Hill Rd.

Ord Rd.

Southcote Rd.

⑨

College Rd.

③

Belmont Golf Course

Tribe Rd. No. 1

Harvey Rd.

Tribe Rd. No. 5

⑦ **⑧**

⑩

Longford Rd.

Warwick Pond

Tribe Rd. No. 2 South

Marley Beach Close

②

Rocklands Rd.

Spice Hill Rd.

South Rd.

Astwood Park

ATLANTIC OCEAN

Warwickshire Rd.

①

Warwick Long Bay

Bay City Guest House, **17**	Granaway Guest House, **3**	Robin's Nest, **20**
Clairfont Apts., **1**	Grape Bay Cottage, **11**	Royal Palms Hotel, **19**
Coco Reef Hotel, **10**	Greenbank Cottages, **5**	Salt Kettle House, **6**
Edgehill Manor, **18**	Horizons & Cottages, **7**	Sandpiper Apartments, **2**
Elbow Beach Hotel, **8**	Little Pomander Guest House, **13**	Serendipity, **12**
The Fairmont Hamilton Princess, **16**	Oxford House, **14**	Waterloo House, **15**
Fourways Inn, **4**	Paraquet Guest Apts., **9**	

★ **Fodor's**Choice ⌂**Waterloo House.** Its charms are as many as its
$$$–$$$$ years of service (Waterloo has been enchanting guests since
1929). Descriptives like warm, elegant, intimate, charming,
tranquil, and indulgent will roll readily off your tongue as
you walk the rooms and grounds of this lovely property.
Blessed with one of the island's best chefs, and an interna-
tional, service-oriented staff, this place fares just fine on
its own, but you get the additional value of the use of its
sister properties on and near the south shore. This means
you can play golf at Horizons and sign up for water sports
at the otherwise private Coral Beach & Tennis Club. You
can dine here as well with the $50 MAP supplement—a
great deal. Rooms are individually fashioned: curtains, car-
pets, and fabrics are chosen by the owner, a woman who
clearly is entranced by detail. Most rooms are in the main
house, all have water views. ■TIP→**Lunch on the sunny lawn
at the marina's edge should not be missed. PROS:** stylish,
intimate, right in the heart of Hamilton. **CONS:** not on a
beach. ⊠*100 Pitts Bay Rd., Hamilton HM 11 ✆Box HM
333, Hamilton HM BX* 🖃*441/295–4480, 800/468–4100
in U.S.* ⊕*www.waterloohouse.com* ➪*23 rooms, 6 suites*
♿*In-room: safe, refrigerator, Wi-Fi. In-hotel: restaurant,
bars, pool, no elevator, laundry service, public Internet,
public Wi-Fi* ⊟*AE, MC, V* ⍁*BP, MAP.*

$$$ ⌂**The Fairmont Hamilton Princess.** The reigning royalty of
Bermuda lodging, the Princess boasts some of the most
comfortable rooms on the island, especially at the higher
end. The hotel seems to have no problem selling out all of
its rooms consistently, as it caters to and pampers business guests like no other hotel in the capital can; indeed,
it's the only full-service resort in Hamilton. It's steps away
from the shops and liveliness of Front Street, as well as the
principal insurance offices, on the edge of Hamilton Harbour. Classy, contemporary rooms and suites have elegant
hardwood furnishings and marble bathrooms. Fairmont
Gold, the chain's exclusive boutique hotel within the larger
property, is memorable for its regal lounge, set in the former ballroom. ■TIP→**Take posh afternoon tea here complete
with silver pots and fine china.** Although at the Princess, as
in all Hamilton hotels, there's no beach, you can walk off
the dock onto a fun, twice-daily ferry (followed by a shuttle ride) to Fairmont's south shore beach. Because it caters
to business, prices are lower on weekends. **PROS:** reli-
able first-rate rooms, only full-service resort in the capital,
attractive harborfront location. **CONS:** mainly corporate

guests, ferry or cab necessary to reach beaches. ✉*76 Pitts Bay Rd., Hamilton HM 08 ⌂Box HM 837, Hamilton HM CS ☎441/295–3000 or 800/441–1414 ⊕www.fairmont.com ⏎368 rooms, 42 suites ⌂In-room: safe, Ethernet, Wi-Fi. In-hotel: 2 restaurants, room service, bars, pools, gym, spa, diving, laundry service, concierge, executive floor, public Internet, public Wi-Fi, some pets allowed ▭AE, DC, MC, V.*

$$$ 🏨**Willowbank.** Six acres of lovely waterfront property taper into a corner promontory, splitting two fine beaches, and leading to a wooden walk over the water. This scenic lookout has to be one of the more refreshing vistas on the island. Practicing Christians may appreciate knowing that this former estate was converted to a family-style hotel by a Christian trust. Morning devotions are held in a lounge and grace is said before supper (announced by an ancient ship's bell), which is served in the Loaves and Fishes dining room. But there's no proselytizing. Willowbank is simply a serene and restful alternative to glitzier resorts, with wonderful views and marvelous beaches. Guest rooms, many right on the ocean, have contemporary furnishings, but purposefully are devoid of phones and TVs. ■**TIP➔A free summer children's program includes crafts and trips around the island. PROS:** beautiful setting, two beaches, expansive grounds. **CONS:** religious environment might make some uncomfortable. ✉*126 Somerset Rd., Sandys Parish MA 06 ⌂Box MA 296, Sandys MA BX ☎441/234–1616 or 800/752–8493 ⊕www.willowbank.bm ⏎64 rooms ⌂In-room: no phone, refrigerator, no TV, Ethernet, Wi-Fi (some). In-hotel: restaurant, tennis courts, pool, beachfront ▭MC, V �🍴MAP.*

$$–$$$ 🏨**9 Beaches.** But who's counting? A campus of 84 small, freestanding solar-powered cabanas, each angled for dramatic sea views, will make some travelers feel, despondently, like they are at a deluxe summer camp on the beach, while others will rejoice at the simplicity and direct engagement with nature. Plainly furnished cabanas have verandas, wicker ceiling fans, and sides and ceilings made of a canvas material that rustles in the breeze like sailcloth. Guests swear by these—or at them (depending on how they sleep). The half dozen cabanas perched over the water have glass floor panels that reveal the clear shallow waves underfoot. Though water sports (take a fishing tour and the chef will cook your catch for dinner) are the name of the game here, technology is nicely integrated with Wi-Fi hot spots, com-

plimentary iPods, and cell phones to reach staff from any location. Kids under 16 stay free. This is Bermuda's only truly informal resort. **PROS:** scenic, great for water sports, nice beach. **CONS:** the name of the resort may oversell its small beaches. ⊠*4 Daniel's Head Lane, Sandys Parish MA 04* ☎*441/232–6655 or 866/841–9009* ⊕*www.9beaches. com* ↶*84 cabanas* ♿*In-room: safe, refrigerator, no TV, Wi-Fi. In-hotel: restaurant, bars, tennis court, pool, gym, beachfront, water sports, bicycles, concierge, children's programs (ages 1–12), laundry service, public Internet, no-smoking rooms* ⊟*AE, MC, V* ⏀*CP.*

★ **Fodor's**Choice ⬚**Royal Palms Hotel.** You have to love a hotel
$$–$$$ that takes its gardens with a botanist's seriousness and yet has enough sense of humor to leave a rubber ducky on your bath mat. Royal Palms is a winner for having high standards, great service, and a welcoming touch, too—fresh-from-the-garden flowers celebrate your arrival. The best perch might well be the front swing, from which you can survey the lush grounds, including two tall royal palms that give the hotel its name. Also wonderful is the sunny, all-glass breakfast room where you eat at 90-year-old Bermudian cedar tables. If you're looking for privacy, there are three buildings set around the gardens of the main 1903 building; many rooms here have private entrances. It's clear that brother-and-sister owners Richard Smith and Susan Weare put more detailed care into their property, and manage it better than just about anyone else in Bermuda. A final touch is Ascot's—one of the island's best restaurants. **PROS:** beautiful gardens, wonderful breakfast, terrific service, great restaurant. **CONS:** no pool, no beach, 10-minute walk to Hamilton. ⊠*24 Rosemont Ave., Pembroke Parish HM 06* ✉*Box HM 499, Hamilton HM CX* ☎*441/292–1854, 800/678–0783 in U.S. and Canada* ⊕*www.royalpalms.bm* ↶*27 rooms* ♿*In-room: safe, dial-up, Wi-Fi. In-hotel: restaurant, bar, pool, no elevator, laundry service* ⊟*AE, MC, V* ⏀*CP.*

$$ ⬚**Bay City Guest House.** Business guests will find this bright blue mansion—the island's newest hotel—a great value downtown. Bank executive Bernadette Footé purchased, renovated, and reopened the hotel in late 2005 to target business travelers looking for a good value in a small upscale hotel. Suites 9–12 have fine views of the harbor across the street, and are recommended; room 9 has a hot tub and nearly 180-degree views; room 12 (for $295, a relative bargain on the island) is a grand corporate suite

with an ornamental fireplace surmounted by a 37-inch plasma screen, a king-size bed, and the dark wood and carpeting you can find throughout the hotel. Downstairs, the comfortable breakfast room, which also looks onto the harbor, is a pleasant place to start the day. For self-service types there's a shared kitchen. **PROS:** across from the harbor in Hamilton, spacious rooms. **CONS:** no pool, no beach, reception not always present. ⊠*53 Pitts Bay Rd., Hamilton HM 06* ☎*441/295–1275* ⊕*www.baycity.bm* ⤶*10 rooms, 2 suites* ⚐*In-room: safe, Wi-Fi. In-hotel: bar, public Internet, public Wi-Fi* ⊟*AE, MC, V* ❘⊙❘*CP.*

COTTAGE COLONIES

★ Fodor'sChoice ⚏**Cambridge Beaches.** Cambridge Beaches has a
$$$$ coat of arms that reads PRIMA ET OPTIMA, or First and Best. The First? Yes—it's the island's oldest cottage colony. The Best? Well, if you want a pervasive sense of tranquillity and relaxed refinement, then that's a fact, too. No other Bermuda resort uses its privileged setting better—its 25 acres on a peninsula near the western end of the island creates a sense of meandering expansiveness. Many large properties on the island are centered around one main beach, but Cambridge has five, including beautiful Long Bay Beach and Morning Beach (backed by a chic infinity pool unveiled in 2007). The complimentary daily tea service is a civilized affair, set in a beautiful lounge overlooking Mangrove Bay. The varying sizes, styles, and locations of the cottages and rooms make for a wide range of prices. Less-expensive rooms open onto lawns and gardens, but overlook the same wide ocean. Ocean Spa is among the very best in Bermuda. **PROS:** private, gamut of activities and beaches to choose from, beautiful grounds and beaches. **CONS:** far removed from rest of island, very expensive. ⊠*30 King's Point Rd., Sandys Parish MA 02* ☎*441/234–0331, 800/468–7300 in U.S.* ⊕*www.cambridgebeaches.com* ⤶*66 rooms, 25 suites, 3 2-bedroom cottages* ⚐*In-room: safe, refrigerator, DVD (some), Ethernet. In-hotel: 2 restaurants, room service, bars, tennis courts, pools, gym, spa, beachfront, diving, water sports, laundry service, public Internet, no kids under 5* ⊟*AE, DC, MC, V* ❘⊙❘*BP, MAP.*

★ $$$$ ⚏**Horizons and Cottages.** Horizons is a dying breed of old Bermuda—in fact, at the time of this writing, the Four Seasons was rumored to be ready to purchase it and its sister property across the street, the Coral Beach and Tennis Club. Although some things at Horizons (like the nine-hole course) could use an upgrade to get back to its former Relais & Chateaux polish, it's worth a stay to experience the former plantation estate's core cottage colony experience. For decades vacationers before you have soaked up the convivial and social environment, highlighted by drinks in the curious downstairs pub with its vintage billiard games and dinner served in the main clubhouse. Rooms don't have TVs; a game of tennis and a swim across the street at Coral Beach will suffice instead. Although Horizons has many similarities to Cambridge Beaches, this property is more clubby. Oriental rugs, polished wood floors, cathedral ceilings, and open fireplaces are elegant reminders of the 18th century, when the main house in this resort was a private home. Most guest cottages have a large common room with a fireplace, a library, and board games, and all have terraces. **PROS:** beautiful grounds, two-in-one hotel stay courtesy of sister property, gorgeous beach. **CONS:** golf course in bad shape, upkeep is slacking while the hotel waits to sell. ⊠*33 S. Shore Rd., Paget Parish PG 04* ☏*Box PG 198, Paget PG BX* ☎*441/236–0048, 800/468–0022 in U.S.* ⊕*www.horizonscottages.com* ➾*40 rooms, 5 suites* ⚿*In-room: safe, kitchen (some), refrigerator (some), no TV, dial-up. In-hotel: restaurant, bar, golf course, tennis courts, pool, gym, laundry facilities, laundry service, public Internet* ⊟*AE, MC, V* ⚏*BP, MAP.*

★ **$$$$** 📷**Pink Beach Club & Cottages.** Pink Beach Club is a Bermuda original. This secluded cottage colony, on the west side of the island, a few minutes from Mid Ocean and Tucker's Point golf courses, opened in 1947. The main house, where you'll find the reception restaurant, looks like a private club, with dark-wood paneling, a large fireplace, and beam ceilings. Paved paths wind through 16½ acres of gardens, leading to two pretty, private beaches and 25 pink cottages. Single-room suites are expansive, with king-size beds, pullout couches, and sitting areas. One- and two-bedroom suites have separate living rooms, and some have two bathrooms. All have French doors that open onto a balcony or terrace and most have ocean views. **PROS:** near Mid Ocean and Tuckers Point golf courses and the airport, classic cottage colony, very formal and private, no TV. **CONS:** isolated from populated parts of island and other vacationers, more formal, no TV. ⊠*1016 S. Shore Rd., Tucker's Town, Smith's Parish HS 01* ☏*Box HM 1017, Hamilton HM DX* ☎*441/293–1666, 800/355–6161 in*

U.S. and Canada ⊕*www.pinkbeach.com* ⌐⌐*94 suites* ⅍*In-room: safe, no TV, refrigerator, Ethernet (some), dial-up. In-hotel: restaurant, room service, bar, tennis courts, pool, gym, beachfront, water sports, bicycles, no elevator, laundry service, public Internet* ⊨*AE, MC, V* ⊚*MAP.*

$$$ ⊞ **The St. George's Club.** This time-share complex, which looks and feels like a 1990s condo community, is the closest thing to a modern hotel room in St. George's. The grounds are tidy, ample, and perched high above St. George's. A walk (or drive) down a gardened path takes you into town from the 18-acre campus. Clean one- and two-bedroom cottages come with a fully equipped kitchen and views of the ocean, one of three pools, or a public golf course designed by Robert Trent Jones. The sleek, three-story main building holds the lobby, business center, a convenience store where you can buy champagne and sunblock, and two restaurants: Griffin's, serving contemporary food, and Blackbeard's Hideout Beach Club, a summer-only pub by Tobacco Bay public beach and the golf course. **PROS:** only non-B&B in St. George's, nice views walking to town, private. **CONS:** no activities outside of the pool, feels more like a suburban development than a vacation spot, far from the rest of the island. ⊠*6 Rose Hill, St. George's Parish GE O5* ⌐*Box GE 92, St. George's GE BX* ☎*441/297–1200* ⊕*www.stgeorgesclub.bm* ⌐⌐*72 cottages* ⅍*In-room: safe, kitchen, refrigerator, DVD (some), Wi-Fi. In-hotel: 2 restaurants, bars, tennis courts, pools, gym, laundry facilities, laundry service, public Internet* ⊨*AE, MC, V.*

$$ ⊞ **Fourways Inn.** The main edifice at this mid-island cottage colony is a family home, which belonged to the owners of Harvey's Bristol Crème in the 1700s. It's with this gastronomic tradition in mind that this pretty but otherwise unextraordinary cottage colony comes to life. Like most on the island, the colony is set amid a profusion of greenery and flowers around a pool; its suites have marble floors and balconies or patios. In short, it's pleasant. The main draws are its top-notch Continental restaurant, which brings formal patrons to its large dining room and 6,000-bottle wine list; and its small pub, the Peg Leg Lounge, which, partly situated in the old home's kitchen, manages to feel like a classic old-world redoubt, with unpolished bronze chandeliers and an enormous fireplace, the home's former woodstove. **PROS:** inexpensive, can walk to beaches, great dining. **CONS:** middle of the island, no beach. ⊠*1 Middle Rd., Paget Parish PG 01* ⌐*Box PG 294, Paget*

PG BX ☎*441/236–6517, 800/962–7654 in U.S.* ⊕*www.
fourwaysinn.com* 🖥*6 rooms, 4 suites* ⚬*In-room: kitchen,
refrigerator. In-hotel: restaurant, bar, pool, laundry service,
no-smoking rooms* ▭*AE, MC, V* ⦿*CP.*

HOUSEKEEPING COTTAGES & APARTMENTS

★ **Fodors**Choice ⊡**Grape Bay Cottage.** Down a long and mean-
$$$ dering private estate road lined with hibiscus-fronted
mansions, you can find this perfectly simple, laughably
cute cottage perched right at the edge of the soft sands of
Grape Bay Beach. The two-bedroom cottage has an open
fireplace, hardwood floors, a full-size kitchen, a king-size
bed, a pull-out couch, and a lawn patio overlooking the
beach. The area is quiet and secluded, ideal for beach-lov-
ers who like to cook for themselves and do serious sand-
and-surf time. The cottages are a bit costly for one couple
(though cheaper than any resort in Bermuda), but for two
or even three couples sharing expenses (extra cots are pro-
vided), this is an eminently affordable choice. Gwen, the
friendly housekeeper, has welcomed guests here for years,
and recounts with familial joy the latest news in the lives of
regular visitors. Although you can't perhaps afford to pur-
chase a beachfront home in Bermuda, this may be the next
best thing. **PROS:** sharable with friends or family, beach-
front, quiet. **CONS:** no pool. ✉*Grape Bay Dr., Paget Par-
ish* 🏠*Box HM 1851, Hamilton HM HX* ☎*441/295–7017,
800/637–4116 in U.S.* 🖷*441/296–0563* 🖥*1 cottage* ⚬*In-
room: kitchen, refrigerator, no TV. In-hotel: beachfront,
laundry facilities* ▭*AE, MC, V.*

$$ ⊡**Edgehill Manor.** The first thing you notice is the color: pea
green. It takes your eyes a minute to adjust to the grand
colonial-style house, built around the turn of the 20th century, and its newer wing. But then you see the order that's
kept here: spotless grounds, with notes of hung flower pots,
an inviting pool surrounded by lush greenery, and handsome
simple and clean rooms, all with private balconies. Central Hamilton is a short 10-minute walk downhill. French
country–style furniture, small flat-screen TVs, and lots of
bright florals fill the guest and common rooms. **PROS:** nice
pool, well maintained, clean rooms. **CONS:** not a leisure
destination, no beach. ✉*36 Rosemont Ave., Hamilton HM
EX* 🏠*Box HM 1048, Hamilton HM EX* ☎*441/295–7124*
⊕*www.bermuda.com/edgehill* 🖥*14 rooms* ⚬*In-room: safe,*

3

kitchen (some), refrigerator (some), VCR (some), Wi-Fi. In-hotel: pool, no elevator, public Wi-Fi ⊟*AE, MC, V* ⊙*CP.*

★ **Fodor's**Choice ⊞**Clairfont Apartments.** Clairfont offers one of
$ Bermuda's best values, and it's probably the island's best
buy if you're on a budget and don't mind a five-minute
walk to one of the island's best beaches. Furnishings, while
not exactly fancy, are the best in this price category. Rooms
offer a great value for spaciousness as well. But above all
you'll want to kiss the finicky, cleaning-crazy manager Cor-
rine Simons because the property is spotless. Kitchens and
baths were upgraded in 2007. Choose between two studios
or six one-bedrooms—all with fully equipped kitchens. The
studios ($130 year-round) have king-size beds and separate
kitchens. The four sunny upstairs units have balconies,
and the downstairs apartments have patios, leading onto
a communal lawn and a nice pool. The property welcomes
a lot of families with children during the summer months
and Warwickshire Long Bay Playground is a few minutes'
walk away. Monthly rates in winter are an astonishingly
low $1,250. Early booking is recommended. **PROS:** cheap,
very clean and well maintained, large units. **CONS:** not
beachfront. ⊠*6 Warwickshire Rd., Warwick Parish WK 02*
⌁*Box WK 85, Warwick Parish WK 02* ☎*441/238–3577*
⊕*www.clairfontapartments.bm* ⌁*8 apartments* ⌂*In-room:*
*kitchen, refrigerator, DVD, Ethernet. In-hotel: pool, laun-
dry service* ⊟*AE, MC, V.*

$ ⊞**Garden House.** Hospitable owner and manager, the eccen-
tric Rosanne Galloway is a fervent gardener, and spends
much time on this large property planting and pruning.
The grounds aren't flawless; indeed there's a relaxed work-
in-progress approach that is evident, but for the right traveler, the result is an underpriced stay with more space than
you'll know what to do with. You'll have to walk a ways
to a beach, but the long lawn extends to a path that reaches
Ely's Harbour where you can swim, as long as you don't
mind diving into deep water right off the shore. There are
other exciting aspects of this oft-overlooked corner of the
island: Wreck Road, a marvelous mansion-lined residential
street that skirts Ely's Harbor, has a small beach at the far
end; and Somerset Bridge is reached from a dirt path that
leads to Middle Road. Rooms are furnished with Persian
rugs and antique furniture. All units have patios that lead
out to the gardens. Children under 12 stay free. **PROS:**
inexpensive cottages and rooms, quiet, interesting corner
of the island to explore, friendly hostess. **CONS:** few ser-

vices, not beachfront. ✉4 Middle Rd., Sandys Parish SB 01 ☎441/234–1435 🖷441/234–3006 ⌖3 apartments, 2 cottages ♿In-room: safe, kitchen, refrigerator, DVD (some), VCR. In-hotel: pool, laundry facilities ⊟No credit cards ⊘Closed Dec.–Feb.

★ Fodor'sChoice🖪**Granaway Guest House.** One of the island's
$ best values, Granaway is a 1734 manor house with villa-like lawn and gardens leading to a clear and well-maintained pool. Any of the outdoor chairs and lounges are great places to relax. The pink house is across the street from Hamilton Harbour and ferries to Hamilton. South shore beaches are a 30-minute walk, or a jaunt of a cab ride, so it's an affordable option if you don't have be on the beach. All rooms are distinct; the "yellow room" features original cedar beams, and the "pink room" has a private terrace with harbor views. A private cottage, which maxes out at $280 a night in peak season, gives you your own small home with kitchen. **PROS:** great value, gardened terrace, relaxing lawn and pool area, historic property. **CONS:** not waterfront or easy walk to beaches, only Continental breakfast. ✉Harbour Rd., Warwick WK 533 ☎441/236–3747 U.S. ⊕www.granaway.com ⌖5 rooms, 1 cottage ♿In-room: kitchen (some), refrigerator. In-hotel: pool ⊟AE, MC, V ⦿CP.

$ 🖪**Greenbank Cottages.** Greenbank has been family-run for 50 years, and this is what Bermuda vacations were like back then: by way of entertainment you had a due-west pier with two chairs to watch the sunset. A stay at Greenbank is a slow, relaxed experience. There's no beach here (and no TVs). Instead, you sit out on the harborfront lawn and take in the sun, or use the private dock for deepwater swimming. Or catch the ferry, just steps across the road, to explore the island. The waterside cottages, especially Salt Winds, have lovely harbor views. No two are alike—some were converted from old horse and buggy stations once used in transporting salt. All are clean and updated, with kitchens, private entrances, and shaded verandas. **PROS:** close to ferry, secluded neighborhood, relaxed place. **CONS:** no pool or beach. ✉17 Salt Kettle Rd., Paget Parish PG 01 ✆Box PG 201, Paget PG BX ☎441/236–3615 ⊕www.greenbankbermuda.com ⌖4 cottages, 5 studios, 2 rooms ♿In-room: kitchen (some), refrigerator, no TV, Wi-Fi. In-hotel: public Wi-Fi ⊟AE, MC, V.

CLOSE UP

Bermudian Architecture

The typical Bermudian building is built of limestone block, usually painted white or a pastel shade, with a prominent chimney and a tiered, white-painted roof that Mark Twain likened to "icing on the cake." More than just picturesque, these features are proof that "Necessity" really is "the Mother of Invention." Limestone, for instance, was a widely available building material—and far better able to withstand hurricane-force winds than the old English-style "wattle and daub."

The distinctive roof, similarly, was not developed for aesthetic reasons. It's part of a system that allows Bermudians to collect rainwater and store it in large tanks beneath their houses. The special white roof paint even contains a purifying agent. If your visit includes some rainy days, you may hear the expression, "Good day for the tank!" This is rooted in the fact that Bermuda has no freshwater. It relies on rain for drinking, bathing, and cooking water, as well as golf-course and farmland irrigation. So residents are careful not to waste the precious liquid. The island has never run out of water, though the supply was stretched during World War II, when thousands of U.S. soldiers were stationed in Bermuda.

"Moongates" are another interesting Bermudian structural feature, usually found in gardens and walkways around the island. These Chinese-inspired freestanding stone arches, popular since the late 18th century, are still often incorporated into new construction. Thought to bring luck, the ring-shape gates are favored as backdrops for wedding photos.

Other architectural details you may notice are "welcoming arms" stairways, with banisters that seem to reach out to embrace you as you approach the first step, and "eyebrows" over window openings. Also look for "butteries": tiny, steep-roofed cupboards, separate from the house, and originally built to keep dairy products cool in summer. If you wonder why, in this warm climate, so many houses have fireplaces in addition to air-conditioners, come in January, when the dampness makes it warmer outside than in.

—revised by Susan MacCallum-Whitcomb

$ ▥**Paraquet Guest Apartments.** For those not picky about the room they stay in, Paraquet (pronounced "parakeet") provides a centrally located, motel-like, no-frills stay. Rooms are simple, clean, and unadorned. The biggest draw is, at its price, proximity to Elbow Beach, one of the prettiest beaches on the island—a mere five-minute walk away! The Para-quet Restaurant is reasonably priced and—surprise!—is an American-style diner, with milk shakes, straws in old jars, and low counter stools. You can also walk to the nearby supermarket and cook your own meals in one of nine rooms with kitchenettes. **PROS:** convenient diner, affordable, close to the beach. **CONS:** no views, no pool, no amenities. ⊠*72 South Rd., Paget Parish PG 04* ⊕*Box PG 173, Paget PG BX* ☎*441/236–5842* ⊕*www.paraquetapartments.com* ⌖*18 rooms* ⚬*In-room: no phone (some), kitchen (some), refrig-erator. In-hotel: restaurant, laundry facilities* ⊟*MC, V.*

$ ⊡**Robin's Nest.** This well-maintained valley property is a tad off the beaten path, in a quiet residential neighbor-hood about a mile north of Hamilton and within walking distance to a secluded beach cove. Behind the main house up a flight of stairs you'll likely be surprised to find the guest rooms in what looks like a two-story urban apart-ment complex. Studios here are new, with spacious and modern kitchenettes; upstairs studios have balconies, and the ground-floor studios open onto tranquil, intimate gar-dens and a pool. The small number of rooms means you're more than likely to enjoy the good-size pool and patio all to yourself. A short bus ride can take you to Hamilton, Admiralty Park, or north-shore snorkeling sites. To find Robin's Nest, take Ingham Vale from North Shore Road. **PROS:** well-kept rooms and grounds, pool. **CONS:** out of the way location. ⊠*10 Vale Close, Pembroke HM 04* ☎*441/292–4347* ⊕*www.robinsnestbda.com* ⌖*11 studio apartments* ⚬*In-room: kitchen, refrigerator. In-hotel: pool* ⊟*No credit cards.*

$ ⊡**Sandpiper Apartments.** The brochure for this simple, apartment-style property boasts "the finest in luxury." Well, ahem, Sandpiper is probably the *least* luxurious choice in all of Bermuda. That said, it's not bad if you're looking for an easygoing do-it-yourself kind of stay within walking distance to all south shore beaches. Spacious and basically decorated, the 14 whitewashed units include five one-bedroom apartments with full kitchens and nine stu-dios with kitchenettes. Each has either a balcony or patio. Most can accommodate up to four people. Choose from rooms with names outside that read Estascy [sic], Lover's Lair, Twiddle-dom (Unit 5) or Twiddle-dee (Unit 5A). **PROS:** convenient to south shore beaches, inexpensive, pool. **CONS:** not beachfront, limited services. ⊠*S. Shore*

Rd., Warwick Parish ⬧*Box HM 685, Hamilton HM CX*
☎*441/236–7093* ⊕*www.sandpiperbda.com* ⌖*14 apart-*
ments ⬧*In-room: safe, kitchen (some). In-hotel: pool,*
laundry facilities ⊟*AE, MC, V.*

$ ☎**Serendipity.** These two studio apartments in residential
Paget don't appear on official Bermuda Department of
Tourism accommodation catalogs; hence, perhaps, the
name. For budget travelers who stumble upon one of these
two rooms offered by Albert and Judy Corday, fortune is
smiling. Judy's family has been on the island since 1612,
and she welcomes return guests as part of that extended
family. The real genius of this place, however, is value. Both
ground-floor apartments are clean and spacious, if decorated on the older, homier side. They have fully equipped
kitchenettes and private patios that overlook the pool and
yard, which is canopied in summer by the red blooms of
two magnificent poincianas. Grape Bay beach is a lovely
12-minute walk away. The home is next to the Railway
Trail, and across the street from the Paget Nature Reserve.
PROS: clean, private, friendly, spacious, cheap. **CONS:**
have to walk to beach, no hotel-style services. ⬦*6 Rural*
Dr., Paget Parish PG 06 ☎*441/236–1192* ⌖*2 apartments*
⬧*In-room: safe, kitchen, refrigerator. In-hotel: pool* ⊟*No*
credit cards.

BED & BREAKFASTS

★ $$ ☎**Oxford House.** Oxford House is the only true bed-and-
breakfast in the capital, and one imagines that even if it
had competition, it would still be the best. Even executives
staying in town should be impressed by the elegant pale-
pink two-story town house, which is two blocks from the
capital's shops, ferries, and buses. Rooms have Internet and
desks. The 1938 inn is family-owned and -operated, and
each room is individually decorated with pretty, matching
fabrics and antique and reproduction furniture. Polished
cedar floors, a fireplace, and handsome Chippendale chairs
lend warmth to the breakfast room, where you can sam-
ple scones each morning. There are coffeemakers in the
rooms as well. **PROS:** friendly and attentive service, clean
and updated rooms, right in Hamilton. **CONS:** rooms
more executive than cozy, no beach, no pool. ⬦*20 Wood-*
bourne Ave., Hamilton ⬧*Box HM 374, Hamilton HM BX*
☎*441/295–0503, 800/548–7758 in U.S., 800/272–2306 in*
Canada ⊕*www.oxfordhouse.bm* ⌖*12 rooms* ⬧*In-room:*

LODGING ALTERNATIVES

APARTMENT & VILLA RENTALS

If you want a home base that's roomy enough for a family, consider renting a private house or apartment. Furnished rentals can save you money, especially if you're traveling with a group. **BermudaGetaway** (⊕*www.bermudagetaway.com*) lists a selection of high-standard properties but does not accept reservations. For that, you can contact the property owner directly. **Bermuda Accommodations** (☎*877/730–1352 or 416/232–2243* ⊕*www.bermudarentals.com*) maintains an up-to-the-minute listing of available properties all over the island *and* makes reservations. The Web site has photos and good descriptions of what you can expect to find. **Coldwell Banker JW Bermuda Realty** (☎*441/292–1793* ⊕*www.bermudarealty.com*) requires you to register with the company before an agent will help you find a property that meets your requirements. You can also make reservations with **Villas International** (☎*415/499–9490 or 800/221–2260* ⊕*www.villasintl.com*).

BED & BREAKFASTS

B&Bs in Bermuda range from grand, converted Victorians to a couple of rooms with shared bath in a small home. Breakfasts, too, run the gamut, though light Continental breakfasts with fresh fruit are more common than hearty bacon-and-eggs meals. Sometimes there is a pool on the property, but to get to the beach, you usually have to travel by bus or scooter. **Bermuda Accommodations** (☎*877/730–1352 or 416/232–2243* ⊕*www.bermudarentals.com*) lists and takes reservations for rooms available in B&Bs.

HOME EXCHANGES

If you would like to exchange your home for someone else's, join a home-exchange organization, which will send you its updated listings of available exchanges for a year and will include your own listing in at least one of them. It's up to you to make specific arrangements. **HomeLink International** (☎*954/566–2687 or 800/638–3841* ⊕*www.homelink.org*) charges $90 yearly for a listing. Searching properties is free.

Ethernet, Wi-Fi (some). In-hotel: restaurant, no elevator, laundry service ⊟*AE, MC, V* ⊙|*CP.*

$ ⊡ **Little Pomander Guest House.** You're welcomed to this circa-1600 house—one of the island's oldest—by a quaint driftwood sign above the door. "Little Pomander" has indeed modest ambitions, perhaps a natural extension of its mellow owner, Pat Harvey. It's on a quiet one-way residential street that edges along a narrow inlet of Hamilton harbor. The backside of the cottage has a lawn looking over the water to town; lawn chairs are set out and some guests make use of the barbecue. One much-requested room has a patio with steps leading down to the lawn. Another room with water views is divided by a large unlikely bulge—which turns out to be the house's old wood stove. Quirkiness ends at breakfast—with its humble selection of bagels and toast. **PROS:** inexpensive, residential area makes you feel like part of a community, nice waterfront views of Hamilton, 10-minute walk to Hamilton or beaches. **CONS:** no beach, rooms slightly aging, linens clean but not contemporary. ⊠ *16 Pomander Rd., Paget Parish PG 02* ⬧*Box HM 384, Hamilton HM BX* ☎*441/236–7635* ⊕*www.littlepomander.com* ⊸*6 rooms* ⚘*In-room: refrigerator, Wi-Fi. In-hotel: public Wi-Fi* ▱*AE, MC, V* ⊚*CP.*

★ **Fodor'sChoice** ⊡ **Salt Kettle House.** Innkeeper Hazel Lowe has
$ the warmth and personality that B&B aficionados dream about. This, coupled with the fact that her house and its cottages rest directly on a secluded bay adjoining Hamilton Harbour, make Salt Kettle House the most memorable stay on the island. Besides Ms. Lowe, dramatis personae include her friendly cats Willy and Milly; two ducks; books, which are everywhere; and returning patrons, who constitute 90% of guests. A cozy lounge inside the main entrance has a real fireplace where you can gather for cocktails and conversation. First-timers, "whether they like it or not," are given insightful tips by Ms. Lowe on the best of Bermuda. Four waterside cottages have shaded patios and lounge chairs, bedrooms, sitting rooms, and full kitchens. You can fish here and cook your catch, read on a lawn hammock, or have tea with Ms. Lowe, B&B rock star. **PROS:** steps from ferry, wonderful private setting, beautiful gardens, great hospitality. **CONS:** no beach, no pool. ⊠ *10 Salt Kettle Rd., Paget Parish PG 01* ☎*441/236–0407* ⊟*441/236–8639* ⊸*3 rooms, 4 cottages* ⚘*In-room: safe, kitchen, refrigerator, no TV (some). In-hotel: laundry facilities, public Wi-Fi* ▱*No credit cards* ⊚*BP.*

Nightlife & the Arts

WORD OF MOUTH

"I was told that Bermuda's nightlife is low-key but I went with a group of girlfriends and we had soooooooooo much fun. I guess you make your own fun. We danced till we dropped at Splash nightclub in Hamilton—great DJs! Another night we got to chat (and sing!) with the locals at the Pickled Onion. Bring the right attitude and you'll have fun wherever you go. We want to go back again for the Bermuda Music Festival in October."

—jemiejac

Updated
by Andrew
Raine

BERMUDIANS LOVE TO DRINK. That's the title of a popular local song, and it hits the nail right on the head. Yes, the island that gave the world the Dark 'n Stormy and the rum swizzle might not have the largest selection of hot spots in which to party the night away, but what Bermuda lacks in venues it makes up for in attitude. Tourists, expats, and locals all mix together to create a melting-pot social scene, especially on Friday nights—the unofficial party day for just about everyone living on the Rock. The vibe is civilized but still fun and friendly, and if you're not sure where you want to go, just ask around; people will be more than happy to give you their thoughts—they might even buy you a drink!

If you prefer your nightlife have more culture than rum concoctions, there's still plenty to do. Hubie's Bar is host to the island's finest jazz artists, and City Hall provides a venue for visiting artists on an ad hoc basis. Dramatic productions take place across a variety of venues—anywhere from a hotel auditorium to the back of a Front Street pub.

For a rundown of what's hot and happening in Bermuda, pick up the Bermuda Calendar of Events brochure at any Visitor Information Centre. The free monthly *Preview Bermuda* magazine also lists upcoming island events and can be accessed online at ⊕*www.previewbermuda.com*. *The Bermudian* ($5), a monthly magazine, has a calendar of events, as does *RG* magazine, which is included free in the *Royal Gazette* newspaper on the first Thursday of the month. *This Week in Bermuda,* another free magazine, describes arts and nightlife venues. The *Bermuda Sun* newspaper has a Scene section on Friday, which includes an events calendar. It's also a good idea to check ⊕*www.boxoffice.bm* for upcoming show information.

Some hotels carry a TV station that broadcasts information about the island's cultural events and nightlife. Radio VSB, FM 1450, gives a lineup of events daily at 11:15 AM. You can also dial 974 for recorded information. Because the arts scene in Bermuda is so casual, many events and performers operate on a seasonal or part-time basis. Bulletin boards are also a good spot to check for upcoming events.

NIGHTLIFE

Hamilton is the island's central nightlife hub, with a smattering of decent bars and clubs, featuring live music and drink promotions. Outside of the city there's a thriving nightlife scene within the hotels. In summer, weekly cruises and beach bashes add to the party scene.

Don't overlook the work of local musicians: Bermuda has a long tradition of producing superb jazz artists and hosts an annual jazz festival in fall. One of the best places to catch a jam session is at Hubie's Bar on Friday night; it's a typical jazz bar that caters to the forty-plus crowd. Everyone knows where Hubie's is, so a cab can easily get you there—and it's the kind of place where your neighbor at the bar could be a mail carrier or a member of Parliament.

As a general rule, both men and women tend to dress smart-casual for clubs. This means you may not want to wear T-shirts, ratty jeans, or running shoes. Pubs and clubs begin to fill up around 9:30 or 10.

BARS & LOUNGES

Most bars serve light pub fare in addition to a mean rum swizzle or a Dark 'n Stormy, two local rum-based drinks. Too lazy to call a cab and too elegant to ride your moped? Some of the island's best nightlife takes place at hotel bars—so check yours. Nonhotel guests are always welcome, too.

HAMILTON

Owned and operated by a local comedian and radio personality, **Bootsie's Comedy Club** (✉ *123 Front St.* ☎ *441/737–2668*) is worth a visit as much for the music as for the laughs. Talented jazz–reggae artists offer an authentic Bermuda experience and the crowd is mostly local, so it's good for a true taste of Bermudian nightlife.

★ **Fodor's**Choice Egyptian-theme **Cafe Cairo** (✉ *93 Front St.* ☎ *441/292–4737*) is probably the most popular of Hamilton's nightspots. Decorated with North African furnishings, it's a great place for an early-evening meal. Eating later may lead to indigestion, as after 10 PM it transforms into a jumping nightclub that's often packed with both locals and tourists. Food and drink is served until 3 AM or later on weekends and there's a covered outside area where the adventurous can try smoking the water pipe.

With a trendy Bermudian restaurant in front and an even trendier sushi bar called Yashi in the back, **Coconut Rock** (⊠*20 Reid St.* ☎*441/292–1043*) has a relaxed and friendly buzz. Don't confuse this place with Coconuts, the upscale restaurant at the Reefs resort in Southampton.

★ **Fairmont Hamilton Princess** (⊠*76 Pitts Bay Rd.* ☎*441/295–3000*) is the life of the island on Friday nights from May through October, when management sets up an outdoor buffet, offers special drink prices, and occasionally schedules bands. The magnificent lawns of the famous hotel are packed with locals and tourists who equally enjoy a cold drink and an ogle at the elegant yachts in the harbor. The vibe is trendy, so save your most stylish duds for this night.

Flanagan's Irish Pub & Restaurant (⊠*69 Front St.* ☎*441/295–8299*), on the second floor of the Emporium Building, is a favorite for folks who like to dance and talk over drinks. Lots of exotic, fun beverages, like frozen mudslides, are served up and there's often live music or a DJ on weekends. Adjoining the Irish pub is its sister bar **Legend's Sports Bar,** at the same address. Giant screens flicker with live sports action and walls are plastered with photographs of sporting heroes. There's a pool table and a thriving poker league based at the bar. Both are open from 11 AM to 1 AM.

★ **Fresco's Wine Bar & Restaurant** (⊠*2 Chancery Lane* ☎*441/295–5058*) has the largest selection of wine-by-the-glass in Bermuda, plus desserts to die for. It's just undergone extensive renovations that have made it one of the trendiest places to start a Friday evening out. The crowd is sophisticated but buttoned down. If the weather's nice, try the outdoor bar where you can sip away and chat with your friends under the stars. Dinner is served at the bar until 10:30.

Small, cozy **Hog Penny**, aka the *Cheers* bar (⊠*5 Burnaby Hill* ☎*441/292–2534*), was the inspiration for the Bull & Finch Pub in Boston. With dark-wood paneling and pub fare like steak-and-kidney pie and bangers and mash, the Hog Penny will likely remind you more of an English country pub than a Boston hangout. A singer plays most nights in summer (just Friday and Saturday in winter), when the floor is cleared for dancing. It's open nightly until 1, and it can be very busy.

Lemon Tree Café (⊠7 Queen St. ☎441/292–0235) is a popular happy-hour spot on Friday nights from around 9 PM to midnight. It's a good place to continue the party after Hamilton Princess's happy hour. Lemon Tree caters to a mixed crowd of expats, locals, and tourists who come either to dance to the DJ's disco-style tunes or to sit and chat in the outside area overlooking Victoria Park.

The Pickled Onion (⊠53 Front St. ☎441/295–2263) is a restaurant and bar that caters to a well-heeled crowd of locals and visitors. It's recently undergone a refurbishment that's glammed up the place and given it a cleaner, more sophisticated feel. Live music—usually jazz and pop—plays nightly from about 10:30 to 1 in high season and irregularly off-season.

OUTSIDE HAMILTON

After winter renovations, **Café Lido** and **Mickey's Beach Bar** (⊠Elbow Beach Hotel, 60 S. Shore Rd., Paget Parish ☎441/236–9884) are again open for business and look better than ever. With intimate dining areas and expansive bars, both establishments overlook the cool blue waters just beyond the south shore's Elbow Beach. This complex is perfect for a quiet evening for two.

Frog & Onion Pub (⊠Cooperage Bldg., Sandys Parish ☎441/234–2900) serves a splendid variety of down-to-earth pub fare in a dark-wood, barnlike setting. If you're spending the day at Dockyard, it's a great place to recharge your batteries. It's also one of only two places on the island where you can buy Bermudian-brewed beer.

★ **Henry VIII** (⊠69 S. Shore Rd., Southampton Parish ☎441/238–1977) is a popular restaurant and bar with rich oak paneling, polished brass, and a good program of local or visiting entertainment almost every night. You can also find one of the island's most popular entertainers, piano player and singer Dave Bootel, here. The Sunday night Henry VIII–Southampton Princess Wine Cellar combination is a big crowd puller.

★ **Jasmine** (⊠Fairmont Southampton, 101 S. Shore Rd., Southampton Parish ☎441/238–8000) draws the smartly dressed to its lounge and dance floor. Definitely check out the Joe Wylie Trio in season. Sandwiches, salads, and other light fare are served until 1 AM.

The **Michael Douglas Bar** (⊠Ariel Sands Beach Resort, 34 S. Shore Rd., Devonshire Parish ☎441/236–1010), in the resort's clubhouse, is decorated with publicity photos of the actor and his family. That might sound a little bizarre, but it's not—the resort is owned by the famous actor's Bermudian ancestors, and given that Mr. Douglas spends large amounts of time at his Warwick home with wife Catherine Zeta-Jones, it's not impossible that you might see the real thing walking past the photos. Pull up a stool or relax on a couch beside the giant central fireplace while you wait.

As well as being a relaxed and traditional pub and restaurant, the **North Rock Brewing Company** (✉ *10 S. Shore Rd., Smith's* ☎*441/236–6633*) is one of only two places on the island to get a genuine Bermuda-brewed ale. Try a sampler for a taste of all six of North Rock's famous beers—ranging from the sharp St. David's Light Ale to the head-spinning Whale of Wheat. You might want to book a taxi back to your hotel.

Salt Rock Grill (✉*27 Mangrove Bay Rd., Sandys Parish* ☎*441/234–4502*) keeps locals and visitors alike coming back for more, with its fine cuisine (which includes sushi), water views, and reasonable prices. The cheap happy-hour drinks will lure you in, but the friendly staff and intimate dance floor will keep you there all night.

★ **Fodor'sChoice Swizzle Inn** (✉*3 Blue Hole Hill, off North Rd., Bailey's Bay, Hamilton Parish* ☎*441/293–1854*) has business cards from all over the world tacked on the walls, ceilings, and doors. "Swizzle Inn, swagger out" is the motto. As the name suggests, it's the best place on the island for a jug of rum swizzle. An acoustic guitarist plays a repertoire of classics most nights and even invites brave members of the audience to get up and sing with him. This place is famous and is an absolute must-do.

The **Veranda Bar** (✉*Elbow Beach Hotel, 60 S. Shore Rd., Paget Parish* ☎*441/236–3535*) has a jazz-lounge feel and an outdoor patio, extensive rum menu, and separate cigar room. It's perfect for enjoying a relaxing drink while gazing over the south shore views, or into that special someone's eyes. Get your groove going to DJs on Wednesday and Friday nights and a live band on Saturday in summer.

White Horse (✉*8 King Sq., St. George's* ☎*441/297–1838*) is probably the most popular bar outside Hamilton. It's great for an afternoon pint on the wooden terrace overlooking the water, where swarms of fish fight for scraps thrown from the tables. There are large-screen TVs for sports fans and nightly entertainment for everyone else. It's packed every Tuesday night in summer, when the cruise ships are in port.

The Wine Cellar Bar (✉ *Fairmont Southampton, 101 S. Shore Rd., Southampton Parish* ☎*441/238–8000*) is a nightclub and sports bar within the Southampton Princess hotel. It's an authentic stone cellar with a decent-size dance floor that vibrates to the sound of live music and DJs on a nightly basis throughout the summer. The place is particularly popular on Sunday and draws a mixed crowd of locals and hotel guests. Entertainment by either the popular live-music duo Prestige or DJs goes until 3 AM.

4

MUSIC & DANCE CLUBS

Bermuda's musicians have suffered in recent years with some of the mainstream bars now tending to rely on solo singers with backing tracks, but there's still quality, professional music to be found in some of the less obvious places. Hubie's Bar on Court Street in the "back of town" area is the surest place to find top-quality musicians, while Elbow Beach hotel also often hosts jazz nights. The island's clubs cater to a diversified local and visiting crowd, so you'll be sure to find something to suit your musical taste—be it reggae, calypso, hip-hop, or techno. International artists occasionally perform in Bermuda, especially during the annual Bermuda Music Festival, which usually takes place during the first weekend in October.

If you're looking for something a little more fast-paced than a pub or lounge, there's a thriving party scene with various organizers competing to host top nights out. Unite, Siren Productions, and Volcanic all cater to a trendy, friendly crowd with events ranging from beach parties to opulent color-theme extravaganzas at the Fairmont Southampton. There's no strict schedule or venue for these parties, so look for ads in the local press or check out ⊕*www.volcanic.bm* and ⊕*www.unite.bm*.

HAMILTON

The **Bermuda Folk Club** hosts monthly get-togethers, which usually take place at 8:30 PM on the first Saturday of the month and are often done on an open-mike basis. Note that musicians might perform any number of musical styles besides folk. Drinks are often served at happy-hour prices, and the cover is $6, but can rise to more than $20 for off-island acts. It's worth calling to inquire about nights other than first Saturdays, too, as unpublicized gigs and events sometimes pop up. Venues vary, call ☎ 441/799–2020 or check ⊕ www.folkclub.bm for details.

★ **Fodor'sChoice Hubie's Bar** (⊠ *10 Angle St., off Court St.* ☎*441/293–9287*) books the best jazz bands on the island for weekly sessions on Fridays from 7 to 10. Other kinds of live music or poetry readings might be on the schedule other nights—whatever it is, it's bound to be good. There's a $5 cover. The area is a bit dodgy, so it's best to take a cab to and from the bar.

Level Nightclub (⊠*Bermuda House La., off Front St.* ☎*441/292–4507*) is a European-style dance club that fills up late on Friday and Saturday. An open-air courtyard with a video screen for larger than life music videos keeps the party going until 3 AM daily. When it rains, a canvas roof is pulled over the terrace.

Splash (⊠ *10 Bermudiana Rd.* ☎*441/296–3849*) is Bermuda's hottest nightclub. With a guest DJ spinning tunes each week in a variety of styles including techno, reggae, and dance, this Hamilton club is usually jam-packed and hopping by 11. The door policy is strict for nonmembers so you'll want to dress to impress. The cover charge is $20.

OUTSIDE HAMILTON

★ At **The Deep** (⊠*Elbow Beach Hotel, 60 S. Shore Rd., Paget Parish* ☎*441/232–6969*) you can dance the night away and sip drinks at tables overlooking the dance floor. The island's top DJs and bands often make appearances here, and the music and the comprehensive champagne, wine, and cocktail menu attract the fashionable people of Bermuda's social register. Dance the night away to techno or house music on Sunday night when large numbers of the island's hospitality staff gather to party. Entrance fees can vary depending on the day and your sex; females are usually not charged, males usually have to cough up $20.

The Don't-Stop-the-Carnival-Party at **Hawkins Island** (⊕*www.hawkinsisland.com*) in the Great Sound is a hugely popular party night. It runs throughout the summer and features a boat cruise to and from the island, an open bar, a sumptuous barbecue dinner, Reggae from Tropical Heat, and a show from the new Dark 'n Stormy Carnival limbo dancers. A boat leaves the main ferry terminal at Albouy's Point at 7 PM on Tuesday, Wednesday, Friday, and Saturday, returning at 10:30 PM. The all-inclusive price is $90 per person with tickets available at the **BIC** (⊠*Somers Bldg., 15 Front St., Hamilton* ☎*441/292–8652*).

THE ARTS

Bermuda's arts scene is concentrated in a number of art galleries—Masterworks in the Botanical Gardens, City Hall in Hamilton, and the Arts Centre in Dockyard are the best known—a handful of performance venues, and a few gathering spots, like Rock Island Coffee Café on Reid Street. For dramatic and musical performances, the City Hall Theatre and the Ruth Seaton James Auditorium host the country's best, including Bermuda Festival events. It's also home to the annual Bermuda Idol competition based on the popular American show.

DANCE

The **Bermuda Civic Ballet** (☎*441/293–4147*) performs classical ballet at various venues during the academic year. Internationally known artists sometimes appear as guests.

The **Bermuda School of Russian Ballet** (☎*441/293–4147 or 441/295–8621*) has been around for half a century and presents unique ballet and modern-dance performances. Showtimes and venues vary, so call for details.

The **National Dance Foundation of Bermuda** (☎*441/236–3319* ⊕*www.dancebermuda.org*) funds workshops and develops local talent as well as attracting international dancers and putting on shows and fund-raisers. It draws support from all over the island and enjoys the patronage of Bermuda's most famous resident, Catherine Zeta-Jones.

FILM

☾ Kids love Movie Day at the Youth Branch of the **Bermuda National Library** (⊠*74 Church St., Hamilton* ☎*441/ 295–0487*).

Liberty Theatre (⊠*Union and Victoria sts., Hamilton* ☎*441/291–2035*) is a 270-seat cinema with four daily showtimes, including a matinee. The area immediately outside the theater is safe during the day, but you should not linger in this neighborhood after dark.

The **Little Theatre** (⊠*Queen St., Hamilton* ☎*441/292–2135*) is a 173-seater across the street from Casey's Bar. There are usually three showtimes per evening.

Neptune Cinema (⊠*The Cooperage, Dockyard* ☎*441/291–2035*) is a 118-seat cinema that typically shows feature films twice nightly, with matinees Friday, Saturday, and Sunday.

Southside Cinema, the island's largest theater, is on the former U.S. military base near the airport. Showtime is usually 7:30. Advance tickets are available at **Unlimited Supplies** (⊠*2 Woodlands Rd., Hamilton* ☎*441/295–9229*).

MUSIC

The **Bermuda School of Music** (☎*441/296–5100* ⊕*www.musicschool.bm*) was formed when the country's two leading music schools merged in 2001. Concerts are presented periodically at various venues. There's a guitar festival in May and various other events throughout the year.

THEATER

The **Bermuda Musical & Dramatic Society** (⊠*11 Washington St., Hamilton* ☎*441/292–0848 or 441/295–5584* ⊕*www.bmds.bm*) has some good amateur actors on its roster. Formed in 1944, this active theater society stages performances year-round at their Daylesford headquarters, one block north of City Hall. The Christmas pantomime is always a sellout, as are most other performances. Visit or call the box office at Daylesford, on Dundonald Street, for reservations and information. Tickets are about $10.

Bermuda is the only place outside the United States where Harvard University's **Hasty Pudding Theatricals** (⊠*City Hall, 17 Church St.* ☎*441/295–1727*) performs. For almost 30 years this satirical troupe has entertained the island during Bermuda College Weeks (March through April). Produced by the Bermuda Musical & Dramatic Society, each of these Bermuda-based shows incorporates political and social issues of the past year. They're all staged at the **City Hall Theatre**. Tickets are about $20.

Beaches, Sports & the Outdoors

WORD OF MOUTH

"There is a little cove on the right of the main Horseshoe Bay beach where you can just stand in the water and see fish swim by. Cool but crowded. We walked left past the main beach and there are several smaller beaches (Chaplin and Stonehall Bay beach). Very scenic and not crowded. There are lots of huge boulders scattered in the water and on the beach. The waves were a bit strong but we had a fabulous time. Make sure to take your camera."

—mnag

Updated
by Keisha
Webb-
Gibbs

Long before your plane touches down in Bermuda, the island's greatest asset becomes breathtakingly obvious—the crystal clear, aquamarine water that frames the tiny, hook-shape atoll. So clear are Bermuda's waters that, in 1994, the government nixed a local scuba-diving group's plan to create a unique dive site by sinking an abandoned American warplane in 30 feet of water off the island's East End, fairly close to the end of the airport's runway. The government feared that the plane would be easily visible from above—to arriving passengers—and could cause undue distress. It's the incredible clarity of the water that makes Bermuda one of the world's greatest places for exploratory scuba diving and snorkeling, especially among the age-old shipwrecks off the island. The presence of these sunken ships is actually one of Bermuda's ironies—as translucent as the water is, it wasn't quite clear enough to make Bermuda's treacherous reefs visible to the hundreds of ship captains who have smashed their vessels on them through the centuries.

Thanks to Bermuda's position near the Gulf Stream, the water stays warm year-round. In summer the ocean is usually above 80°F, and it's even warmer in the shallows between the reefs and shore. In winter the water temperature only occasionally drops below 70°F, but it seems cooler because the air temperature is usually in the mid-60s. There's less call for water sports December through March, not because of a drop in water temperature, but because of windy conditions. The wind causes rough water, which in turn creates problems for fishing and diving boats, and underwater visibility is often clouded by sand and debris.

In high season, mid-April through mid-October, fishing, diving, and yacht charters fill up quickly. Three major water-sports outfitters on the island—Blue Hole Water Sports, Somerset Bridge Watersports, and Windjammer Watersports—provide most of the rentals. Many boats carry fewer than 20 passengers, so it's advisable to sign up as soon as you arrive on the island. The shoulder seasons are March through mid-April and mid-October through November. During the "golf and spa season," December through February, many operators close to make repairs and perform routine maintenance. Though a few operators stay open on a limited basis, most will only schedule an outing when there are enough people to fill a boat.

nearby paved road is great for evening strolls, small children's playground keeps kids busy, great beach to spot turtles, picnic area. **CONS:** lots of vehicle traffic, bathrooms can be stinky and often run out of toilet paper. ⊠*Cooper's Island Rd., St. David's Island* Ⓜ*Bus 10 from Hamilton.*

★ **Fort St. Catherine Beach.** Fort St. Catherine is one of the larger north-shore beaches, and the water's deep enough for a serious swim. There's also beach rentals and a snack bar. If and when you get beach-bummed out, head over to the military fort next door, for which this beach is named. Nearby Blackbeard's Hideout is a great place for a refueling meal. **PROS:** beach snack shop and nearby restaurant are convenient, fort tours are great for a beach break. **CONS:** beach is far from nearest bus stop. ⊠*Coot Pond Rd., St. George's Parish* Ⓜ*Bus 1, 3, 10, or 11 from Hamilton.*

☺ **Shelly Bay Beach.** Known for its sandy bottom and shallow water, Shelly Bay is a good place to take small children. It also has shade trees, a rarity at Bermudian beaches. A playground behind the beach attracts hordes of youngsters on weekends and during school holidays. A nearby soccer and cricket practice field and a public basketball court are handy when you want to blow off some steam. **PROS:** shallow beach and adjoining playground for kids, on-site Jamaican food eatery, fun water rentals. **CONS:** noisy street traffic, lots of kids during summer camps, good swimming spots are hard to find during low tide. ⊠*North Shore Rd., Hamilton Parish* Ⓜ*Bus 10 or 11 from Hamilton.*

Somerset Long Bay. Popular with Somerset locals, this beach is on the quiet northwestern end of the island, far from the bustle of Hamilton and major tourist hubs. In keeping with the area's rural atmosphere, the beach is low-key. Undeveloped parkland shields the beach from the light traffic on Cambridge Road. The main beach is long by Bermudian standards—nearly ¼ mi from end to end. Although exposed to northerly storm winds, the bay water is normally calm and shallow—ideal for children. The bottom, however, is rocky and uneven, so it's a good idea to put on water shoes before wading. **PROS:** low-key. **CONS:** rocky bottom. ⊠*Cambridge Rd., Sandys Parish* Ⓜ*Bus 7 or 8 to Dockyard or Somerset from Hamilton.*

Tobacco Bay Beach. The most popular beach near St. George's— about 15 minutes northwest of the town on foot—this small north-shore strand is huddled in a coral cove. Its beach house has a snack bar, equipment rentals, toilets,

BEACHES

Bermuda's south-shore beaches are more scenic than those on the north side, with fine, pinkish sand, and limestone dunes topped with summer flowers and Bermuda crabgrass. The water on the south shore does get a little rougher when the winds are from the south and southwest, but mainly the pale-blue waves break at the barrier reefs offshore and roll gently upon the sandy shoreline. Because the barrier reefs break up the waves, surfing has not really taken off in Bermuda, though many locals—especially children—love to bodysurf at Horseshoe Bay. Kite-surfing is also becoming increasingly popular. Most Bermudian beaches are relatively small compared with ocean beaches in the United States, ranging from about 15 yards to half a mile or so in length. In winter, when the weather is more severe, beaches may erode—even disappear—only to be replenished as the wind subsides in spring.

The Public Transportation Board publishes *Bermuda's Guide to Beaches and Transportation,* available free in all visitor information centers and most hotels. A combination map and bus-and-ferry schedule, the guide shows beach locations and how to reach them. The Bermuda telephone directory, available in hotels, also has maps and public-transportation schedules, plus many other tips for how to get around and what to see.

Few Bermudian beaches offer shade, but some have palm trees and thatched shelters. The sun can be intense, so bring a hat and plenty of sunscreen. You can rent umbrellas at some beaches, but food and drink are rare, so pack snacks and lots of water.

NORTH-SHORE BEACHES

☾ **Clearwater Beach.** On the eastern tip of the island in St. David's Clearwater is a long sandy strip of beach that's popular with serious swimmers and triathletes who use it as a training ground. But don't be intimidated, the young and old also flock here to wade in the shallow water, and there are buoy markers that identify where the beach becomes deeper. Clearwater is one of the few beaches in Bermuda that has an adjoining café, serving kid favorites such as burgers and fries. There's also an in-house bar when the five-o'clock-somewhere mood strikes. Beach bathrooms and lifeguards during the tourist season (April through September) make this a great choice for families. **PROS:**

showers, changing rooms, and ample parking. It's a 10-minute hike from the bus stop in the town of St. George's, or you can flag down a St. George's Minibus Service van and ask for a lift ($2 per person). In high season the beach is busy, especially midweek, when the cruise ships are docked. **PROS:** beautiful rock formations in the water. **CONS:** so popular it becomes overcrowded. ✉ *Coot Pond Rd., St. George's Parish* ☎ *441/297–2756* Ⓜ *Bus 1, 3, 10, or 11 from Hamilton.*

★ **Turtle Beach.** Down a stretch from Clearwater Beach, Turtle Beach offers the same tranquillity, but with a bit less traffic. The water's also a deeper turquoise color here. If you're lucky, you might even spot a turtle. There's also a lifeguard station with a guard on duty. When your tummy grumbles, it's a short walk to Gombey's Restaurant. **PROS:** quiet beach, popular for turtle sightings. **CONS:** little parking, moped traffic. ✉ *Cooper's Island Rd., St. David's Island* Ⓜ *Bus 10 from Hamilton.*

5

SOUTH-SHORE BEACHES

Astwood Cove & Park. On the weekends, you can find lots of children and families at this popular beach. The Astwood Park area is shady and grassy, which makes it popular among locals for birthday parties and family picnics. **PROS:** shady park area. **CONS:** short walk from the park down to the beach area. ✉ *Off South Shore Rd., Warwick Parish* Ⓜ *Bus 7 from Hamilton.*

Chaplin and Stonehole Bays. In a secluded area east along the dunes from Horseshoe Bay Beach, these tiny adjacent beaches almost disappear at high tide. An unusual high coral wall reaches across the beach to the water, perforated by a 10-foot-high, arrowhead-shape hole. Like Horseshoe Bay, the beach fronts South Shore Park. Wander farther along the dunes and you can find several other tiny, peaceful beaches before you eventually reach Warwick Long Bay. **PROS:** low-key atmosphere, adjoining beaches. **CONS:** beach shoes needed. ✉ *Off South Rd., Southampton Parish* Ⓜ *Bus 7 from Hamilton.*

★ ♻ **Elbow Beach.** Swimming and bodysurfing are great at this beach, which is bordered by the prime strand of sand reserved for guests of the Elbow Beach Hotel on the left, and the ultra-exclusive Coral Beach Club beach area on the right. It's a pleasant setting for a late-evening stroll, with the lights from nearby hotels dancing on the water, but the romance dissipates in daylight, when the beach is

Beaches

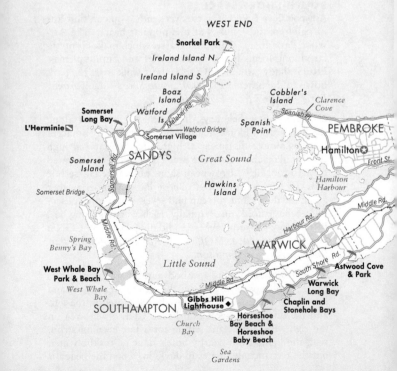

0   2 miles

0   3 km

ATLANTIC OCEAN

◣ **Constellation**

WEST END

Snorkel Park ◣
Ireland Island N.

Ireland Island S.

*Boaz
Island*

*Cobbler's
Island*

*Clarence
Cove*

Spanish Rd.

**Somerset
Long Bay**

*Watford
Is.*

Malabar Rd.

*Spanish
Point*

PEMBROKE

L'Herminie ◣

Watford Bridge
Somerset Village

*Somerset
Rd.*

Hamilton ⊙

SANDYS

Great Sound

Front St.

*Somerset
Island*

Somerset Bridge

*Hawkins
Island*

*Hamilton
Harbour*

Middle Rd.

Middle Rd.

Harbour Rd.

WARWICK

*Spring
Benny's Bay*

Little Sound

South Shore Rd.

**Astwood Cove
& Park**

**West Whale Bay
Park & Beach**

*West Whale
Bay*

Middle Rd.

**Warwick
Long Bay**

SOUTHAMPTON

**Gibbs Hill
Lighthouse** ◆

**Chaplin and
Stonehole Bays**

*Church
Bay*

**Horseshoe
Bay Beach &
Horseshoe
Baby Beach**

*Sea
Gardens*

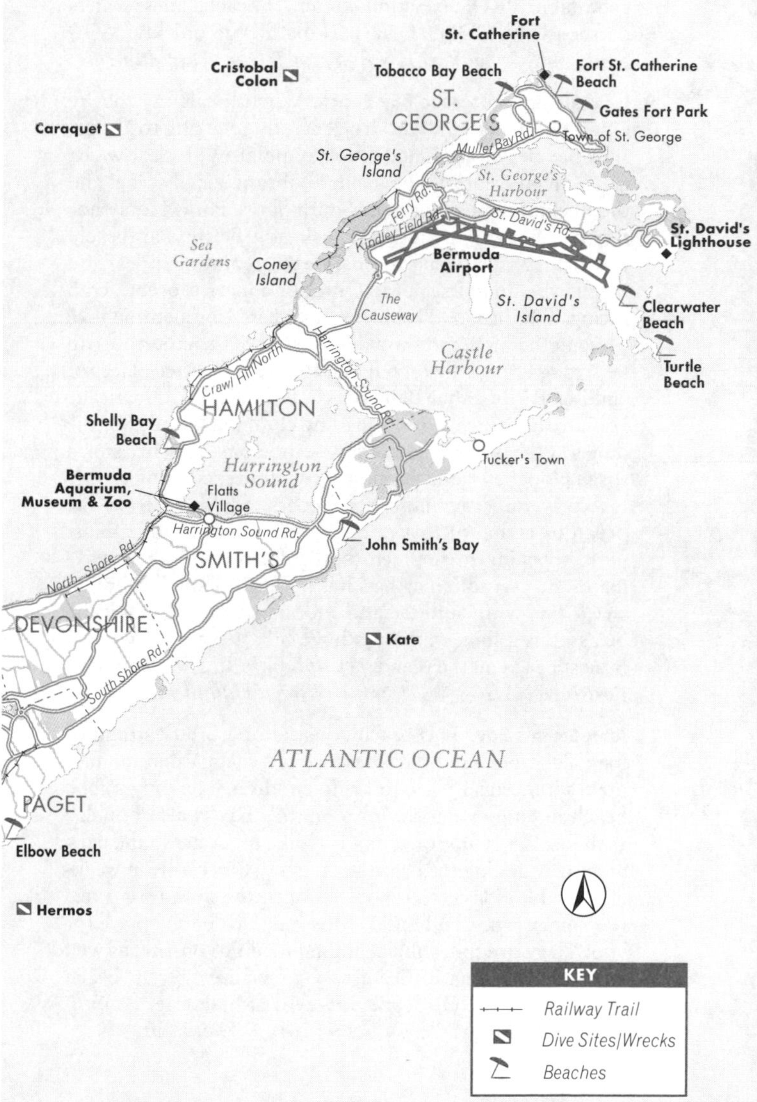
Fort St. Catherine
Cristobal Colon
Tobacco Bay Beach
Fort St. Catherine Beach
ST. GEORGE'S
Gates Fort Park
Caraquet
Town of St. George
Mullet Bay Rd.
St. George's Island
St. George's Harbour
Ferry Rd.
St. David's Rd.
Kindley Field Rd.
St. David's Lighthouse
Sea Gardens
Coney Island
Bermuda Airport
The Causeway
St. David's Island
Clearwater Beach
Harrington Sound Rd.
Castle Harbour
Turtle Beach
Crawl Hill/North
HAMILTON
Shelly Bay Beach
Tucker's Town
Harrington Sound
Bermuda Aquarium, Museum & Zoo
Flatts Village
Harrington Sound Rd.
John Smith's Bay
North Shore Rd.
SMITH'S
DEVONSHIRE
Kate
South Shore Rd.
ATLANTIC OCEAN
PAGET
Elbow Beach
Hermos
KEY
Railway Trail
Dive Sites/Wrecks
Beaches

noisy and crowded. Protective coral reefs make the waters the safest on the island, and a good choice for families. A lunch wagon sells fast food and cold drinks during the day, and Mickey's beach bar (part of the Elbow Beach Hotel) is open for lunch and dinner, though it may be difficult to get a table. **PROS:** beautiful stretch of beach, safest waters on the island. **CONS:** busy, parking fills up quickly. ⊠*Off South Rd., Paget Parish* Ⓜ*Bus 2 or 7 from Hamilton.*

★ FodorsChoice **Horseshoe Bay Beach.** When locals say they're
Ⓒ going to "the beach," they're generally referring to Horseshoe Bay Beach, the island's most popular. With clear water, a 1/3-mi crescent of pink sand, a vibrant social scene, and the uncluttered backdrop of South Shore Park, Horseshoe Bay has everything you could ask of a Bermudian beach. A snack bar, changing rooms, beach-rental facilities, and lifeguards add to its appeal. Outdoor concerts, events, crab racing, and the Good Friday Annual Kite Competition take place in the high and shoulder seasons. The undertow can be strong, especially on the main beach. A better place for children is **Horseshoe Baby Beach.** Before 2003's Hurricane Fabian, this beach was reached by climbing a trail over the dunes at the western end of Horseshoe Bay. Fabian's storm surge ploughed right through those dunes, creating a wide walkway for eager little beachgoers. Sheltered from the ocean by a ring of rocks, this cove is shallow and almost perfectly calm. In summer, toddlers can find lots of playmates. **PROS:** adjoining beach is perfect for small children, snack bar with outdoor and indoor seating. **CONS:** the bus stop is a long walk up a huge hill, gets very crowded, busiest beach on the island. ⊠*Off South Rd., Southampton Parish* ☎*441/238–2651* Ⓜ*Bus 7 from Hamilton.*

Ⓒ **John Smith's Bay.** This beach consists of a pretty strand of long, flat, open sand. The presence of a lifeguard in summer makes it an ideal place to bring children. The only public beach in Smith's Parish, John Smith's Bay is also popular with locals. Groups of young folk like to gather in the park area surrounding the beach for parties, especially on weekends and holidays, so if you're not in the mood for a festive bunch with loud radios, this may not be the place for you. There are toilet and changing facilities on-site, as well as moped parking. **PROS:** grassy picnic area, serene beach in the evening. **CONS:** rough waves at high tide. ⊠*South Shore Rd., Smith's Parish* Ⓜ*Bus 1 from Hamilton.*

✪ **Snorkel Park.** This is a popular spot among local families who like to treat their children to a sandy white beach and pristine views of the water. Food and bar amenities are on-site with beach equipment rentals for the kids as well as parents. If your cruise ship docks in Dockyard, Snorkel Park is a short walk from the cruise terminal. A children's playground is just outside the park. Before you leave be sure to stop in the Clocktower Mall and the Craft Market. Also nearby is the Bone Fish Bar & Grill, the Frog & Onion Pub, and an ATM. **PROS:** park is perfect for children, nearby shopping area and restaurants. **CONS:** must rent beach equipment to use beach, can be busy with summer children's camps. ⊠ *31 Freeport Rd., Dockyard* ☎ *441/234–6989* Ⓜ *Bus 7 or 8 from Hamilton.*

Warwick Long Bay. Different from the covelike bay beaches, Warwick Long Bay has about a ½-mi stretch of sand—the longest of any beach here. Its backdrop is a combination of steep cliffs and low grass- and brush-covered hills. The beach is exposed to some strong southerly winds, but the waves are usually moderate because the inner reef is close to shore. A 20-foot coral outcrop less than 200 feet offshore looks like a sculpted boulder balancing on the water's surface. South Shore Park, which surrounds the bay, is often empty, a fact that only heightens the beach's appealing isolation and serenity. In summer, the Bermuda Department of Tourism hosts "Movies at The Beach." **PROS:** summer movies on the beach. **CONS:** strong southerly winds in winter months. ⊠ *Off South Rd., Southampton Parish* Ⓜ *Bus 7 from Hamilton.*

★ **West Whale Bay.** This beach can be a secluded oasis if you go at the right time: sunset. To get to the beach, you need to cross a huge field and walk down a natural rock formation path. **PROS:** romantic. **CONS:** a bit of a walk from the parking area. ⊠ *Off Whale Bay and Middle Rds., Southampton Parish* Ⓜ *Bus 7 or 8 from Hamilton.*

SPORTS & THE OUTDOORS

BICYCLING

The best and sometimes only way to explore Bermuda's nooks and crannies—its little hidden coves and 18th-century tribe roads—is by bicycle or motor scooter. Arriving at the small shore roads and hill trails, however, means first navigating Bermuda's rather treacherous main roads. They are narrow, with no shoulders, and often congested with traffic (especially near Hamilton during rush hours). Fortunately, there's another, safer option for biking in Bermuda: the Railway Trail, a dedicated cycle path blissfully free of cars.

Despite the traffic, bicycle racing is a popular sport in Bermuda, and club groups regularly whir around the island on evening and weekend training rides. Be prepared for some tough climbs—the roads running north and south across the island are particularly steep and winding—and the wind can sap even the strongest rider's strength, especially along South Shore Road in Warwick and Southampton parishes. Island roads are no place for novice riders. Helmets are strongly recommended on pedal bikes (it's illegal to ride without them on a motor scooter), and parents should think twice before allowing preteens to bike here.

BIKE PATHS

★ **The Railway Trail.** Running intermittently the length of the old Bermuda Railway (old "Rattle 'n' Shake"), this trail is scenic, paved, and restricted to pedestrian and bicycle traffic. You can ask the staff at any bike-rental shop for advice on where to access the trail. One especially lovely route starts at Somerset Bridge and ends 2½ mi later near the Somerset Country Squire pub. You can take your bike onto the ferry for a pleasant ride from Hamilton or St. George's to the Somerset Bridge stop. From there, bike to the bridge on the main road, turn right, and ride uphill for about 50 yards until you reach the sign announcing RAILWAY TRAIL. Turning onto the trail, you find yourself along a course with spectacular views of the Great Sound. Along the way you pass old Fort Scaur, several schools, and the large pink Somerset Cricket Club. Toward the end of the trail segment, you'll find yourself on Beacon Hill Road opposite the bus depot. Here you can turn around and head back to Somerset Bridge, or, for refreshment, turn left and ride to the main road (you can see Somerset Police Station), and make a sharp right turn to find Mangrove Bay Beach and the Somerset Country Squire pub and restaurant. Because the Railway Trail is somewhat isolated and not lighted, you should avoid it after dark.

South Shore Road. This main island road passes absolutely gorgeous ocean views. South Shore Road—also known as South Road—is well-paved and, for the most part, wider than Middle Road, North Shore Road, and Harbour Road, with relatively few hills. However, it's one of Bermuda's windiest and most heavily traveled thoroughfares.

Tribe Road 3. Tribe roads are small, often unpaved side roads, some of which date to the earliest settlement of Bermuda. They make for good exploring, though many are quite short and lead to dead ends. Beginning at Oleander Cycles in Southampton, Tribe Road 3 steeply climbs the hillside just below Gibbs Hill Lighthouse, with views of the south shore below. It eventually leads to a point from where you can see both the north and south shores.

BIKE RENTALS

In Bermuda, bicycles are called pedal or push bikes to distinguish them from the more common motorized two-wheelers, which are also called bikes. Some of the cycle liveries around the island rent both, so make sure to specify whether you want a pedal or motor bike. If you're sure you want to bicycle while you're in Bermuda, try to reserve rental bikes a few days in advance. Rates are around $25 a day, though the longer you rent, the more economical your daily rate. You may be charged an additional $15 for a repair waiver and for a refundable deposit.

Riding a motor scooter for the first time can be disconcerting, wherever you are. Here you have the added confusion that Bermudians drive on the left, and though the posted speed limit is 35 kph, the unofficial speed limit is actually closer to 50 kph (while many locals actually travel faster than that). At most rental shops, lessons on how to ride a motor scooter are perfunctory at best—practice as much as you can before going on to the main road. Though many tourists can and do rent motor scooters, the public transportation system (ferries and buses) is excellent and should not be ruled out.

Eve's Cycle Livery. In three convenient locations around the island, Eve's rents standard-size mountain bikes, as well as motor scooters, including your mandatory helmet. The staff readily supplies advice on where to ride, and there's no charge for a repair waiver. Eve's Cycles on Water Street is convenient if you arrive in Bermuda on a cruise docking in St. George's—the shop is literally a few yards away from the cruise terminal. ✉ *110 Middle Rd., near South Shore Rd., Paget Parish* ☎*441/236–6247* ✉*1 Water St., St. George's* ☎*441/236–0839* ✉*Reid St., Hamilton* ☎*441/236–4491.*

Oleander Cycles. Known primarily for its selection of motor bikes, Oleander Cycles also rents mountain bikes, though none for kids. A repair waiver is charged. Oleander Cycles' Southampton location is convenient to Pompano Beach resort guests; it's next door to the resort. ⊠*8 Middle Rd., west of fire station, Southampton Parish* ☎*441/234–0629* ⊕*www.bermuda.com/oleander* ⊠*Middle Rd. at Valley Rd., Paget Parish* ☎*441/236–2453.*

Smatt's Cycle Livery. Smatt's has two locations—one in Hamilton, next to the Fairmont Hamilton Princess, and the other on the west end of the island at the Fairmont Southampton Resort. The shop offers standard moped rentals with helmet. Before a moped is rented, you'll be asked to take a riding test for your safety. ⊠*74 Pitts Bay Rd., Hamilton* ☎*441/295–1180* ⊠*Fairmont Southampton Resort* ☎*441/238–7800.*

Wheels Cycles. If you're staying in one of Bermuda's large resorts, chances are there's a Wheels Cycles right in the hotel. And even if you're not in a resort you may find a location nearby. The store has several branches all over the island, with mountain bikes for children and adults. ⊠*Front St., near docks, Hamilton* ☎*441/292–2245* ⊕*www.bermuda.com/wheels*

BIKE TOURS

★ **Fantasea Cruises.** This comprehensive outfitter offers a 1½-hour bike tour along the Railway Trail. Your day will start with a short boat cruise to the trail, where you can pick up your bikes. After the ride, finish with a cool-off swim and a drink at 9 Beaches Resort in Somerset. Depending on the day, the tour will start from either Albuoy's Point, Dockyard, or the Waterlot Inn at the Fairmont Southampton. The total trip, including the cruise and biking, lasts three hours. The cost is $65 per person and includes equipment and drinks. ⊠*Albuoy's Point, Hamilton* ☎*441/236–1300* ⊕*www.fantasea.bm.*

CHARTER BOATS & BOAT TOURS

Bermuda is gorgeous by land, but you should take to the water to fully appreciate its beauty. You can either rent your own boat *(see Aquatic Adventures)* or charter one with a skipper. There's literally scores of options to suit all tastes from champagne cruises at sunset to cruise and kayak ecotours.

CHARTER BOATS

More than 20 large power cruisers and sailing vessels, piloted by local skippers, are available for charter. Primarily 30 to 60 feet long, most charter sailboats can carry up to 30 passengers, sometimes overnight. Meals and drinks can be included on request, and a few skippers offer dinner cruises for the romantically inclined. Rates generally range from $300 to $450 for a three-hour cruise, or $650 to $1,500 for a full-day cruise, with additional per-person charges for large groups. Where you go and what you do—exploring, swimming, snorkeling, cruising—is usually up to you and your skipper. Generally, however, cruises travel to and around the islands of the Great Sound. Several charter skippers advertise year-round operations, but the off-season schedule can be haphazard. Skippers devote periods of the off-season to maintenance and repairs or close altogether if bookings lag. Be sure to book well in advance; in the high season do so before you arrive on the island.

Adventure Enterprises. A 36-foot motorized timaran, the *Argo II,* can carry up to 36 people and rents for $250 per hour for sightseeing tours ⊠ *Ordnance Island, St. George's* ☎ *441/335–1382.*

★ **Bermuda Barefoot Cruises.** Skipper Doug Jones will accommodate your every need. He has two 32-foot boats, the *Minnow* and the *Veebyes,* available strictly by private charter, and he'll pick you up and take you anywhere you like. It's like hiring a limousine for a tour of a city, instead of taking a bus. Rates vary depending on the length of the sail. ☎ *441/236–3498* ⊕ *www.bermudabarefootcruises.com.*

Restless Native Tours. Fresh batches of cookies baked on board at every sailing and washed down with lemonade or rum swizzles are the delicious trademark of this family-owned and -operated charter company. Restless Native is also unique in its educational approach to chartering—they offer a crash course on Bermuda's fish and a guided snorkeling trip. The 50- by 30-foot boat is excellent for dinner charters, evening cocktail cruises, birthday parties, and weddings. The owners can pick you up at any wharf on the island. ☎ *441/734–8149 or 441/234–1434.*

★ **Rising Son Cruises.** The *Rising Son II* is a beautiful, 60-foot, 80-passenger catamaran with a full bar. Besides offering sailing, swimming, and snorkeling trips, Captain William "Beez" Evans and the accommodating crew can arrange for you to spend part of the day on Jet Skis, in kayaks, or

Good Cheap Fun!

Bermuda is notoriously expensive, so if you've blown most of your inheritance getting here you needn't splash the rest of it on having a good time.

Walking Along the South-Shore Beaches. There's a 2-mi stretch from Horseshoe Bay in Southampton right down to Warwick Long Bay, which with a bit of clambering and the odd paddle in the ocean you can comfortably negotiate. The quiet secluded spots along the rocks are great for bird-watching and there are a number of tiny coves where you can stop for a picnic.

Cup Match. If you want a real Bermuda experience come to the island during the annual Cup Match holiday—either the last weekend in July or the first weekend in August. It's essentially the all-star cricket game between the best of the west and the best of the east, but you don't have to like cricket to enjoy the atmosphere. Half the island trots through the ground at some stage during the four-day holiday to listen to the sound of the drums, sample the fried chicken, and wave a flag for Somerset or St. George's. It's also the one time of year when gambling is legal and thousands pack the Crown & Anchor tents to roll the dice

for Bermuda's own unique version of the casino favorite—craps. Entry is $10.

Snorkeling at Tobacco Bay. You don't have to rent a boat or even swim very far offshore to get a close-up look at some of Bermuda's wonderful marine life. Tobacco Bay in St. George's is a favorite spot, where colorful sergeant majors, parrot fish, and clown fish can be seen in the crystal clear water close to the rocks. John Smith's Bay in Smith's parish, where shoals of tiny fish cast large dark shadows across the bay, is another great spot.

Wildlife Photography. From a patient day's vigil with an ultralong lens, waiting for a shot of a humpback whale, to a frantic pursuit of a pair of longtails dancing in the summer sky, Bermuda is an amateur photographer's dream.

Rent a Bike. On an island where the speed limit is 20 mph there's no need to worry about renting a car. Bermuda's strict traffic control rules mean you're not allowed to anyway. A bicycle is the best way to discover for yourself the hidden nooks and crannies and secret beaches that the bus routes and the tourist cabs just won't take you to. It costs about $25 a day.

with a parasailing outfitter. Rates start at $800 for the first hour and go up to $2,000 for four hours depending on the number of passengers (up to 80). You can also book one of the popular cruises, such as the Turtle Bay Catamaran Beach Trip. The boat cruises over a turtle sanctuary before anchoring off a quiet sandy bay for snorkeling and kayaking. The price is $65 a head. ⊠ *Town Sq., St. George's* ☎ *441/232–5789* ⊕ *www.charterbermuda.com.*

Tam-Marina. Founded in 1969, Tam-Marina has a reputation for lively dinner and cocktail cruises on a fleet of elegant white ships. *Lady Erica* and *Lady Tamara* often accommodate large private parties on the Great Sound, whereas *Lady Charlotte* is smaller and more luxurious. You can book online. ⊠ *61 Harbour Rd., Paget Parish* ☎ *441/236–0127* ⊕ *www.ladyboats.com.*

CRICKET

Cricket is the number one pastime on this sports-mad island, a fact that was seen with the national celebrations that followed the island's qualification for the Cricket World Cup in 2007. Bermuda is the smallest country ever to make the finals of the competition and its cricketers are treated as heroes in their homeland.

★ Fodor'sChoice On the local scene, **Cup Match** in late July or early August is *the* summer sporting event, played over two days. The event celebrates the emancipation of slaves in Bermuda, with the top players from around the island competing in two teams: the East End team and the West End team. Although the match is taken very seriously, the event itself is a real festival, complete with plenty of Bermudian food and music. Bermuda's only venue for legal gambling, the Crown & Anchor tent is pitched at the field each year. Thousands of picnickers and partyers show up during the two-day match. Although the players wear only white, fans wear colors to support their team—blue on blue represents the East End and navy on red represents the West End. A $10 entry fee is charged per day.

The regular cricket season runs from April through September. Contact the **Bermuda Cricket Board** (⊠ *Gorham Rd., Hamilton* ☎ *441/292–8958* ⊕ *www.bermudacricketboard. com*) for information about the match and other events throughout the year. A welcome addition to the local cricket calendar is the **20/20 World Cricket Classic** (⊕ *www.*

worldcricketclassic.bm/index.html) held on the island for the first time in April 2006. It's an annual event that attracts former stars for a weeklong festival of cricket. Tickets go from $35 and up.

FISHING

Bermuda's proximity to the deep ocean makes it one of the best places in the world for deep-sea fishing. Many of the International Fishing Association's world-record catches were hauled in a few miles off the Bermuda coastline. July and August is marlin season and anglers from all over the world come to the island in a bid to try and hook monster blue marlin in excess of 1,000 pounds. Deep-sea fishing is not just for the experts, though. Most charter companies are happy to teach amateurs how to hook and reel in a catch—whether it's tuna, wahoo, or even marlin. Some of the charter fishermen let you keep your catch but they're not obliged to do so. Many of the fishermen rely on sales to restaurants to bolster their businesses, so unless it's a good day they might not give much away. And don't be surprised to find fish you pulled out of the ocean that day on the menu in one of Bermuda's many restaurants that evening. As well as deep-sea fishing, shore fishing is also popular, while some fishermen trawl inside the reefs. If you've got the cash there's no substitute for the thrill of the open ocean. Scores of operators are on the island, about 20 of which are regularly out on the water. A full list is available at ⊕*www.bermudatourism.com/fishing_charter.html*. Prices vary depending on the size and quality of the boat.

REEF & OFFSHORE FISHING

Three major reef bands lie at various distances from the island. The first is anywhere from ½ to 5 mi offshore. The second, the Challenger Bank, is about 12 mi offshore. The third, the Argus Bank, is about 30 mi offshore. As a rule, the farther out you go, the larger the fish—and the more expensive the charter.

Most charter-fishing captains go to the reefs and deep water to the southwest and northwest of the island, where the fishing is best. Catches over the reefs include snapper, amberjack, grouper, and barracuda. Of the most sought-after deepwater fish—marlin, tuna, wahoo, and dolphin-fish—wahoo is the most common, dolphinfish the least. Trawling is the usual method of deepwater fishing, and charter-boat operators offer various tackle setups, with test-line weights ranging from 20 pounds to 130 pounds. The boats, which range from 31 feet to 55 feet long, are fitted with gear and electronics to track fish, including depth sounders, global-positioning systems, loran systems, video fish finders, radar, and computer scanners.

Half-day and full-day charters are offered by most operators, but full-day trips offer the best chance for a big catch because the boat has time to reach waters that are less often fished. Rates are about $600 per boat for half a day (four hours), $1,000 per day (eight hours). For more information about chartering a fishing boat, you can request or pick up a copy of *What to Do: Information and Prices* at the Bermuda Department of Tourism.

★ **Atlantic Spray Charters.** Half-day and full-day year-round charters are available on Atlantic's 40-foot *Tenacious*. Rates are $650 for the four-hour half day, $850 for six hours, and $1,000 for the eight-hour full day, including all the equipment you need, soda and water, and, most important, the knowledge you need to catch the big fish. ⊠ *St. George's* ☎ *441/735–9444* ⊕ *www.atlanticspraycharters.bm.*

Fish Bermuda. Allen DeSilva is one of Bermuda's most knowledgeable skippers. His Web site is a great source of information on fishing conditions in Bermuda and he guarantees a fun day out for beginners or serious anglers on his DeMako boat, based out of Mill Creek near Hamilton. It costs $1,600 to charter the boat for a nine-hour day. ∎ TIP→ **Check out DeSilva's Web site for yummy recipes on how to cook up your local catch.** ⊠ *Mill Creek, Pembroke* ☎ *441/295–0835 or 441/505–8626* ⊕ *www.fishbermuda.com.*

Overproof. Skipper Peter Rans is a regular in the big-game classic and a master at hooking monster marlin. He can take you to the best spots and help you reel in whatever game fish is in season. His rates vary from $850 for half a day to $1,350 for nine hours of serious marlin hunting. ⊠ *136 Somerset Rd., Somerset* ☎ *441/238–5663 or 441/335–9850* ⊕ *www.overprooffishing.com.*

Playmate Fishing Charters. Father-and-son team Keith and Kevin Winter boast a combined total of 75 years fishing Bermuda's waters so you won't be stuck for experience on a Playmate charter. Rates go from $900 for half a day to $1,300 for the full day with extra costs for tournament fishing. ⊠ *4 Mills Point Lane, Pembroke* ☎ *441/292–7131 or 441/335–5172* ⊕ *www.playmatefishing.com.*

SHORE FISHING

The principal catches for shore fishers are pompano, bonefish, and snapper. Excellent sport for saltwater fly-fishing is the wily and strong bonefish, which hovers in coves, harbors, and bays. Among the more popular spots for bonefish are West Whale Bay and Spring Benny's Bay, which have large expanses of clear, shallow water protected by reefs close to shore. Good fishing holes are plentiful along the south shore, too. Fishing in the Great Sound and St. George's Harbour can be rewarding, but enclosed Harrington Sound is less promising. Ask at local tackle shops about the latest hot spots and the best baits. You can also make rental arrangements through your hotel or contact Windjammer Watersports.

Windjammer Watersports. Rods and reels rent for $20 a day (credit card required to secure the rental). Squid bait and weights are sold here, and it's open seven days a week. ✉*Dockyard Marina* ☎*441/234–3082* ✉*Cambridge Beaches, Sandys Parish* ☎*441/234–0250.*

GOLF

For descriptions of and information about Bermuda's nine golf courses, see Chapter 6.

HELMET DIVING

A different, less technical type of diving popular in Bermuda is helmet diving, offered between April and mid-November. Although helmet-diving cruises last three hours or more, the actual time underwater is about 25 minutes, when underwater explorers walk along the sandy bottom in about 10 to 12 feet of water (depending on the tide), wearing helmets that receive air through hoses leading to the surface. Underwater portraits are available for an extra charge. A morning or afternoon tour costs about $50 for adults and includes wet suits when the water temperature is below 80°F. Note that not all outfitters permit children to helmet dive.

Bermuda Bell Diving. Trips are scheduled daily at 10 and 2, and cost $60 per person. It's recommended that you make reservations one month ahead of time, although they're willing to accommodate you on short notice if there's room on the boat. ✉*Flatts Village, Smith's Parish* ☎*441/292–4434* ⊕*www.belldive.bm.*

One Fish, Two Fish, Red Fish, World Cup Fish

Bermuda's angling competitions attract top fishermen from all over the world. The Bermuda Blast tournament over the July 4 weekend coincides with the World Cup—where anglers across the globe compete to land the largest fish on the planet between 8 AM and 4:30 PM. Each year more and more boats descend on Bermuda over the holiday weekend, with the winners having been pulled out of the island's waters three times since 2002. The biggest local tournament is the Bermuda Big Game Classic with many of the World Cup fishermen sticking around to take part in the three-day festival. The dates vary depending on when the weekend falls but it's usually around July 15. The lure of monster marlin in excess of 1,000 pounds keeps them coming for the third leg of the Bermuda Triple Crown, the Seahorse Anglers Club tournament, the following week. Marlin season is what a lot of Bermuda's sport fishermen live for. "It's the biggest, baddest fish in the ocean—there's no feeling like landing a marlin," explains Sloane Wakefield of Atlantic Spray Charters. The **Bermuda Sport Fishing Association** at ☎441/295–2370 is a good source of information about tournaments.

Greg Hartley's Under Sea Adventure. The Hartleys schedule two diving trips per day, usually at 10 and 1:30, six days per week, in high season. Dives cost around $60 per person. Nondivers are not allowed to snorkel or swim in the same area as the divers, the theory being that fish that are used to helmet divers and approach them for food may endanger themselves by becoming used to snorkelers, swimmers, and eventually fisherfolk. ✉ *Watford Bridge, Sandys Parish* ☎ *441/234–2861* ✇ *www.hartleybermuda.com.*

Peppercorn Diving. Affiliated with Triangle Diving, Peppercorn offers an introduction to the underwater world if you're not ready to take on scuba diving. ✉ *Grotto Bay Beach Hotel, 11 Blue Hole Hill, Hamilton Parish* ☎ *441/293–7319.*

PARASAILING

Parasailing outfitters operate in the Great Sound and in Castle Harbour from May through October. The cost is about $45 per person for an eight-minute flight. Want to sail through the sky with your significant other under a single parachute? Two-person trips costs around $80.

Skyrider Bermuda. Skyrider tours over the Great Sound depart every hour on the hour and cost $50 ($15 if you just want to ride in the boat). ⊠*Dockyard Marina, Sandys Parish* ☎*441/234–3019.*

St. George's Parasail Water Sports Ltd. Open seven days a week, it's $50 for a short ride, $35 for children. ⊠*Somers Wharf, St. George's* ☎*441/297–1542.*

RUNNING & WALKING

Top runners flock to the island in January for the Bermuda International Race Weekend, which includes a marathon and 10-km races. Many of the difficulties that cyclists face in Bermuda—hills, traffic, and wind—also confront runners. Be careful of traffic when walking or running along Bermuda's narrow roads—most don't have shoulders.

Bermuda International Marathon, Half Marathon, and 10K Race. Part of International Race Weekend, held in mid-January, these races attract world-class distance runners from several countries, but they're open to everyone. ☎*441/236–6086.*

The Railway Trail. Runners who like firm pavement are happiest and safest along this former train route, one of the most peaceful stretches of road in Bermuda.

South-Shore Beaches. If you like running on sand, head for the south shore. The trails through South Shore Park are relatively firm. A large number of serious runners can be seen on Horseshoe Bay Beach and Elbow Beach early in the morning and after 5 PM. Another beach for running is ½-mi Warwick Long Bay, the island's longest uninterrupted stretch of sand. The sand is softer here than at Horseshoe and Elbow, so it's difficult to get good footing, particularly at high tide. By using South Shore Park trails to skirt coral bluffs, you can create a route that connects several beaches. Note that the trails can be winding and uneven in some places.

SAILING & YACHTING

Bermuda has a worldwide reputation as a yacht-racing center. The sight of the racing fleet, with brightly colored spinnakers flying, is striking even if it's difficult to follow the intricacies of the race. The racing season runs from March to November. Most races are held on weekends in the Great Sound, and several classes of boats usually compete. You can watch from Spanish Point and along the Somerset shoreline. Anyone who wants to get a real sense of the action should be on board a boat near the race course. The Gold Cup race is held in October, and International Race Week is held at the end of April. In June in alternating years, Bermuda serves as the finish point for oceangoing yachts in three major races starting in the United States.

RACES & EVENTS

Bermuda Ocean Race. This race, from Annapolis, Maryland, takes place every other year in June, with one in 2008. For information, contact **St. George's Dinghy & Sports Club** (☎441/297–1612).

King Edward VII Gold Cup. This is the event of choice if you're more interested in racing than gawking at expensive yachts. Managed by the **Royal Bermuda Yacht Club** (☎441/295–2214), the October tournament hosts many of the world's top sailors—some of whom are America's Cup skippers—and includes the elite among Bermudians in a lucrative chase for thousands in prize money.

Newport (RI)-to-Bermuda Ocean Yacht Race. Powerhouse yachtsmen flock to this event in June. The race takes place every two years, with one in 2008. Be sure to attend the after-race party—it's open to the public and is always extremely well attended. Contact the **Royal Bermuda Yacht Club** at (☎441/295–2214).

Non-Mariners Race. Though not as prestigious as the rest, this annual race, which takes place in early August during Cup Match weekend (the annual cricket holiday), is one of the highlights of the year. Held out of the **Sandys Boat Club** (☎441/234–2248 or 441/234–4137) at Mangrove Bay, the goal of this race is simple: to see whose boat (constructed on the beach minutes before) can make it out of the harbor without sinking. Easy to watch as the boats never get very far from land, this race sets the stage for an afternoon of music, barbecue, local political satire, and merrymaking. Legend has it that someone even tried to float an old bus one year. A good viewpoint from which to watch the race is the **Somerset Country Squire Pub** (☎441/234–0105).

RENTALS

Outfitters like **SurfShack** and **Windjammer** *(see Aquatic Adventures)* have a range of crafts to rent and also offer lessons for beginners. It's also worth checking out **Paget Dinghy Club,** which is the main center for sailors in Hamilton and offers lessons for beginners. If you know what you're doing and fancy taking part in some amateur racing, this is the place to be on a Wednesday evening. Just turn up at the dock—skippers are always looking for willing crew members. ✉*Mangroville, Paget* ☎*441/236–3077* ⊕*www. rhadc.com.*

SCUBA DIVING

Bermuda has all the ingredients for classic scuba diving—reefs, wrecks, underwater caves, a variety of coral and marine life, and clear, warm water. Although you can dive year-round (you will have to bring your own gear in winter, when dive shops are closed), the best months are May through October, when the water is calmest and warmest. No prior certification is necessary. Novices can learn the basics and dive in water up to 25 feet deep on the same day. Three-hour resort courses ($95–$110) teach the basics in a pool, on the beach, or off a dive boat, and culminate in a reef or wreck dive.

The easiest day trips involve exploring the south-shore reefs that lie inshore. These reefs may be the most dramatic in Bermuda. The ocean-side drop-off exceeds 60 feet in some places, and the coral is so honeycombed with caves, ledges, and holes that opportunities for discovery are pretty much infinite. Despite concerns about dying coral and dwindling fish populations, most of Bermuda's reefs are still in good health. No one eager to swim with multicolor schools of fish or the occasional barracuda will be disappointed. ⚠**In the interest of preservation the removal of coral is illegal and subject to hefty fines.**

Dive shops around Bermuda prominently display a map of the outlying reef system and its wreck sites. Only 38 of the wrecks from the past three centuries are marked. They're the larger wrecks that are still in good condition. The nautical carnage includes some 300 wreck sites—an astonishing number—many of which are well preserved.

As a general rule, the more recent the wreck or the more deeply submerged it is, the better its condition. Most of the well-preserved wrecks are to the north and east, and dive depths range between 25 feet and 80 feet. Several wrecks off the western end of the island are in relatively shallow water, 30 feet or less, making them accessible to novice divers and even snorkelers.

Blue Water Divers Ltd. The major operator for wrecks on the western side of the island, Blue Water Divers offers lessons, tours, and rentals. The lesson-and-dive package for first-time divers, including equipment, costs $99. From the Elbow Beach Hotel location, you can ride a diver-propulsion vehicle (DPV), which is like an underwater scooter, past a wreck and through caves and canyons. A one-tank dive for experienced divers costs $60, and a two-tank dive is $85. With two tanks you can explore two or more wrecks in one four-hour outing. For all necessary equipment—mask, fins, snorkel, scuba apparatus, and wet suit (if needed)—plan to spend about $40 more. Night dives are available, too. This operator is not to be confused with Dive Bermuda, despite the Web address. ⊠*Elbow Beach Hotel, Paget Parish* ☎*441/232–2909* ⊠*Robinson's Marina, Somerset Bridge, Sandys Parish* ☎*441/234–1034* ⊕*www.divebermuda.com.*

Dive Bermuda was awarded National Geographic Dive Centre status in 2006 and is the only center on the island to offer courses sanctioned by the world-renowned environmental magazine. It also offers PADI (Professional Association of Diving Instructors) instructor-level courses for divers who want to take the next step in their training. Formerly known as Nautilus Diving, it has locations on the south shore and Hamilton Harbour out of the famous Fairmont hotels. A lesson-and-dive package typically costs $115 including equipment, the same as a single-tank dive. A double-tank dive costs $135. Group rates and multiple dives cost less. ⊠*Fairmont Hamilton Princess Hotel* ☎*441/295–9485* ⊠*Fairmont Southampton Hotel* ☎*441/238–2332* ⊕*www.bermudascuba.com.*

★ **Fodor'sChoice Triangle Diving.** For East End diving among wrecks and coral reefs, head for this outfitter in the Grotto Bay Beach Hotel. A range of dive tours is offered, as well as PADI certification courses. Friendly staff who really know their stuff and who never get tired of sharing their vast knowledge of Bermuda's wrecks make diving with this company all the more fun. The location also offers great access to one of Bermuda's most beautiful reefs at North Rock. At press time, the company was planning to bring cage-diving for sharks by January 2008. Give them a call and see if they're ready for you to get up close and personal with the most fearsome predators in the ocean. ⊠*Grotto Bay Beach Hotel, 11 Blue Hole Hill, Hamilton Parish* ☎*441/293–7319* ⊕*www.trianglediving.com.*

SNORKELING

The clarity of the water, the stunning array of coral reefs, and the shallow resting places of several wrecks make snorkeling in the waters around Bermuda—both inshore and offshore—particularly worthwhile. You can snorkel year-round, although a wet suit is advisable for anyone planning to spend a long time in the water in winter, when the water temperature can dip into the 60s. The water also tends to be rougher in winter, often restricting snorkeling to the protected areas of Harrington Sound and Castle Harbour. Underwater caves, grottoes, coral formations, and schools of small fish are the highlights of these areas.

Some of the best snorkeling sites are accessible only by boat. As the number of wrecks attests, navigating around Bermuda's reef-strewn waters is no simple task, especially for inexperienced boaters. If you rent a boat yourself, stick to the protected waters of the sounds, harbors, and bays, and be sure to ask for an ocean-navigation chart. These charts point out shallow waters, rocks, and hidden reefs.

For trips to the reefs, let someone else do the navigating—a charter-boat skipper or one of the snorkeling-cruise operators. Some of the best reefs for snorkeling, complete with shallow-water wrecks, are to the west, but where the tour guide or skipper goes often depends on the tide, weather, and water conditions. For snorkelers who demand privacy and freedom of movement, a boat charter (complete with captain) is the only answer, but the cost is considerable— $650 a day for a party of 18. By comparison, half a day of snorkeling on a regularly scheduled cruise generally costs $45 to $65, including equipment and instruction.

★ **Fodor'sChoice Church Bay.** When Bermudians are asked to name a favorite snorkeling spot, they invariably rank Church Bay in Southampton (at the western end of the south-shore beaches) at, or near, the top of the list. A small cove cut out of the coral cliffs, the bay is full of nooks and crannies, and the reefs are relatively close to shore. Snorkelers should exercise caution here (as you should everywhere along the south shore), as the water can be rough. A small stall often sells snorkeling equipment, underwater cameras, and fish food.

☼ **Snorkel Park.** Off a rocky beach surrounded by the walls of the fort in Dockyard, the snorkel park is a cool place for kids. With a sunken cannon and other underwater features it's worth a look if you're in the West End. There's a bar and you can rent umbrellas and snorkel gear for a small fee. The site is closed November through April.

Tobacco Bay. This beautiful bay is tucked in a cove near historic Fort St. Catherine's beach. Tobacco Bay offers wonderful snorkeling, public facilities, and equipment rentals, and there's a snack bar near the shore. This site is the most popular in St. George's.

Warwick Long Bay. On south shore in Warwick, this ½ mi of beach is usually secluded and quiet. After Hurricane Fabian in 2003, formerly popular snorkeling spot Church Bay was closed to the public and the snorkeling concession stand there (featuring a popular DJ) was moved to Warwick Long Bay until Church Bay could be reopened.

SNORKELING CRUISES

Snorkeling cruises, offered from April to November, are a less expensive albeit less personal way to experience the underwater world. Some boats carry up to 40 passengers to snorkeling sites but focus mostly on their music and bars (complimentary beverages are usually served on the trip back from the reefs). Smaller boats, which limit capacity to 10 to 16 passengers, offer more personal attention and focus more on the beautiful snorkeling areas themselves. Guides on such tours often relate interesting historical and ecological information about the island. To make sure you choose a boat that's right for you, ask for details before booking. Most companies can easily arrange private charters for groups.

Hayward's Snorkeling & Glass Bottom Boat Cruises. Groups of about 35 people board Hayward's 54-foot glass-bottom *Explorer* for 3¾-hour snorkeling trips. Access into and out of the water from the boat is easy. Special excursions are arranged during the spring migration of the humpback whales. ⊠*Adjacent to Hamilton Ferry Terminal* ☎*441/236–9894* ▧*$50* ☉*Daily 9:45 and 1:30.*

Jessie James Cruises. Half-day trips aboard the 40-passenger luxury Chris Craft *Rambler* cost $50, including gear and instruction. ⊠*47 Front St., Hamilton* ☎*441/236–4804* ⊕*www.jessiejames.bm.*

★ **Restless Native Tours.** Captain Kirk Ward has regularly scheduled sailing and snorkeling trips to the outer reefs on a 50-by-30-foot catamaran. With a crash course in Bermuda's marine life, plus fresh cookies on board, it's hard to resist this popular outfitter. The tours depart from wharfs all over the island. ☎*441/234–8149 or 441/234–1434.*

SNORKELING EQUIPMENT RENTALS

Snorkeling equipment and sometimes underwater cameras are available for rent at most major hotels and at several marinas, as well as from the snorkeling concession stand at Warwick Long Bay. The Grotto Bay Beach Hotel & Tennis Club and Fairmont Southampton have dive operators on-site. A deposit or credit-card number is usually required when renting equipment.

Pompano Beach Club Watersports Centre. Equipment at Pompano rents for $8 per day, or $4 per hour, for a mask, snorkel, and flippers. Each piece is also available separately. ⊠*36 Pompano Beach Rd., Southampton Parish* ☎*441/234–0222.*

Windjammer Watersports. You can rent mask, snorkel, and flippers here for $20 per 24-hour period. Two of three pieces cost just $10. ⊠*Dockyard Marina, Sandys Parish* ☎*441/234–0250.*

TENNIS

Bermuda has one tennis court for every 600 residents, a ratio that even the most tennis-crazed countries would find difficult to match. Many are private, but the public has access to more than 70 courts in 20 locations. Courts are inexpensive and seldom full. Hourly rates for nonguests are about $10 to $16. You might want to consider bringing along a few fresh cans of balls, because balls in Bermuda cost $6 to $7 per can—two to three times the rate in the United States. Among the surfaces used in Bermuda are Har-Tru, clay, cork, and hard composites, of which the relatively slow Plexipave composite is the most prevalent.

Despite Bermuda's British roots, the island has no grass court.

Wind, heat (in summer), and humidity are the most distinct characteristics of Bermudian tennis. From October through March, when daytime temperatures rarely exceed 80°F, play is comfortable throughout the day. But in summer, the heat radiating from the court (especially hard courts) can make play uncomfortable between 11 AM and 3 PM, so some clubs take a midday break. Most tennis facilities offer lessons, ranging from $25 to $30 for 30 minutes of instruction, and racket rentals for $4 to $6 per hour or per play.

Coral Beach & Tennis Club. Introduction by a member is required to play at this exclusive club, which is the site of the annual XL Capital Bermuda Open tournament in April. Coral Beach has eight clay courts, three of which are floodlit. It's open daily from 8 to 8. Resident pro Derek Singleton is the man to talk to about scheduling lessons, which run $45 for a half hour. Tennis whites are required. ⊠ *Off South Shore Rd., Paget Parish* ☎ *441/236–2233.*

Elbow Beach Hotel. This facility is fortunate to have as its director of tennis David Lambert, who is also a former president of the Bermuda Lawn Tennis Association. There are five Plexipave courts on hand, three with lights, and hours of play are 8 AM to 9 PM daily. Courts cost $12 per hour. Lessons and match play can be arranged for hotel guests or other visitors at $30 per half hour. ⊠ *Off South Shore Rd., Paget Parish* ☎ *441/236–3535.*

The Fairmont Southampton. Despite their position at the water's edge, the Plexipave hard courts here are reasonably shielded from the wind, although the breeze can be swirling and difficult. Six courts are at hand, with fees ranging from $12 to $16 per hour on any of the three courts that have lighting. Hours of service are daily from 8 AM to 6 PM, extended until 8 in summer. Lessons from pro Mark Cordeiro are available at $40 per half hour or $75 per hour. ⊠ *South Shore Rd., Southampton Parish* ☎ *441/238–1005.*

Government Tennis Stadium. These are the busiest of Bermuda's tennis courts, their inland location ideal for combating strong winds. Of the eight all-weather courts available, five are Plexi-Cushion and three are Har-Tru. Three courts in the main stadium have floodlights. Hours are from 8 AM to 10 PM weekdays and from 8 to 6 on weekends. Rates are

$8 per hour during the day and $16 per hour at night. Tennis attire is required, and lessons are available starting at $30 per half hour and $50 per full hour. ⊠*2 Marsh Folly, Pembroke Parish* ☎*441/292–0105.*

Pomander Gate Tennis Club. There are five hard courts available (four with lighting) at this scenic club located off Hamilton Harbour. Temporary membership is available for $30 per couple per week. Hours of play are 7 AM to 11 PM on weekdays, until 10 PM on weekends. ⊠*Pomander Rd., Paget Parish* ☎*441/236–5400.*

Port Royal Golf Course. Port Royal has four hard courts, two of which are floodlit. A host of pros are on hand to offer instruction. Rates for court play are the cheapest on the island; $10 per hour in the day and $14 per hour at night—it's open until 10 PM. Arrangements can be made through the golf club from 10 AM. ⊠*Off Middle Rd., Southampton Parish* ☎*441/238–9430.*

TENNIS TOURNAMENTS

Bermuda Lawn Tennis Association. Established in 1964, the association hosts all the important tennis events on the island. Ask for an events calendar. ☎*441/296–0834* ⊕*www.blta.bm.*

XL Capital Bermuda Open. In April, the clay courts at the Coral Beach & Tennis Club host this ATP Tour, a USTA-sanctioned event with the world's top professionals. Big names, such as Patrick Rafter and Todd Eldridge, have played in this event, as well as several of Bermuda's own tennis stars, such as James Collieson. In November there's back-to-back tournament activity at the club, too. The action begins with the Bermuda Lawn Tennis Club Invitational followed by the Coral Beach Club Invitational.

Golf

WORD OF MOUTH

"Port Royal is a nice course, and the 16th hole is the whole enchilada. I had to hit my tee shot toward the ocean because of the wind. I would also recommend St. George's. It's a short course but the views are awesome. One hole (mulligan hole, definitely) you can either hit your tee shot over an inlet (about 260 yards) or hit around it."

—iamawfull

Updated
by Dale
Leatherman

GOLF IS AN IMPORTANT FACET of Bermuda sporting life, where golf courses make up nearly 17% of the island's 21.6 square mi. The scenery on the courses is quite often spectacular, with trees and shrubs decked out in multi-color blossoms against a backdrop of brilliant blue sea and sky. The layouts may be shorter than what you're accustomed to, but they're remarkably challenging, thanks to capricious ocean breezes, daunting natural terrain, and the clever work of world-class golf architects.

Of the seven 18-hole courses and two 9-hole layouts on Bermuda, five are championship venues: Belmont Hills, the Mid Ocean Club, Port Royal, Riddell's Bay, and Tucker's Point. All are well maintained, but you should not expect the springy bent grass fairways and fast greens typical of U.S. golf courses. The rough is coarse Bermuda grass that will turn your club in your hands. Because the island's fresh water supply is limited, watering is usually devoted to the greens and tees, which means the fairways are likely to be firm and give you lots of roll. Expect plenty of sand hazards and wind—*especially* wind.

Most clubs have TifEagle or Tifdwarf greens—finer-bladed grasses that are drought-resistant and putt faster and truer than Bermuda grass. However, the greens at St. George's Golf Club are seashore paspalum grass, a fine-bladed, salt-resistant variety that is popular in the Caribbean. It's a user-friendly putting surface once you get used to the fact that the ball doesn't break as much as you expect. In any case, you'll want to spend time on the practice greens to get a better feel.

Most courses overseed with rye grass sometime between late September and early November to maintain color and texture through the cooler winter months. Some courses use temporary greens, whereas others keep their regular greens in play during the reseeding process. This makes for inaccurate putting situations, so if you're visiting in fall, call ahead to find out the condition of the greens. Though all courses now have carts, there's often a "cart path only" rule in force to protect the fairways, so expect to do some walking.

Many Bermudian tracks have holes on the ocean or atop seaside cliffs. They're wonderfully scenic, but the wind and that big natural water hazard can play havoc with your game.

All courses in Bermuda have dress codes: long pants or Bermuda (knee-length) shorts and collared shirts for both men and women. Denim is not allowed. All courses require soft spikes. ■TIP→ **Bermudian men always wear color-coordinated knee-high socks with their shorts on other occasions, but it's okay to go bare-legged on the golf course.**

Courses in Bermuda are rated by the United States Golf Association (USGA), just as they are in the States, so you can tell at a glance how difficult a course is. For example, a par-72 course with a rating of 68 means that a scratch golfer (one who usually shoots par) should be four under par for the round. High handicappers should score better than usual, too.

Reserve tee times before you leave home or ask your hotel concierge to do so as soon as you arrive. This is especially necessary to access the private courses. "Sunset" tee times, available at lower greens fees, generally start at 3 PM, but call ahead to be sure.

Lessons, available at all courses, cost $35 to $60 for a half hour, and $60 to $100 for an hour. Club rentals cost $25 to $45 (except on the Horizons and Cottages "mashie" course, where $5 will get you the few irons and putter needed). Caddies are available only at the Mid Ocean Club, where you'll pay $30 per golf bag or $35 for a double carry, plus a tip of 10 to 15 percent.

DID YOU KNOW? Bermuda does not have rivers and streams, and has very few natural ponds, so any water hazards you encounter (other than the ocean) are likely man-made.

GOLF COURSES & CLUBS

BELMONT HILLS GOLF CLUB
18 holes. 6,017 yards. Par 70. Rating: blue tees, 68.4; white tees, 66.8; red tees, 69.

Belmont Hills, opened in June 2003, was designed by California architect Algie Pulley Jr. and built on the site of the former Belmont Manor and Golf Club, a haven for celebrities in the early 1900s. "Hills" was added to the course name to reflect the dramatic design features that Pulley used to replace the previous, rather mundane layout. This is now a real shot-making test, heavily contoured and with more water than most other Bermuda courses. The sand in the bunkers is the same used at the famed Augusta National, site of the Masters. A waterfall connects two man-made

Secrets from a Golf Pro

Golf courses elsewhere are often designed with the wind in mind—long downwind holes and short upwind holes. Not so in Bermuda, where the wind is anything but consistent or predictable. Quirky air currents make play on a Bermudian course different every day. The wind puts a premium on being able to hit the ball straight, and grossly exaggerates any slice or hook.

The hard ground of most Bermudian courses means you must abandon the strategy you use on heavily watered tracks. Your ball will run a lot in the fairway, so don't overestimate the distance to hazards. Around the greens, it's wise to run the ball to the hole rather than chipping. Not only will you find it difficult to get under the ball on the firm fairways, but your shot will be subject to the vagaries of the wind. If you're in the clinging Bermuda grass rough, your club face is likely to turn if you try to swing through it.

So, how should you prepare for a Bermuda trip? Practice run-up shots from close-cropped lies using a 5- or 6-iron—or a putter from just off the green. Use mid-irons to practice punching shots from the rough, angling back into the fairway rather than trying to advance the ball straight ahead and risk landing in the rough again. Putting surfaces are often undulating and grainier than bent grass, so putts will break less than you expect. They'll also die much more quickly unless you use a firm stroke.

lakes that can come into play on several holes. The final four holes are particularly challenging because of their tight landing areas bordered by out-of-bounds stakes. A bad hit or intervention by the ever-present wind can lead to lost balls and penalties. The pressure continues until the ball is in the hole, because the greens are heavily bunkered and multitiered. Putting surfaces are well-maintained TifEagle grass. Fairways are attractively defined by palm trees, and an automated irrigation system keeps everything lush. The course has the island's only double green, a 14,000-square-foot putting surface on holes 1 and 10.

Highlight Hole: The 7th hole, a 178-yard par 3, is bordered by a waterfall.

Clubhouse: The main clubhouse stands on the site of the former Belmont Hotel, close to the 9th hole. The building has lovely views of the Great Sound and Hamilton Harbour, plus an airy lounge, bar, pro shop, and restaurant. **Blu'** (☎441/232–2323) is an extraordinary dining experience. Its eclectic menu includes fork-tender Angus steaks; innovative seafood dishes such as salmon, crab, shrimp, and avocado wrapped in a tortilla; and irresistible desserts. ✉97 Middle Rd., Warwick Parish ☎441/236–6400 ⊕www.belmonthills.com ⌨Greens fees $103 daily, $60 sunset (walking only after 2 PM). Mandatory cart rentals $27 per person. Pull cart rentals (sunset only) $10. Shoe rentals $15. Club Rentals $45. Lessons $60 for 30 minutes, $100 per hour.

BERMUDA GOLF ACADEMY

When you just want to practice or have some fun teaching the kids how to play golf in a relaxed environment, head for the Bermuda Golf Academy. The 320-yard driving range is floodlit at night until 10 (weekdays) or 10:30 (weekends) and there are 40 practice bays. ■TIP→If you get a rainy day, fine-tune your game in one of the 25 covered bays. Elevated target greens are placed 75 to 230 yards from the tees. You can also work on sand shots in the practice bunker or sharpen your putting on a 3,000-square-foot practice green.

Especially attractive for families is the 18-hole miniature golf course, which features pagodas, a waterfall, waterways—even a drawbridge to hit over on the 16th hole. The minicourse is lighted at night and takes 45 to 80 minutes to complete. Adjacent is a new restaurant and small café, **East Meets West** (☎441/238–8580). As the name implies, the cuisine includes Japanese, Chinese, Balinese, English, Caribbean, Indian, and American. The café side has a wide range of hot sandwiches, wraps, salads, meins, noodles, and Indian dishes, plus full breakfasts. ✉10 Industrial Park Rd., off Middle Rd., Southampton Parish ☎441/238–8800 ⌨Driving range $5, $6 after 5 PM. Miniature golf $10 adults, $8 children. Lessons $40 a half hour, $70 per hour, or $100 per hour with a video analysis.

FAIRMONT SOUTHAMPTON GOLF CLUB
18 holes. 2,684 yards. Par 54. Rating: 53.7.

Spreading across the hillside below the high-rise Fairmont Southampton, this executive golf course is known for its steep terrain, giving players who opt to walk (for sunset tee times only) an excellent workout. The vertical drop on the first two holes alone is at least 200 feet, and the rise on the 4th hole makes 178 yards play like 220. The Ted Robinson design is a good warm-up for Bermuda's full-length

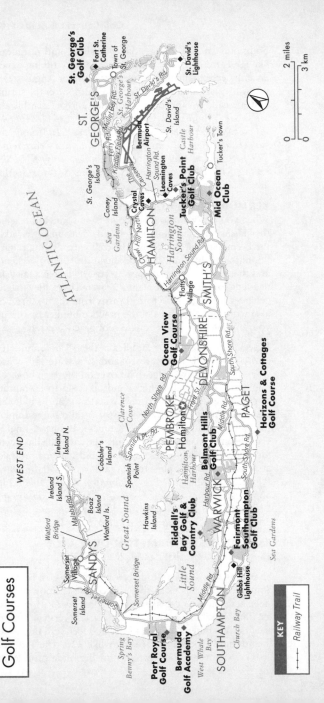

Golf Courses

KEY

—+— Railway Trail

ATLANTIC OCEAN

WEST END

Ireland Island N.

Ireland Island S.

Cobbler's Island

Coney Island

Sea Gardens

St. George's Island

ST. GEORGE'S

St. George's Golf Club ◆

◆ Fort St. Catherine

Town of St. George

St. George's Harbour

Ferry Rd.

Mullet Bay Rd.

Kindley Field Rd.

St. David's Rd.

St. David's Lighthouse ◆

Bermuda Airport

St. David's Island

Crawl Hill

North Shore Rd.

Crystal Caves

Leamington Caves ◆

Harrington Sound Rd.

The Causeway

Castle Harbour

Harrington Sound

Tucker's Point Golf Club ◆

Mid Ocean Club ◆

Tucker's Town

HAMILTON

Flatts Village

SMITH'S

DEVONSHIRE

North Shore Rd.

Ocean View Golf Course ◆

Front St.

PEMBROKE

Hamilton

Clarence Cove

Spanish Point

Spanish Pt. Rd.

Hamilton Harbour

Harbour Rd.

Middle Rd.

South Shore Rd.

Belmont Hills Golf Club ◆

PAGET

Horizons & Cottages Golf Course ◆

Great Sound

Hawkins Island

Little Sound

Watford Bridge

Watford Island

Boaz Island

Malabar Rd.

Watford Is.

Somerset Island

Somerset Village

SANDYS

Somerset Rd.

Somerset Bridge

Spring Benny's Bay

West Whale Bay

Port Royal Golf Course ◆

Bermuda Golf Academy ◆

Gibbs Hill Lighthouse

Church Bay

Middle Rd.

SOUTHAMPTON

Riddell's Bay Golf & Country Club ◆

WARWICK

Fairmont Southampton Golf Club ◆

South Shore Rd.

Sea Gardens

0 — 2 miles

0 — 3 km

courses, offering a legitimate test of wind and bunker play. The front nine has almost constant views of the ocean and is more difficult than the back nine, with tight holes calling for careful club selection.

Highlight Hole: The signature hole is the 214-yard 14th, but the most striking is the 174-yard 16th hole, which sits in a cup ringed by pink oleander bushes. The Gibbs Hill Lighthouse, less than a mile away, is the backdrop.

Clubhouse: Because the hotel and its restaurants are so close, there's no golf clubhouse per se, just a 10th-hole Golf Hut for snacks and drinks. The golf shop has a fine selection of quality golf wear and any essentials you might forget to bring. On the level above the golf shop is **Bacci** (☎441/238–8000), a fine Italian restaurant overlooking the course. If you have a yearning for steak, catch the hotel shuttle to the bottom of the hill, where the 320-year-old **Waterlot Inn** (☎441/238–8000) sits on the edge of the marina. It's unassuming from the outside, but inside it's all elegance, romance, and comfort, with beamed ceilings and windows overlooking the water and terrific sunsets. The Angus steaks here are among the best on the island and the seafood is delectable, too. Try the seared scallop appetizer and the surf and turf. Both restaurants are open evenings only, from 6 to 10. ✉*Fairmont Southampton, South Rd., Southampton Parish* ☎*441/239–6952* ⊕*www.fairmont. com/Southampton* ⛳*Greens fees $79 with mandatory cart, $39 sunset walking. Pull-cart rental $7.50. Shoe rentals $10. Titleist-club rentals $25. Lessons $40 a half hour, $80 per hour.*

HORIZONS & COTTAGES GOLF COURSE
⛳ *9 holes. 756 yards. Par 27. Rating: none.*

On the grounds of the Horizons & Cottages colony, this "mashie" (irons only) course is a fun place to practice your short game or expose your kids to play on a nicely maintained quick course. Do keep up the pace of play, though, so as not to disturb those following you. Golf carts are not available—understandably, since the longest hole (4th) is just 122 yards and the shortest (7th) a mere 51. Hit a hole in one and your name will be added to the plaque in the Pub Bar, which, dating to 1710, is the oldest part of the main building.

Highlight Hole: The 8th green is the highest point on the property, with great views of the well-tended resort and the south shore. But don't be too distracted. The upcoming 9th hole is very tight.

Clubhouse: There's no clubhouse, but on the floor above the Pub Bar is a nameless delightful Relais & Chateau restaurant (☎441/236–0048). Enjoy a full English or Continental breakfast here 7:30 to 10 AM. Lunch is served on the Pool Terrace, Ocean Terrace, or main dining room from 12:30 to 3 PM, and dinner is from 7 to 9 on the Ocean Terrace, Barbeque Terrace, or in the Middleton Room. Fresh Bermudian fish is, of course, a highlight of the extensive menu, which also includes beef, duck, lamb, and lobster. ✉ *33 South Rd., Paget Parish* ☎*441/236–0048* ⊕*www.horizonscottages. com* ▱*Greens fees: $25 weekdays, $30 weekends. Club rentals $5. Lessons $35 a half hour, $60 per hour.*

MID OCEAN CLUB

★ *18 holes. 6,548 yards. Par 71. Rating: blue tees, 72.8; white tees, 70.7; red tees, 74.6.*

The elite Mid Ocean Club is a 1921 Charles Blair Macdonald design revamped in 1953 by Robert Trent Jones Sr. *Golf Digest* ranked it 45th in the top 50 courses outside the United States. Patrons include celebrities and politicians such as Michael Douglas and Catherine Zeta-Jones, New York City Mayor Michael Bloomberg, and Michael Jordan. Presidents Eisenhower, Bush Sr., and Clinton have also played here. The club has a genteel air, and a great sense of history. Even though it's expensive, you must play it at least once, walking it with a caddy to savor the traditional golf experience and the scenery.

There are many holes near ocean cliffs, but you'll want to linger on the back tee of the last hole, where the view up the coast is spectacular. You'll come away with memories of the course's many elevation changes and tight doglegs. One in particular is the 5th hole, Cape, where Babe Ruth is said to have splashed a dozen balls in Mangrove Lake as he tried to land too far down the fairway on the other side. Because Mid Ocean is the second-longest course on the island, the average woman player may have trouble reaching greens in regulation—and some men, too, especially when the wind is up.

If you haven't been here since 2006, you'll find the layout is now irrigated and the TifEagle greens are truer and faster than ever. Many trees were pruned or removed to increase airflow and encourage grass growth. This all happened in

2007 in preparation for the televised PGA Grand Slam, which the club hosted that October, and will host again in 2008. The tournament was held for years in Hawaii, so this was a coup for Mid Ocean and Bermuda.

Highlight Hole: The 433-yard 5th is a par-4 dogleg around Mangrove Lake. The elevated tees sit atop a hillside of flowering shrubbery, with the lake below. It's tempting to take a big shortcut over the water, but remember the Babe's experience. To the left of the green, a steep embankment funnels balls down into a bunker, setting up a delicate sand shot to the putting surface.

Clubhouse: Overlooking the 18th hole and the south shore, the Mid Ocean's peach-and-white clubhouse is classically Bermudian down to the interior cedar trim. You'll get a logo towel for your hefty greens fees, and there are other goodies available in the pro shop. Several of the club's rooms commemorate famous American and British 20th-century politicians who played the course—there's the Churchill Bar, the Eisenhower Dining Room, and the MacMillan Television Room. The latter two are for members only, but you can have a drink in the bar and choose from an international menu in the **Eden Room** (☎441/293–0330), which is open to nonmembers for breakfast and lunch on Monday, Wednesday, and Friday. The menu includes a wide selection of salads, soups, and sandwiches. ⊠*Mid Ocean Dr., off S. Shore Rd., Tucker's Town* ☎*441/293–0330* ⊕*www.themidoceanclubbermuda.com* ✆*Greens fees $210 ($70 when playing with a member). Nonmembers must be sponsored by a club member (your hotelier can arrange this); nonmember starting times available Mon., Wed., and Fri. until noon, except holidays. After noon, every second tee time is available to nonmembers. Caddies $30 per bag, single, or $35 per bag, double (tip not included). Cart rental $25 per person. Shoe rentals $6. Club rentals $40. Lessons $40 a half hour, $80 per hour.*

OCEAN VIEW GOLF COURSE
9 holes. 2,940 yards. Par 35. Rating: 68 playing white then blue tees, 68.7 playing yellow then red tees.

If you want to play with locals or just mingle to talk golf, Ocean View is the place to be after the workday ends. Only 10 minutes from Hamilton, it's very popular. Switch tees on your second loop of the 9 holes for an 18-hole round playing 5,658 yards to a par of 70. The first hole is a tough par 5 with a long, tight fairway flanked by a coral wall on one side and a drop-off to the shore on the other. The course is aptly named; there are panoramas from many holes as well as from the clubhouse and the restaurant patio. The club has a 260-yard driving range where the wind is often at your back, giving you a pleasant feeling that your drives are longer than they really are.

Highlight Hole: The green on the 192-yard, par-3 9th hole is cut into a coral hillside that's landscaped with colorful plants. It's a demanding shot when the wind is gusting from the north or west.

Clubhouse: Inside Ocean View's modest clubhouse is the **Out of Bounds Restaurant and Bar** (☎*441/295–9093*) overlooking the north shore. Open for breakfast and lunch, the small dining room has a menu with the usual burgers, sandwiches, and salads, as well as Bermudian favorites such as fish chowder and fish-cake sandwiches. ✉ *2 Barker's Hill, off N. Shore Rd., Devonshire Parish* ☎*441/295–9092* ⊕*www.oceanview.bm* ⚑*Greens fee (18 holes) $85 with cart, $60 walking before 3 PM, $60 sunset with cart or walking. Club rentals $25. Lessons $50 for half hour.*

PORT ROYAL GOLF COURSE

★ *18 holes. 6,561 yards. Par 71. Rating: blue tees, 72.6; white tees, 70.1; red tees, 73.7.*

You've probably heard about it and seen pictures of the 16th hole at Port Royal, arguably Bermuda's best-known golf hole. The green of the 176-yard par 3 occupies a treeless promontory with a backdrop of the blue waters and pink sands of Whale Bay. When the wind is blowing hard onshore, as it frequently does, this can be a tough green to reach. The holes leading up to the 16th are the icing on the cake, with ocean views on 7, 8, 9, and 15. One of three government-owned courses (Ocean View and St. George's are the others), Port Royal is a perennial favorite of locals and visitors. The 1970 Robert Trent Jones Sr. layout has many elevated tees and greens and some clever doglegs. There are plenty of hills, on the back nine in particular.

Highlight Hole: Like the much-photographed 16th hole, the 387-yard, par-4 15th skirts the windswept cliffs along Whale Bay. The well-preserved remains of the Whale Bay Battery, a 19th-century fortification, stand next to the fairway.

Clubhouse: With its coral walls and white roof and shutters, the Port Royal clubhouse has all the charm of a traditional Bermudian house. Open for breakfast and lunch (until 5 PM) is the **Eagle View Restaurant & Bar** (☎441/234–5078). Bermuda cedar beams run the length of the dining room, and there's a patio that overlooks the 9th and 18th greens and the sea beyond. Fresh Bermuda fish, burgers, peas and rice, and pasta are always on the menu. The bar, open from 11 AM to 8 PM Monday through Thursday, and later on weekends, has two flat-screen TVs, usually tuned to sports events. ⊠*Off Middle Rd., Southampton Parish* ☎*441/234–0974, 441/234–4653 for automated tee-time reservations* ⊕*www.portroyalgolf.bm* ⚑*Greens fees: $140 including cart and practice balls. Sunset rates are $85 with cart, $70 walking in summer (Apr.–Oct.); and $65 with cart, $50 walking in winter (Nov.–Mar.). Pull cart rentals $10. Shoe rentals $15. Club rentals $37. Lessons $50 for half hour.*

RIDDELL'S BAY GOLF & COUNTRY CLUB
18 holes. 5,854 yards. Par 70 (72 for women). Rating: blue tees, 68.5; white tees, 66.9.

Opened in 1921, Riddell's Bay is Bermuda's oldest course and one of the island's "must plays" for its scenery and precise shot-placing demands. Designed by Devereaux Emmett, who went on to plot the Congressional Golf Club near Washington, D.C., it receives periodic fine-tuning and upgrading at the hands of Ed Beidel. Don't let the 5,800-yard length fool you; this tight layout is cleverly woven into a peninsula that is only 600 yards wide in some places. The first hole, a 424-yard par 4 (par 5 for women) doglegs to an elevated green, serving notice of difficulty to come. Positioned between Riddell's Bay and the Great Sound, and with Popplewell's Pond in the interior, the course has water views and a fair number of water encounters. For instance, the sea lies all along the right side of dogleg on hole 8, and the 9th demands a drive across an inlet. The 10th tee box perches above a beautiful inlet where boats are moored.

Highlight Hole: The 8th hole, a 360-yard par 4, doglegs along the water to a green near the brink. With a tailwind, big hitters often go for the green. The Gibbs Hill Lighthouse is a distant backdrop.

Clubhouse: The Riddell's Bay clubhouse, a 150-year-old farmhouse refurbished in 1998, has locker rooms, a well-stocked pro shop, a bar made of Bermuda cedar, a lounge overlooking the 18th green and 1st tee, and the **Riddell's Bay dining room** (☎*441/238–1060 Ext. 112*), open for breakfast and lunch. On the menu are salads (including a nice

From Tee Time to Bed Time

If you stay in a hotel with its own golf course or one that has agreements with some of the golf clubs, it cuts out much of the planning you'll have to make on your own. For instance, the Fairmont Southampton Princess has its own 18-hole executive course and access agreement with Riddell's Bay Golf & Country Club. Tee times are blocked for hotel guests and a shuttle is provided to and from the hotel.

At the Tuckers Point Club, which has a new hotel and spa opening at the end of 2008, you can contrast the old and the new in golf course designs without straying very far from the resort. On-site is Roger Rulewich's fabulous design, laid down atop the old Castle Harbour Golf Club, designed by his mentor, Robert Trent Jones Sr. Literally next door is the classic Mid Ocean Club, a Charles Blair Macdonald track redesigned by Jones in 1953. You will have seen Mid Ocean on television during the 2007 PGA Grand Slam, and you'll be anxious to try your luck.

Then there's Cambridge Beaches, the island's oldest cottage colony, which occupies 25 acres on a promontory at the island's western end. Last year the hotel launched a Fairway to Heaven package that includes three rounds of golf at any of the island's courses, a golf massage, dinner on a private island and other extras. If you're staying at the Horizons & Cottages colony (see lodging listing page), a Relais & Chateaux property, you can sharpen your short game on the property's mashie course in preparation for playing one of the major tracks.

When you make your lodging arrangements, check to see what golf packages and perks are available. Many hoteliers are also members at the clubs and are happy to facilitate arrangements.

smoked salmon and goat cheese plate), sandwiches (the Riddell's Bay Fishcake is a signature dish), burgers and, of course, a fine fish chowder. The dining room is open 10 AM to 3 PM weekdays and 8 AM to 4 PM weekends. ✉ *Riddell's Bay Rd., Warwick Parish* ☎ *441/238–1060* ⊕ *www. riddellsbay.com* ✐ *Greens fees $145, including mandatory cart. Shoe rentals $15. Club rentals $40. Lessons $50 for half hour, $90 for hour.*

ST. GEORGE'S GOLF CLUB

18 holes. 4,043 yards. Par 62. Rating: blue tees, 62.8; white tees, 61.4; red tees, 62.8.

What a delight this short but daunting course is. The Robert Trent Jones Sr. creation dominates a secluded headland at the island's northeastern end, with views of the Atlantic on every hole. It's the only course in Bermuda with greens turfed in seashore paspalum, a fine-bladed grass that thrives on saltwater. It putts faster and truer than Bermuda, but the breaks are not as pronounced. In early 2007, the bunkers were refurbished. Wind—especially from the north—sweeps and swirls over these short holes with their small, aggressively bunkered greens, confounding club selection. St. George's has light traffic midweek, so if you play then you'll be able to pause to enjoy the views.

Highlight Hole: The 9th hole is aptly named "Salt Spray." A par 3 playing 143 yards from the back tees and 106 yards from the forward tees, it's right on the ocean, so any ball to the left ends up in the Atlantic.

6

Clubhouse: Overlooking the 18th hole is the clubhouse, with locker rooms, pro shop, and **Mulligan's Restaurant** (☎441/297–1836). The cozy dining room-bar and patio, which are tended by a friendly and efficient staff, have a fine view of the north shore and the ramparts of Fort St. Catherine. Breakfast and lunch are served daily 8 AM to 4 PM, and dinner after 6 PM on Friday. The menu includes sandwiches and salads as well as many local favorites such as fish-and-chips, grilled fresh fish, steaks, the award-winning Alfred's Fish Chowder, and St. David's fish cake (a codfish-and-mashed-potato concoction flavored with parsley and thyme). ✉ *1 Park Rd., St. George's Parish* ☎441/297–8353 *pro shop, 441/234–4653 tee times* ⊕*www.stgeorgesgolf. bm* ⚑*Greens fees $90 including cart, sunset $70 including cart. The same fees apply to walking, which is not allowed on weekends and holidays until after 3 PM. Shoe rentals $15. Club rentals $35. Lessons $50 half hour.*

TUCKER'S POINT GOLF CLUB

★ **Fodor's**Choice *18 holes. 6,361 yards. Par 70. Rating: blue tees, 71.5; white tees, 68.9; red tees, 68.5.*

If you remember the old Castle Harbour Golf Club, you'll recognize some of the views, but not the holes. Roger Rulewich, a former senior designer for the late Robert Trent Jones Sr., mapped out a stunning site layout in 2002, making the most of elevation changes and ocean views. It's longer than nearby Mid Ocean, and holds more surprises. On many holes, you tee off toward the crest of a hill, not knowing what lies beyond. Topping the rise reveals the challenge, often involving a very elevated, sculpted green with a scenic vista. The course is fully irrigated and beautifully groomed. The final resort components—the Harbour Court Waterfront Villas and the 88-room Tucker's Point Hotel & Spa—are scheduled to open in fall 2008 and spring 2009, respectively.

Highlight Holes: There are many outstanding holes, but the par-4 17th is one of the most picturesque in Bermuda, with sweeping views of Tucker's Town and Castle Island. A rival is hole 13, where the perspective is the north coast and the Royal Navy Dockyard 20 mi away on the island's western tip.

Clubhouse: The 20,000-square-foot Tucker's Point Golf Clubhouse, a traditional Bermudian British–colonial design with covered verandas and tray ceilings, stands on a hilltop with a commanding view. Within are posh locker rooms, a large pro shop, and superb dining. You can relax with a cocktail or dine alfresco on the second-floor veranda while enjoying a panorama of Castle Harbour and Tucker's Town. **The Grill** (☎441/298–6983), an elegant yet comfortable dining area, has an extensive menu that includes sublime fish chowder, lamb, salmon, and tuna tartare, as well as catch-of-the-day and omelet specials. Breakfast is served on weekends, lunch every day, and dinner Tuesday through Saturday in winter. In summer dinner is served at the Beach Club. ✉ *9 Paynters Rd., St. George's Parish* ☎*441/298–6970* ⊕*www.tuckerspoint.com* ⛳*Greens fees $224 with cart, $119 with cart for members' guests. Shoe rentals, $10. Club rentals $45. Lessons $55 for half hour, $90 for hour.*

Shopping

WORD OF MOUTH

"My favorite inexpensive souvenirs are cedar Christmas ornaments from the Bermuda Crafts Market in Dockyards, linen tea towels with Bermudian flowers, cottages, or birds from the Irish Linen Shop, and cute hand-painted pieces from the Island House. The Bermuda perfumery is great, too."

—cmcfong

By Suzy
Buckley

If you're accustomed to shopping in Neiman Marcus, Saks Fifth Avenue, and Bergdorf Goodman, the prices in Bermuda's elegant shops won't come as a surprise. Designer clothing and accessories, from MaxMara to Louis Vuitton, tend to be sold at prices comparable to those in the United States, but without the sales tax. Crystal, china, watches, and jewelry are often less expensive here and sometimes even on par with American outlet-store prices. Perfume and cosmetics are often sold at discount prices, and there are bargains to be had on woolens and cashmeres in early spring, when stores' winter stocks must go. The island's unforgiving humidity and lack of storage space means sales are frequent and really meant to sweep stock off the shelves.

Art galleries in Bermuda attract serious shoppers and collectors. The island's thriving population of artists and artisans—many of whom are internationally recognized—produces well-reputed work, from paintings, photographs, and sculpture to miniature furniture, hand-blown glass, and dolls. During your gallery visits, look for Bruce Stuart's abstract paintings, Graeme Outerbridge's vivid photographs of Bermudian architecture and scenery, and Chelsey Trott's slim wood and bronze sculptures.

Bermuda-made specialty comestibles include rum and rum-based liqueurs, and delicious local honey, which you can find in most grocery stores. Condiments from Outerbridge Peppers Ltd. add zip to soups, stews, drinks, and chowders. The original line has expanded to include Bloody Mary mix, pepper jellies, and barbecue sauce.

The duty-free shop at the airport sells liquor, perfume, cigarettes, rum cakes, and other items. You can also order duty-free spirits at some of the liquor stores in town, and the management will make arrangements to deliver your purchase to your hotel or cruise ship. If you choose to shop in town rather than at the airport, it's best to buy liquor at least 24 hours before your departure, or by 9:30 on the day of an afternoon departure, in order to allow enough time for delivery. With liquor, it pays to shop around, because prices vary. Grocery stores usually charge more than liquor stores. U.S. citizens age 21 and older who have been out of the country for 48 hours are allowed to bring home 1 liter of duty-free liquor.

SHOPPING DISTRICTS

Hamilton has the greatest concentration of shops in Bermuda, and Front Street is its pièce de résistance. Lined with small, pastel-color buildings, this most fashionable of Bermuda's streets houses sedate department stores and snazzy boutiques, with several small arcades and shopping alleys leading off it. A smart canopy shades the entrance to the 55 Front Street Group, which houses Crisson's. Modern Butterfield Place has galleries and boutiques selling, among other things, Louis Vuitton leather goods. The Emporium, a renovated building with an atrium, has a range of shops, from antiques to souvenirs.

St. George's Water Street, Duke of York Street, Hunters Wharf, Penno's Wharf, and Somers Wharf are the sites of numerous renovated buildings that house branches of Front Street stores, as well as artisans' studios. Historic King's Square offers little more than a couple of T-shirt and souvenir shops.

In the West End, Somerset Village has a few shops, but they hardly merit a special shopping trip. However, the Clocktower Mall, in a historic building at the Royal Naval Dockyard, has a few more shopping opportunities, including branches of Front Street shops and specialty boutiques. The Dockyard is also home to the Craft Market, the Bermuda Arts Centre, and Bermuda Clayworks.

DEPARTMENT STORES

A. S. Cooper & Sons. With branches in all major hotels, Cooper & Sons is best known for its extensive inventory of crystal and china, with pieces and sets by Waterford, Swarovski, Wedgwood, Royal Doulton, Lladro, and Villeroy & Boch, many sold at 15% to 20% less than U.S. prices. The store also carries tasteful Bermudian souvenirs in the Fine Jewelry & Gifts department on the lower level. In 2007, Cooper & Sons debuted a Cosmetics & Fragrances department in its new Front Street store. The main store also carries its private-label clothing collection for women and a ladies sportswear department, which carries Calvin Klein, Ralph Lauren, and other popular brands. The men's line can be found at the well-stocked A. S. Cooper Man store, just down the street. ⊠ *59 Front St., Hamilton* ☎ *441/295–3961* ⊕ *www.coopersbermuda.*

com ✉*Clocktower Centre, Dockyard* ✉*22 Water St., St. George's.*

A. S. Cooper Children's. This kids' clothing shop has everything you'll need to dress your little one. From shorts and shirts in summer to long pants and jackets for Bermuda's rainy winter, it's all here. ✉*27 Front St., Hamilton* ☎*441/295–3961.*

A. S. Cooper Express. Flirty, bright clothes for junior girls in the know, from DKNY jeans and T-shirts to a great selection by Guess? are stocked in this airy store. A full wall of accessories in a rainbow of colors is one of the many highlights here. ✉*Washington Mall, Reid St., Hamilton* ☎*441/296–6525.*

A. S. Cooper Home. If a housewarming present is what you're looking for, this is the perfect place. Candles, decorative home gifts, and flowers fill this shop, alongside bedding and home accessories by Lladro and Villeroy & Boch. ✉*26 Church St., Hamilton* ☎*441/295–2615.*

★ **Fodor'sChoice A. S. Cooper Man.** This division of the classy department store is first-rate, with a staff that's reserved and courteous, but very helpful when needed. The store is the exclusive Bermuda supplier of Polo Ralph Lauren. ✉*29 Front St., Hamilton* ☎*441/295–3961 Ext. 201.*

Harbourside. A. S. Cooper's ready-to-wear shop stocks women's clothing, including plus sizes, accessories, and its own line of fragrances. Bermuda shell pieces and other locally made gifts can also be found at this location. ✉*Pier 6, Front St., Hamilton* ☎*441/296–1675.*

Gibbons Co. One of Bermuda's oldest retailers (still run by the Gibbons family) is a fairly casual department store that stocks a wide range of men's, women's, and children's clothing, with brands such as Calvin Klein and DKNY. There's a substantial lingerie section, as well as quality handbags, purses, scarves, and Monet fashion jewelry. Gibbons also has a sizable household department and is the exclusive supplier of Denby tableware, which sells at a much lower price than in Canada or the United States. The on-site Peniston Brown perfume shop stocks many French, Italian, and American lines. But most notable are the company's two intimate boutiques next door, housing Nine West and Twenty 5 Reid boutique. ✉*21 Reid St., Hamilton* ☎*441/295–0022.*

KNOW-HOW

Clothing, china, and jewelry in Bermuda are sold at prices similar to those abroad, but since there's no sales tax, you can get good deals, especially on high-end goods. If you see something you like, go ahead and buy it—comparison shopping isn't fruitful on Bermuda, as prices are typically fixed island-wide. In all but a few stores, shoppers leaving the fitting rooms are expected to return unwanted items to the store floor. The island's bounty of craft markets and artists' studios offers a multitude of inexpensive souvenirs, from Bermuda honey to hand-painted pillows. Buyers and sellers don't really bargain, although a vendor may offer a discount if you buy something in bulk.

BUSINESS HOURS

Shops are generally open Monday to Saturday from 9 to 5 and closed on Sunday, although some supermarkets are open from 1 to 5 on Sunday. From April to October, some of the smaller Front Street shops stay open late and on Sunday. The shops in the Clocktower Mall at the Royal Naval Dockyard are usually open from Monday to Saturday 9:30 to 6 (11 to 5 in winter) and Sunday 11 to 5. Some extend their hours around Christmas. Almost all stores close for public holidays. Many of Bermuda's more exclusive shops have branches in the larger resort hotels.

KEY DESTINATIONS

Department stores such as A. S. Cooper & Sons and Gibbons Co. are excellent one-stop shopping destinations, but you may have more fun exploring the boutiques on Front Street, as well as Reid Street and streets branching off it. For crafts, head to the Royal Naval Dockyard, where you can find artisans' studios and a permanent craft market. The town of St. George's has a bit of everything, including lots of small, unique boutiques, where you can find the perfect island outfit or a Bermuda-cedar model of a famous ship.

SMART SOUVENIRS

Small cakes from the Bermuda Rum Cake Company in the Dockyard make popular gifts and cost $9 duty free. Men may want to pick up a pair of real Bermuda shorts, which come in an array of bright colors, such as hot pink or royal blue. They sell for about $30 in department stores. The Outerbridge line of sherry peppers and other sauces is available at grocery stores and souvenir shops. Locals use them to flavor fish chowder, among other dishes.

7

Marks & Spencer. A franchise of the large British chain, Marks and Sparks (as it's called by everyone in Bermuda and England) is usually filled with locals attracted by its moderate prices for men's, women's, and children's clothing. Summer wear, including swimsuits, cotton jerseys, and polo shirts, is a good buy, as is underwear. The chain's signature line of food and treats, plus wine from all over the world, is at the back of the store. On the upper level you'll find a comprehensive selection of the Levi's and Dockers clothing lines. ✉ *18 Reid St., Hamilton* ☎ *441/295–0031.*

SPECIALTY STORES

ANTIQUES

The Bermuda Railway Museum. An extensive collection of historical artifacts from Bermuda's short-lived railway is housed here. The museum shop sells photos, maps, books, prints, antiques, jewelry, coins, stamps, and china. If you take the bus here, get off at the first stop after the Bermuda Aquarium. The shop is open Tuesday to Friday from 10 to 4 or by appointment with Rose Hollis. ✉ *37 N. Shore Rd., Hamilton Parish* ☎ *441/293–1774.*

Thistle Gallery. Antique British furniture, porcelain, china, glassware, and silver are laid out for sale in this large cottage store. ✉ *7 Park Rd., Hamilton* ☎ *441/292–3839.*

ART GALLERIES

★ Fodor'sChoice **Bermuda Arts Centre at Dockyard.** Sleek and modern, with well-designed displays of local art, this gallery is housed in one of the stone buildings of the former Royal Naval Dockyard. The walls are adorned with paintings and photographs, and glass display cases contain exquisitely crafted quilts as well as costume dolls, jewelry, and wood sculpture. Exhibits change frequently. Several artists' studios inside the gallery are open to the public. The center is open daily from 10 to 5. ✉ *Museum Row, Dockyard* ☎ *441/234–2809.*

★ **Bermuda Society of the Arts.** Many highly creative society members sell their work at the perennial members' shows and during a revolving series of special group exhibits. You can find watercolor, oil, and acrylic paintings, and pastel and charcoal drawings, as well as occasional photographs, collages, and sculptures. ✉ *17 Church St., 3rd fl. West Wing, City Hall, Hamilton* ☎ *441/292–3824* ⊕ *www.bsoa.bm.*

Masterworks Foundation Gallery. The foundation, formed in 1987, exhibits art by well-known Canadian, British, French, and American artists, including Georgia O'Keeffe and Winslow Homer, who produced work inspired by Bermuda. The Bermudiana Collection contains more than 400 works in watercolor, oil, pencil, charcoal, and other media. The Bermuda National Gallery locations at City Hall, Camden House, Government House, and Waterloo House all display pieces from this collection. ✉*97 Front St., Hamilton* ✉*Botanical Gardens, 183 South Rd., Devonshire* ☎*441/236–2950* ⊕*www.bermudamasterworks.com.*

Picturesque. If you like photography, check out Roland Skinner's two shops. His shots of Bermuda beach scenes and wildlife sell from $95 to $800. ✉*129 Front St. E, Hamilton* ☎*441/292–1452* ✉*Clocktower Mall, Dockyard* ☎*441/234–3342.*

X-Clue-Sive Creations. Pick up Doris Wade's hand-painted pottery here or indulge your creative side and create your own Bermuda souvenirs. Choose from 100 bare shapes and paint to your heart's content. The studio will glaze and fire the piece in four to seven days. ✉*86 Reid St., Hamilton* ☎*441/296–1676.*

BEAUTY & PERFUME

Bermuda Perfumery. This popular destination has downsized but still remains an interesting, must-see spot. Free, regularly scheduled guided tours of the old St. George's building now housing the factory include an exhibit on the distillation of flowers into perfume and one about fragrance distribution and packaging. At the Lili Boutique gift shop you can purchase perfumes, including the factory's 11 fragrances, as well as imported soaps. ✉*Stewart Hall, 5 Queen St., St. George's* ☎*441/293–0627.*

Peniston Brown Ltd.–The Perfume Shop. In addition to being the exclusive Bermuda agent for Guerlain products, Peniston Brown's boutique stocks an extensive selection of French, American, and Italian perfumes, as well as soaps, bath salts, and bubble bath. The main boutique on Front Street also stocks Guerlain's complete line of cosmetics and skin care. ✉*23 W. Front St., Hamilton* ☎*441/295–0570* ✉*6 Water St., St. George's* ☎*441/297–1525* ✉*Gibbons Co. Perfume Department, 21 Reid St., Hamilton* ☎*441/295–5535.*

7

BOOKSTORES

Bermuda Book Store Ltd. Owner Hannah Willmott has expanded her bright little Hamilton bookstore to a location in the Clocktower Mall. The shops are stocked with best sellers, children's books, and special Bermuda titles (including some out-of-print books). ⊠*3 Queen St., Hamilton* ☎*441/295–3698* ⊠*Clocktower Parade, Dockyard* ☎*441/234–4065.*

The Bookmart. The island's largest bookstore carries plenty of contemporary titles and classics, plus a complete selection of books on Bermuda. Paperbacks and children's books are in abundance, as well as every popular beauty, technology, and men's magazine you can think of. This is also the place to come for greeting cards, balloons, and little gift items. Don't forget to visit the Annex toy department on the lower level. ⊠*Brown & Company, 4 Reid St., Hamilton* ☎*441/295–3838.*

CIGARS

House of Cigars: Chatham House. In business since 1895, this shop looks like an old-time country store. Thick, gray, lusty cigar smoke fills the air, and a life-size statue of a Native American princess greets you as you walk in. You can find top-quality cigars from the Dominican Republic, Jamaica, and Cuba (Romeo y Julieta, Bolivar, Partagas, Punch), Briar and Meerschaum pipes, Dunhill lighters, and Swiss Army knives. Prices for handmade Cubans start at $5. ⊠*63 Front St., Hamilton* ☎*441/292–8422.*

CLOTHING & ACCESSORIES

CHILDREN'S CLOTHING

Family Clothing Shop. This tiny, inexpensive hideaway sells kids' clothes, sandals, and socks—perfect for stocking up on anything you left at home. ⊠*1 Water St., St. George's* ☎*441/297–5517.*

IANA. Fine Italian clothing for girls and boys newborn to age 16 are sold here at prices matching the quality of goods. ⊠*Walker Arcade, 12 Reid St., Hamilton* ☎*441/292–0002.*

Pirate's Port Boys. Casual wear for boys is crowded into this small store and sold at very reasonable prices. **Pirate's Port Girls** has trendy, inexpensive clothes for toddlers to teens. ⊠*Washington Mall, Reid St., Hamilton* ☎*441/292–1080.*

MEN'S CLOTHING

David Winston. An upmarket spot owned by the island's English Sports Shop group, this handsome store carries European-designed men's clothing and accessories. Hugo Boss, Danish brand Matinique, and Profuomo are well represented, and it's a great spot to pick up mens' Italian shirts, ties, and belts. ✉*2 Reid St., Hamilton* ☎*441/295–4866.*

Flatts Mens Wear. Owner Mick Adderley runs the only shop on the island specializing in big-and-tall sizes for men. ✉*13 N. Shore Rd., Flatts Village* ☎*441/292–0360.*

Taylor's. Although the main Archie Brown store in Hamilton is closed, Taylor's is still dedicated entirely to Scottish-made knits. You can also buy tartan by the yard, and mohair knits, skirts, and scarves. ✉*30 Water St., St. George's* ☎*441/297–1626* ✉*49 Front St., Hamilton* ☎*441/295–2672.*

MEN'S & WOMEN'S CLOTHING

Davison's of Bermuda. Davison's offers exactly what you would expect of an island clothing store—light, comfortable cotton shirts, pants, and shorts for adults and children. Sherry peppers, aprons, teddy bears, and a collection of stuffed trolls are among the gift items. There's a branch in the Fairmont Southampton, too. ✉*93 Front St., Hamilton* ☎*441/292–3826* ✉*Water St., St. George's* ☎*441/297–8363* ✉*Clocktower Centre, Dockyard* ☎*441/234–0959.*

English Sports Shop. This shop specializes in British knitwear. The store's own line of cotton sweaters is priced at $29.95, although cashmere sweaters start from $220. Upstairs is a good supply of men's business and formal wear, and children's clothes. Women's clothing and accessories are on the ground level. Another branch is in the Fairmont Southampton. ✉*49 Front St., Hamilton* ☎*441/295–2672* ✉*Water St., St. George's* ☎*441/297–0142.*

Giorgio Beneti. This stylish boutique, opened in October of 2005, sells leather jackets, handbags, wallets, shoes, and belts imported from Argentina. ✉*44 Reid St., Hamilton* ☎*441/296–8097.*

Mambo. Need a slice of Italian chic? Stop by this tiny shop that stocks funky Italian labels such as Dolce & Gabbana, Miss Sixty, Diesel, Von Dutch, Page Premium Denim, and Just Cavalli. ✉*Walker Arcade, 12 Reid St., Hamilton* ☎*441/296–9797.*

7

The Outlet. Reduced-price merchandise from the English Sports Shop, Aston & Gunn, Cecile, and Crown Colony, as well as some U.S. merchandise, are sold here for up to 75% off the usual prices. ✉ *30 Queen St., Hamilton* ☎ *441/295–0084.*

Sasch. Part of the six-store Stefanel group of boutiques, this store brings the very latest, hippest fashions in casual, business, and dress wear from Florence to Bermuda. The clothes are high quality, made of primarily natural fibers in neutral colors. Large men may have trouble finding a good fit—most sizes are for smaller frames, and some styles are body-hugging. There's also a small selection of trendy shoes and handbags. ✉ *12 Reid St., Hamilton* ☎ *441/295–4391.*

WOMEN'S CLOTHING
Boutique C.C. This English Sports Shop–owned store sells quality formal and business wear for women of every age with a flair for fashion, but the selection of evening wear is the highlight of this beautifully renovated store. Look for reasonably priced cocktail dresses and classic suits along with stylish contemporary separates and trendy accessories. ✉ *1 Front St., Hamilton* ☎ *441/295–3935.*

★ **Fodor'sChoice Calypso.** Bermuda's fashionable set comes to this boutique to spend plenty of money on Italian leather shoes and sophisticated designer wear by Graham Kandiah. Calypso has the island's largest selection of swimwear, including Villegriquin. Pick up a straw hat and sunglasses to make the perfect beach ensemble. Eclectic novelty items from Europe make great gifts. Calypso's shop in Butterfield Place, **Voila!,** carries Longchamp handbags and Johnston & Murphy men's shoes. There are branches at the Coral Beach & Tennis Club, Fairmont Southampton, and Clocktower Mall at the Dockyard. ✉ *45 Front St., Hamilton* ☎ *441/295–2112.*

★ **Cecile.** Specializing in upscale European designer fashions, Cecile carries such labels as Valentino Red, Tibi, Pucci, Louis Feraud of Paris, and the perennial resort-wear favorite, Lilly Pulitzer. There's a good selection of evening wear and swimwear, including swimsuits by Gottex. An accessories department carries shoes, scarves, jewelry, handbags, and belts. The boutique offers very favorable prices, often significantly lower than U.S. retail, on some of the world's foremost fashion names. ✉ *15 Front St., Hamilton* ☎ *441/295–1311.*

Eve's Garden Lingerie. Silk and satin panties, boxers, brassieres, and nightgowns, in sizes small to full-figure, are tucked away in this discreet shop at the back of Butterfield Place. You can also find massage oils and an adult section. ⊠*Butterfield Pl., Hamilton* ☎*441/296–2671.*

Frangipani. Owned by A. S. Cooper, this little store sells colorful women's fashions with an island-resort look. Cotton, silk, and rayon leisure wear are the backbone of the stock. Frangipani also sells a collection of hand-strung, brightly colored, beaded necklaces, bracelets, and earrings. ⊠*16 Water St., St. George's* ☎*441/297–1357.*

MaxMara. Prices for this Italian designer's clothing average about 20% less in Bermuda than in the United States, although the accessories sell at much the same as U.S. prices. Although the boutique is much smaller than its counterpart on Madison Avenue, it still has a good selection of conservative-casual wear and evening attire. ⊠*57 Front St., Hamilton* ☎*441/295–2112 Ext. 130.*

★ **Stefanel.** This popular Italian chain is good for simple, stylish, modern women's clothes, mostly made from cotton and other natural fabrics. Its own line of jackets, crocheted sweaters, and camisoles is particularly worth a look. The colors are neutral, sometimes with delicate small prints. Prices are commensurate with quality, but seasonal sales are particularly rewarding. ⊠*12 Walker Arcade, Reid St., Hamilton* ☎*441/295–5698.*

CRAFTS

Bermuda Craft Market. The island's largest permanent craft outlet is the Dockyard's old cooperage building, which dates to 1831. Dozens of artisans show their work here, and you can expect to find baubles and edibles, from Bermuda-cedar hair clips to Bermuda honey and jam. Quilts, decoupage, and hand-painted glassware are among the prettiest souvenirs and gifts in the marketplace. ⊠*The Cooperage, Dockyard* ☎*441/234–3208.*

★ **The Bounty.** The spicy smell of cedar is the first thing to greet you in this tiny shop, where owner Kersley Nanette and his staff handcraft teak and cedar model ships. The focus is on tall ships of the 17th and 18th centuries. Prices range from $150 to $2,000. Models of the *Sea Venture* and *Deliverance* are especially popular. Call for an appointment. ⊠*2A Old Maid's Lane, St. George's* ☎*441/297–2143.*

★ **Fodor'sChoice The Island Shop.** Brightly colored island-theme artwork for ceramics, linens, and pillows are designed by owner Barbara Finsness. A number of her original watercolors are available for purchase. She also stocks the store with cedar-handle handbags embroidered with Bermuda buildings, shell napkin rings, plates, monogrammed guest towels, rugs, chunky jewelry, and elegant gifts, as well as candles and bath products. A smaller selection of her gifts can be found in the Old Cellar on Front Street. ✉ *3 Queen St., Hamilton* ☎*441/292–6307.*

GIFTS & SOUVENIRS

Crackerbox. Shells, shells, and more shells are what you can find in this adorable souvenir shop. Big bins of them invite rummaging, and you can buy just one or a whole handful. Also for sale are charms and jewelry made from shells and sea glass (bits of colored glass worn smooth from tumbling in the ocean or machine-tumbled to look that way). The store has its own line of Tobacco Bay Chocolate Beach Stones (chocolate-candy color to look like beach stones), and Bermuda Summer Breeze candles. ✉ *15 York St., St. George's* ☎*441/297–1205.*

★ **Fodor'sChoice Dockyard Glassworks and Bermuda Rum Cake Company.** This combination micro-bakery and glassblowing shop is a favorite among locals and visitors alike. Pull up an armchair and watch as artists turn molten glass into vases, plates, miniature tree frogs, and other collectibles. Afterward help yourself to the rum-cake samples. Flavors include traditional black rum, rum swizzle (with tropical fruit juices), rum and ginger, and rum and banana. You can buy the cakes duty-free for $11.95, $19.95, and $29.95. If you purchase glassware, the company will pack the purchase and deliver it to your hotel or cruise ship. A small outlet in St. George's sells a collection of glasswork in addition to the cakes. ✉ *1 Maritime Lane, Dockyard* ☎*441/234–4216* ✉ *3 Bridge St., St. George's* ☎*441/297–3908.*

Flying Colours. This family-owned and -operated shop, established in 1937, has the island's largest selection of souvenir T-shirts, with creatively designed logos in hundreds of styles. The shop also carries everything for the beach—hats, towels, sarongs, toys for playing in the sand—plus other quality souvenirs, like shell jewelry. Educational toys are a specialty. ✉ *5 Queen St., Hamilton* ☎*441/295–0890.*

★ **Gosling's Black Seal Gift Shop.** The rum maker's signature shop sells bottles of plain and flavored rum and tins of rum cake, plus T-shirts, ties, hats, and more, all with the Gosling logo, a black seal. ⊠*97 Front St., Hamilton* ☎*441/295–1123.*

Onion Jack's Trading Post. Onion Jack's own line of sweet and spicy sauces is sold here, along with an assortment of flip-flops, beachwear, and sunglasses. ⊠*77 Front St., Hamilton* ☎*441/295–1263.*

Otto Wurz. It's hard to miss this Front Street store. Joke signs proclaiming such witticisms as LAUGH AND THE WORLD LAUGHS WITH YOU, SNORE AND YOU SLEEP ALONE fill its windows. Inside is a collection of model ships, silver and pewter jewelry, children's wood toys, and English silverware. ⊠*3 Front St., Hamilton* ☎*441/295–1247.*

★ **Pulp & Circumstance.** If it's an original, quality gift you're after, look no further. The Reid Street store sells exquisite, modern picture frames in all shapes and sizes and from all over the world, plus candles, bath products, gifts for babies, a great selection of Burt's Bees products, and greeting cards. The Pulp & Circumstance stationery store in Windsor Place, just behind the main one, sells photo albums, pens, and Bermuda-theme stationery. Delicate pastel notepaper engraved with pictures of Gombey dancers or dinghies sells for $35 per box. ⊠*Reid and Queen sts., Hamilton* ☎*441/292–9586* ⊠*Windsor Pl. and Queen St., Hamilton* ☎*441/292–8886.*

★ **Sail On and Shades of Bermuda.** Owned and operated by Hubert Watlington, a former Olympic windsurfer and top local sailor, this shop stocks a gigantic selection of sunglasses, outdoor clothing and swimwear from such brands as Patagonia and Helly Hanson, plus wacky toys and gifts. The store is tucked into a little alley, opposite No. 1 Shed and the cruise-ship dock. A larger selection of women's clothing, including floaty skirts and sundresses, can be found at the store's Washington Mall location on Reid Street. ⊠*Old Cellar Lane, off Front St., Hamilton* ☎*441/295–0808.*

★ ☺ **Treats.** You can find bulk candy in just about every flavor here, but the greatest draw to this tiny store are the fun, seasonal gifts and cute baby toys. Look out for the ladybug rain boots and matching raincoat for kids. A selection of intricately designed Vera Bradley quilted bags is also available. ⊠*Lower level of Washington Mall, Reid St., Hamilton* ☎*441/296–1123.*

★ **Trustworthy Gift Shop.** Proceeds from the sales of Bermuda-inspired coffee-table books, key chains, serving trays, spoons, pens, and bags at this gift shop benefit the Bermuda National Trust. ■TIP→**This is where you can find some of the most upscale gifts to take back home.** ✉47 *Old Cellar Lane, Hamilton* ☎441/296–4164.

GROCERY STORES

Down to Earth, Ltd. This natural-food and health shop sells everything from tea and supplements to organic body products and home cleaners. Don't leave without grabbing a fresh glass of a fruity blend from the juice bar in the corner. ✉*56 Reid St., Hamilton* ☎441/292–5639.

Esso Tiger Market. If you need sundries or munchies in the early hours of the morning, this 24-hour convenience store is the only place to go in Hamilton. Beyond cigarettes and frozen foods, it stocks film, aspirin, and coffee. ✉*37 Richmond Rd., Hamilton* ☎441/295–3776.

Harrington Hundreds Grocery & Liquor Store. Harrington is a must for those observing special diets or seeking unusual ingredients. It has the island's best selection of wheat-free foods, including gluten-free pastas, breads, and cookies. It's close to Spittal Pond and Angel's Grotto, but not within walking distance. ✉*99 S. Shore Rd., Smith's Parish* ☎441/293–1635.

The Marketplace. The island's largest grocery store, and the chain's headquarters, Marketplace offers homemade hot soups, stir-fries, salads, dinners, and desserts for about $7 a pound. This branch is also open Sunday 1–5. ✉*Church St. near Parliament St., Hamilton* ☎441/292–3163.

★ **Miles Market.** Miles is Bermuda's Balducci's, with a large selection of upscale or hard-to-get specialty food items and high-quality imported and local meats and fish. Many items are on the expensive side, but the quality and selection here are unsurpassed in Bermuda. The market delivers anywhere on the island. ✉*Pitts Bay Rd., near Fairmont Hamilton Princess, Hamilton* ☎441/295–1234.

★ **Rock On–The Health Store.** Nutritional supplements, diet books, natural teas, natural remedies, and environmentally friendly toiletries are among the goods offered at one of Bermuda's few health stores. The knowledgeable staff will guide customers in their selections, but there are plenty of books available, too. ✉*Butterfield Pl., 67 Front*

St., Hamilton ☎*441/295–3468* ✉*12 Church St., Hamilton* ☎*441/295–3468.*

Shelly Bay Marketplace. This branch of the Marketplace chain is the only large grocery on North Shore Road. ✉ *110N. Shore Rd., Hamilton Parish* ☎*441/293–0966.*

Somerset Marketplace. The largest grocery store on the island's western end, it's convenient to Whale Bay Inn, but take a moped or taxi. ✉ *48 Somerset Rd., Sandys Parish* ☎*441/234–0626.*

Somers Supermarket. Despite its small size, Somers has a large selection, with hot food, salads, and sandwiches made fresh daily. It offers free delivery service within St. George's, and it's open Monday to Saturday from 7 AM to 9 PM, and Sunday from 8 to 8. ✉ *41 York St., St. George's* ☎*441/297–1177.*

The Supermart. English products, including the Waitrose brand, are the specialties of this store, which stocks all the usual groceries. You can pick up a picnic lunch at the well-stocked salad-and-hot-food bar. ✉*Front St., near King St., Hamilton* ☎*441/292–2064.*

JEWELRY & WATCHES

★ **Astwood Dickinson.** Established in 1904, this store has built a reputation for its exquisite collection of unmounted stones; upmarket jewelry, including designs by Baccarat and Tiffany and Co., and a wide range of Swiss watches. Cartier, Oakley, Gucci, and Tag Heuer watches, among other famous names, are sold for up to 20% less than in the United States. The shop's Bermuda Collection, designed and created in the upstairs workshop, ranges from 18-karat gold charms to bejeweled pendants representing the island's flora and fauna. ✉*83–85 Front St., Hamilton* ☎*441/292–5805* ✉*Walker Arcade, Hamilton* ☎*441/292–4247.*

Crisson's. The only store in Bermuda carrying Rolex, Corum, and Movado, Crisson's attracts well-heeled customers who come here to buy merchandise at prices 20% to 30% off those at home. Earrings are a specialty, and there's a large selection. The gift department carries gold bangles and beads. ✉*55 and 71 Front St., Hamilton* ☎*441/295–2351* ✉*16 Queen St., Hamilton* ☎*441/295–2351* ✉*20 Reid St., Hamilton* ☎*441/295–2351* ✉*Elbow Beach Hotel, S. Shore Rd., Paget Parish* ☎*441/236–9928* ✉*York and Kent sts., St. George's* ☎*441/297–0672* ✉*Water St., St. George's* ☎*441/297–0107.*

7

Everrich Jewelry. This bargain jewelry store stocks countless styles of basic gold and silver chains, earrings, bangles, and rings. ✉*28 Queen St., Hamilton* ☎*441/295–2110.*

Gem Cellar. Jewelers here make Bermuda-theme charms selling for $40 to $200, and they can produce custom-designed gold and silver jewelry in one to two days. ✉*Old Cellar Lane, Hamilton* ☎*441/292–3042.*

Sovereign. This fine-jewelry shop, which also carries a selection of Casio, Citizen, and Timex watches, used to be part of Trimingham's. ✉*13 Reid St., Hamilton* ☎*441/292–7933.*

Solomon's. Manager Allan Porter and his skilled staff custom-design charming, one-of-a-kind pieces costing from $70 to upward of $100,000. ✉*17 Front St., Hamilton* ☎*441/292–4742 or 441/295–1003.*

Vera P. Card. Known primarily for crystal and porcelain figurines, this shop also carries fine and costume jewelry, including an extensive tanzanite ring collection. ✉*11 Front St., Hamilton* ☎*441/295–1729* ✉*9 Water St., St. George's* ☎*441/297–1718.*

★ **Walker Christopher.** *The Bermudian* magazine has named this goldsmith the island's best for fine jewelry. You can work with a jeweler to design your own exclusive piece or choose from classic diamond bands, strands of South Sea pearls, and the more contemporary hand-hammered chokers. Walker Christopher is the only Bermuda retailer carrying the Galatea diamond and pearl collection. The workshop also produces a line of Bermuda-inspired gold jewelry and sterling silver Christmas ornaments. ✉*9 Front St., Hamilton* ☎*441/295–1466* ✉*A. S. Cooper, 59 Front St., Hamilton* ☎*441/295–3961.*

LINENS
House of Linens. A wide collection of hand-embroidered table, bed, and bath linens can be found at this shop, which also sells baby linens and infant wear. ✉*Washington Mall, Reid St., Hamilton* ☎*441/296–0189.*

Irish Linen Shop. In a cottage that looks as though it belongs in rural Ireland, this shop is the place for Irish linen tablecloths. Prices range from less than $10 to more than $3,000. Antique tablecloths can cost nearly $2,000. ■TIP→ **The best buys are the Irish linen tea towels for around $10.** From Madeira come exquisite hand-embroidered handkerchiefs, plus linen sheets and pillowcases, and cotton organdy christening robes with slip and bonnet, hand-embroidered with garlands and tiers of Valenciennes lace (from $220 to more than $800). The store has an exclusive arrangement with Souleiado, maker of the vivid prints from Provence that are available in tablecloths, place mats, and bags, as well as by the yard—the last at a huge savings over U.S. prices. ⊠*31 Front St., Hamilton* ☎*441/295–4089*.

LIQUOR STORES

Bermuda Duty Free Shop. The airport store invites you to put together your own package of Bermuda liquors at in-bond (duty-free) prices. Gosling's Black Seal rum and rum cakes are among the native products. ⊠*Bermuda International Airport, 3 Cahow Way, St. George's* ☎*441/293–2870*.

Burrows Lightbourn. This chain has a comprehensive selection and stores all over the island. ⊠*127 Front St., Hamilton* ☎*441/295–0176* ⊠*Harbour Rd., Paget* ☎*441/236–0355* ⊠*Water St., St. George's* ☎*441/297–0552* ⊠*Main Rd., Somerset* ☎*441/234–0963*.

Gosling Bros. Ltd. The maker of Bermuda's Black Seal rum also stocks a full selection of wines and other liquors at its stores. The helpful and knowledgeable staff provides excellent advice. You can only buy one bottle of Black Seal rum to consume on the island and then another to export—you can even arrange to have it sent to the airport from the shop. The exported bottle will cost you less than the one you plan to drink in Bermuda. ⊠*Front and Queen sts., Hamilton* ☎*441/295–1123* ⊠*York and Queen sts., St. George's* ☎*441/298–7339*.

PHOTO EQUIPMENT

P-Tech. Digital 35mm cameras, point-and-shoot digital cameras, digital photo frames, camcorders, and other small electronics are all here. Brands to look for are Nikon, Canon, Olympus, Minolta, and Pentax. Check out the wide selection of sunglasses as well. ⊠*5 Reid St., Hamilton* ☎*441/295–5496*.

SHOES & HANDBAGS

Boyle, W. J. & Sons Ltd. Bermuda's leading shoe-store chain, Boyle's sells a wide range of men's, women's, and children's shoes. **Trends** on Reid Street has the most up-to-the-minute foot fashions, although the **Sports Locker** has a good stock of running shoes and flip-flops. The Church Street store specializes in children's shoes. ⊠*Queen St., Hamilton* ☎*441/295–1887* ⊠*Mangrove Bay, Somerset* ☎*441/234–*

Yo, Ho, Ho & a Bottle of Rum

One of the distinct pleasures of a visit to Bermuda is getting to sample a bit of island rum and rum-based products. Gosling's Black Seal Rum is perhaps the best-loved by locals. It's darker and thicker than the usual stuff, with a hint of a caramel flavor—especially when mixed with carbonated ginger beer to make a Dark 'n Stormy, a famous Bermuda drink (treat it with respect and caution).

Gosling's is one of Bermuda's oldest companies, and its Hamilton liquor shop was established in 1806. Gosling's Black Seal Rum was sold in barrels until just after World War I and inherited its name from the black sealing wax that sealed the barrel corks. In its 151-proof variety, Black Seal will test the strongest drinker. Many prefer to buy it in the standard 80 proof.

Bermuda's Rum Swizzle, another popular drink, also uses the ubiquitous Black Seal Rum, along with a splash of club soda, lime juice, and sugar. Gosling also produces three liqueurs that are big favorites—Bermuda Gold, Bermuda Banana Liqueur, and Bermuda Coconut Rum. These liqueurs can be ordered everywhere, from poolside bars to late-night jazz clubs. They're even found in cakes, as you soon discover in gift shops and on restaurant menus. Classic Bermuda rum cakes are a delicious, nontoxic way to taste the island's famous export. Fear not if rum's not your thing: Guinness and Heineken are among the widely available imported beers.

0530 ✉ *Water St., St. George's* ☎*441/297–1922* ✉*Trends, the Walkway, Reid St., Hamilton* ☎*441/295–6420* ✉*The Sports Locker, Windsor Place, 18 Queen St., Hamilton* ☎*441/292–3300* ✉*Children's Shop, Church St., Hamilton* ☎*441/292–6360.*

Calypso. Women looking for quirky, snazzy footwear should visit Calypso's main store first. The shoe and bag section is small but with choice, super-trendy, sometimes weird styles and colors. Items may cost a little more than you want to spend but you'll want them anyway. Serious bargains can be had during sales. Calypso has branches at Coral Beach & Tennis Club, Fairmont Southampton, and Clocktower Centre in the Dockyard. ✉*45 Front St., Hamilton* ☎*441/295–2112.*

Louis Vuitton. Come here to find the famous monogram on ladies' handbags, men's and women's briefcases, carry-on luggage, wallets, credit-card cases, and other items. Prices here are the same as in the United States, except there's no tax. Small ladies' handbags start at about $750. Small, soft leather carry-ons cost up to $1,000, and natural cowhide briefcases start at $3,000. ⊠*Butterfield Pl., Front St., Hamilton* ☎*441/296–1940.*

★ **Fodor'sChoice Lusso.** This is the ultimate island boutique for designer shoes and leather goods for men and women. Selections from Prada, Ferragamo, Moschino, and Fendi are stocked in this luxury store. ⊠*51 Front St., Hamilton* ☎*441/295–6734.*

Kay Ri's Children's Shoes. This shop offers trendy, bargain-price shoes for children. The store has a great selection of formal sandals. ⊠*Washington Mall, Reid St., Hamilton* ☎*441/292–9317.*

Quattro. For the latest shoe styles from Florence and Rome, check out this closet-size shoe shop. The men's and women's shoes are beautifully made, but prices can be high. ⊠*12 Reid St., Hamilton* ☎*441/295–9815.*

SPORTING GOODS

★ **The Dive Shop.** The best prices for dive gear are found, naturally, at Bermuda's most complete dive shop. The children's mask-and-snorkel set costs $30. You can find a large selection of wet suits, fishing gear, and camping supplies. ⊠*7 Park Rd., Hamilton* ☎*441/292–3839.*

Fly, Bridge and Tackle. The only island store completely dedicated to fishing supplies, Fly, Bridge and Tackle offers everything a fisherman needs except the fish. Plus, the avid fishermen on staff offer excellent advice about fishing in Bermuda. ⊠*26 Church St., Hamilton* ☎*441/295–1845.*

Sports 'R' Us. This store has Bermuda's largest selection of running shoes, plus gear and equipment for most sports. ⊠*Shoppers Fair Bldg., Church St., near Queen St., Hamilton* ☎*441/292–1891.*

Upstairs Golf & Tennis Shop. Golf clubs, tennis rackets, and the accessories for those sports are the specialties of this store. You can find some of the best brands available, including Ping, Callaway, and Titleist for the golfer, and Yonex and Dunlop for the tennis player. Men's and women's sportswear is also sold. ✉ *26 Church St., Hamilton* ☎ *441/295–5161.*

Wheels Cycles, Ltd. Here's where to rent a single- or double-seat electric scooter to explore Bermuda. The company will pick up and deliver cycles right to your door. ✉ *117 Front St., Hamilton* ☎ *441/292–2245.*

Winners Edge. This store sells exercise wear, water bottles, and helmets, and it's the only store in Bermuda to sell Cannondale, Gary Fisher, and Trek equipment. ✉ *73 Front St., Hamilton* ☎ *441/295–6012.*

STATIONERY & ART SUPPLIES

Artcetera. This is where you can buy pens, paint, charcoal, pastels, sketching pads, canvases, and almost anything else an aspiring artist might need to capture Bermuda in color or black and white. ✉ *34 Burnaby Hill, Hamilton* ☎ *441/295–2787.*

The Royal Gazette Stationery Store. Pens, envelopes, writing paper, and note pads are plentiful at this well-stocked stationery store. ✉ *32 Reid St., Hamilton* ☎ *441/295–4008.*

TOYS

The Annex Toys. This large toy department has one of the best and most up-to-date selections of toys and games for all ages. There's also a good supply of kites and beach toys. ✉ *4 Reid St., Hamilton* ☎ *441/295–3838.*

Jack 'N' Jill's Toy Shop. This cottage near Victoria Park is filled with traditional toys as well as newer, perhaps "cooler" toys. The store is also the island's exclusive retailer of Bruynzeel art supplies. ✉ *7 Park Rd., Hamilton* ☎ *441/292–3769.*

Magic Moments. Party planners will find gift-bag loot, balloons, banners, feather boas, and almost anything else you might need for a theme party. ✉ *Washington Mall, Reid St., Hamilton* ☎ *441/296–8848.*

In Focus Bermuda Essentials

PLANNING TOOLS, EXPERT INSIGHT, GREAT CONTACTS

There are planners and there are those who, excuse the pun, fly by the seat of their pants. We happily place ourselves among the planners. Our writers and editors try to anticipate all the issues you may face before and during any journey, and then they do their research. This section is the product of their efforts. Use it to get excited about your trip to Bermuda, to inform your travel planning, or to guide you on the road should the seat of your pants start to feel threadbare.

GETTING STARTED

We're really proud of our Web site: Fodors.com is a great place to begin any journey. Scan Travel Wire for suggested itineraries, travel deals, restaurant and hotel openings, and other up-to-the-minute info. Check out Booking to research prices and book plane tickets, hotel rooms, rental cars, and vacation packages. Head to Talk for on-the-ground pointers from travelers who frequent our message boards.

▌ RESOURCES

ONLINE TRAVEL TOOLS

All About Bermuda One of the best Bermuda Web sites is ⊕*www.bermuda-online. org.* Supported by the *Royal Gazette,* it has information on every aspect of Bermuda, from history to transportation. The Department of Tourism's Web site ⊕*www.bermudatourism. com* is helpful during the initial stages of vacation planning. ⊕*www.bermuda.com* has a good search engine and links to a number of Bermuda-related Web pages. The Bermuda Hotel Association's ⊕*www. experience-bermuda.com* has a monthly events calendar and a search function that allows users to find events by date or type. Gay visitors to Bermuda might find ⊕*www.gaybermuda. com* useful for finding gay-friendly hotels and nightlife venues. ⊕*BlackandCoke.com*

and ⊕*www.bermynet.com* are online guides to entertainment events in Bermuda. To keep up with current affairs, check out the island's three newspapers: ⊕*www.theroyalgazette. com* for stories from the daily *Royal Gazette* and the weekly *Mid Ocean News,* and ⊕*www. bermudasun.bm* for the twice-weekly *Bermuda Sun.* Visit the Bermuda National Trust at ⊕*www.bnt.bm* for event, tour, and attraction information.

Time Zones Timeanddate.com (⊕*www.timeanddate.com/ worldclock*) can help you figure out the correct time anywhere.

Weather Accuweather.com (⊕*www.accuweather.com*) is an independent weather-forecasting service with good coverage of hurricanes. **Weather.com** (⊕*www. weather.com*) is the Web site for the Weather Channel.

VISITOR INFORMATION

In Bermuda Bermuda Department of Tourism (☎*441/292-0023* ⊕*www.bermudatourism.com*). **St. George's Foundation** (☎*441/297-8043* ⊕*www.stgeorgesfoundation. com*).

In the U.S. Bermuda Department of Tourism (☎*800/223-6106*).

▌ THINGS TO CONSIDER

GEAR

Bermudians dress more formally than most Americans. In the evening, some of the more upscale restaurants and hotel dining rooms require men to wear a jacket and tie and women to dress comparably. However, increasingly, venues are more accepting of the trend toward "smart-casual." In this case, women should be fine with slacks or a skirt and a dressy blouse or sweater. Bermudian men often wear Bermuda shorts (and proper knee socks) with a jacket and tie for formal events and business meetings.

During the cooler months, bring lightweight woolens or cottons that you can wear in layers. A lightweight jacket is always a good idea. Regardless of the season, pack a swimsuit, a beachwear cover-up, sunscreen, and sunglasses, as well as a raincoat (umbrellas are typically provided by hotels). Comfortable walking shoes are a must. If you plan to play tennis, be aware that many courts require proper whites and that tennis balls in Bermuda are extremely expensive, so bring your own.

PASSPORTS

As of January 2007, U.S. citizens arriving by air to Bermuda need a valid passport. U.S. citizens may need a passport as early as January 2008, when traveling by sea. U.S citizens do not need a Visa to enter Bermuda for a period less than 90 days.

■TIP→Before your trip, make two copies of your passport's data page (one for someone at home and another for you to carry separately). Or scan the page and e-mail it to someone at home and/or yourself.

U.S. Passport Information U.S. Department of State (☎877/487–2778 ⊕travel.state.gov/passport).

U.S. Passport & Visa Expediters A. Briggs Passport & Visa Expeditors (☎800/806–0581 or 202/464–3000 ⊕www.abriggs. com). **American Passport Express** (☎800/455–5166 or 603/559–9888 ⊕www.americanpassport.com). **Passport Express** (☎800/362–8196 or 401/272–4612 ⊕www. passportexpress.com). **Travel Document Systems** (☎800/874–5100 or 202/638–3800 ⊕www.traveldocs. com). **Travel the World Visas** (☎866/886–8472 or 301/495–7700 ⊕www.world-visa.com).

TRIP INSURANCE

We believe that comprehensive trip insurance is especially valuable if you're booking a very expensive or complicated trip, or if you're booking far in advance. But whether you get insurance has more to do with how comfortable you are assuming all that risk yourself.

Comprehensive travel policies typically cover trip-cancellation and interruption, letting you cancel or cut your trip short because of a personal emergency, illness, or, in some cases, acts of terrorism in your destination. Some also cover you for trip delays because of bad weather

Trip Insurance Resources

INSURANCE COMPARISON SITES		
Insure My Trip.com	800/487–4722	www.insuremytrip.com
Square Mouth.com	800/240–0369	www.quotetravelinsurance.com
COMPREHENSIVE TRAVEL INSURERS		
Access America	866/807–3982	www.accessamerica.com
CSA Travel Protection	800/873–9855	www.csatravelprotection.com
HTH Worldwide	610/254–8700 or 888/243–2358	www.hthworldwide.com
Travelex Insurance	888/457–4602	www.travelex-insurance.com
Travel Guard International	715/345–0505 or 800/826–4919	www.travelguard.com
Travel Insured International	800/243–3174	www.travelinsured.com
MEDICAL-ONLY INSURERS		
International Medical Group	800/628–4664	www.imglobal.com
International SOS	215/942–8000 or 713/521–7611	www.internationalsos.com
Wallach & Company	800/237–6615 or 504/687–3166	www.wallach.com

or mechanical problems. Another type of coverage to look for is financial default—that is, when your trip is disrupted because a tour operator, airline, or cruise line goes out of business.

If you're going abroad, consider buying medical-only coverage at the very least. Neither Medicare nor some private insurers cover medical expenses anywhere outside of the United States besides Mexico and Canada (including time aboard a cruise ship, even if it leaves from a U.S. port). Medical-only policies typically reimburse you for medical care (excluding that related to preexisting conditions) and hospitalization abroad, and provide for evacuation. You still have to pay the bills and await reimbursement from the insurer.

Expect comprehensive travel insurance policies to cost about 4% to 7% of the total price of your trip (it's more like 12% if you're over age 70). A medical-only policy may or may not be cheaper than a comprehensive policy. Always read the fine print of your policy to make sure that you are covered for the risks that are of most concern to you.

BOOKING YOUR TRIP

Unless your cousin is a travel agent, you're probably among the millions of people who make most of their travel arrangements online.

Is it truly better to book directly on an airline or hotel Web site? And when does a real live travel agent come in handy? Read on.

▐ ONLINE

You really have to shop around. A travel wholesaler such as Hotels.com or HotelClub.net can be a source of good rates, as can discounters such as Hotwire or Priceline, particularly if you can bid for your hotel room or airfare. Indeed, such sites sometimes have deals that are unavailable elsewhere. They do, however, tend to work only with hotel chains (which makes them just plain useless for getting hotel reservations outside of major cities) or big airlines (so that often leaves out upstarts like jetBlue and some foreign carriers like Air India).

Also, with discounters and wholesalers you must generally prepay, and everything is nonrefundable. And before you fork over the dough, be sure to check the terms and conditions, so you know what a given company will do for you if there's a problem and what you'll have to deal with on your own.

Booking engines like Expedia, Travelocity, and Orbitz are actually travel agents, albeit high-volume, online ones. And airline travel packagers like American Airlines Vacations and Virgin Vacations—well, they're travel agents, too. But they may still not work with all the world's hotels.

An aggregator site will search many sites and pull the best prices for airfares, hotels, and rental cars from them. Most aggregators compare the major travel-booking sites such as Expedia, Travelocity, and Orbitz; some also look at airline Web sites, though rarely the sites of smaller budget airlines. Some aggregators also compare other travel products, including complex packages—a good thing, as you can sometimes get the best overall deal by booking an air-and-hotel package.

▐ WITH A TRAVEL AGENT

If you use an agent—brick-and-mortar or virtual—you'll pay a fee for the service. And know that the service you get from some online agents isn't comprehensive. For example Expedia and Travelocity don't search for prices on budget airlines like jetBlue, Southwest, or small foreign carriers. That said, some agents (online or not) *do* have access to fares that are difficult to find oth-

Online Booking Resources

AGGREGATORS

Kayak	www.kayak.com	cruises and vacation packages
Mobissimo	www.mobissimo.com	
Qixo	www.qixo.com	compares cruises, vacation packages, and even travel insurance
Sidestep	www.sidestep.com	compares packages and deals
Travelgrove	www.travelgrove.com	also compares cruises and packages

BOOKING ENGINES

Cheap Tickets	www.cheaptickets.com	a discounter
Expedia	www.expedia.com	online agency
Hotwire	www.hotwire.com	a discounter
lastminute.com	www.lastminute.com	specializes in last-minute travel
Onetravel.com	www.onetravel.com	an online discounter
Orbitz	www.orbitz.com	gives a clear breakdown of fees and taxes before you book
Priceline.com	www.priceline.com	a discounter that allows bidding
Travel.com	www.travel.com	allows you to compare rates
Travelocity	www.travelocity.com	charges a booking fee

ONLINE ACCOMMODATIONS

Hotelbook.com	www.hotelbook.com	focuses on independent hotels
Hotel Club	www.hotelclub.net	good for major cities worldwide
Hotels.com	www.hotels.com	an online wholesaler
Quikbook	www.quikbook.com	"pay when you stay" reservations

OTHER RESOURCES

Bidding For Travel	www.biddingfortravel.com	figure out what you can get and for how much
The Bermuda Hotel Association and Bermuda.com	www.experiencebermuda.com www.bermuda.com	extensive lists of accommodations for varying budgets
Bermuda 4u	www.bermuda4u.com	particularly detailed, with notes on each property

erwise, and the savings can more than make up for any surcharge.

A knowledgeable brick-and-mortar travel agent can be a godsend if you're booking a cruise, a package trip that's not available to you directly, an air pass, or a complicated itinerary including several overseas flights. What's more, travel agents that specialize in a destination may have exclusive access to certain deals and insider information on things such as charter flights. Agents who specialize in types of travelers (senior citizens, gays and lesbians, naturists) or types of trips (cruises, luxury travel, safaris) can also be invaluable.

■ TIP→ **Remember that Expedia, Travelocity, and Orbitz are travel agents, not just booking engines. To resolve any problems with a reservation made through these companies, contact them first.**

Low-cost airfares, particularly from the U.S. east coast, are becoming more prevalent, and with Bermuda's tourism department specifically citing this reduction in price as one of their priorities, prices will likely continue to tumble. That means for those who like to shop around, some great and relatively cheap deals can be found—especially if you're looking to stay in a guesthouse. However, if you're looking to stay in a higher-end resort, significant savings can be made through travel agents, who can also save large groups a fair amount of hassle in terms of travel to and from the airport.

Agent Resources American Society of Travel Agents (☎ 703/739-2782 ⊕ www.travelsense.org).

■ ACCOMMODATIONS

Accommodation standards in Bermuda—whether you prefer a guesthouse or a five-star hotel—are generally high, and strongly regulated by the Bermuda Department of Tourism. However, prices tend to reflect this quality, and you should be warned that there are no true budget options. (Camping is not allowed and there are no hostels on the island.) Staying in a hotel can mean anything from a luxury resort setting to something more similar to a three-star hotel in the U.S. Another option is to stay in more homelike accommodations—either by renting a room in a guesthouse (a commercial establishment roughly similar to a room in a bed-and-breakfast, though some can be very upmarket) or a cottage.

Most hotels and other lodgings require you to give your credit-card details before they will confirm your reservation. If you don't feel comfortable e-mailing this information, ask if you can fax it (some places even prefer faxes). However you book, get confirmation in writing and have a copy of it handy when you check in.

■ TIP→ **Assume that hotels operate on the European Plan (EP, no meals) unless we specify that they use the Breakfast Plan (BP, with full breakfast), Continental Plan (CP,**

Continental breakfast), Full American Plan (FAP, all meals), Modified American Plan (MAP, breakfast and dinner) or are all-inclusive (AI, all meals and most activities).

Be sure you understand the hotel's cancellation policy. Some places allow you to cancel without any kind of penalty—even if you prepaid to secure a discounted rate—if you cancel at least 24 hours in advance. Others require you to cancel a week in advance or penalize you the cost of one night. Small inns and B&Bs are most likely to require you to cancel far in advance. Most hotels allow children under a certain age to stay in their parents' room at no extra charge, but others charge for them as extra adults; find out the cutoff age for discounts.

For price categories, consult the price chart found at the beginning of the "Where to Stay" chapter.

APARTMENT & HOUSE RENTALS

Rental houses, apartments, and villas are all over Bermuda and may be owned by individuals, consortiums, and developers, so booking might be anything from calling the owner in person to booking on a Web site. Bermuda. com ⊕*www.bermuda.com* has a fairly extensive list of the more well-known properties.

Contacts Villas International (☎*415/499–9490 or 800/221–2260* ⊕*www.villasintl.com*).

BED & BREAKFASTS

If you're part of the "no-frills" crowd, guesthouses in Bermuda offer bed-and-breakfast style accommodation. Some have their own Internet sites; most are listed on Bermuda.com ⊕*www. bermuda.com*.

Reservation Services Bed & Breakfast.com (☎*512/322–2710 or 800/462–2632* ⊕*www.bedand breakfast.com*) sends out an online newsletter.

HOME EXCHANGES

With a direct home exchange you stay in someone else's home while they stay in yours. Some outfits also deal with vacation homes, so you're not actually staying in someone's full-time residence, just their vacant weekend place.

Exchange Clubs Home Exchange. com (☎*800/877–8723* ⊕*www.ho-meexchange.com*); $59.95 for a 1-year online listing. **HomeLink International** (☎*800/638–3841* ⊕*www.homelink.org*); $80 yearly for Web-only membership; $125 includes Web access and two catalogs.

▌ AIRLINE TICKETS

Most domestic airline tickets are electronic; international tickets may be either electronic or paper. With an e-ticket the only thing you receive is an e-mailed receipt citing your itinerary and reservation and ticket numbers.

▌TIP→ Discount air passes that let you travel economically in a country or region must often be purchased before you leave home. In some cases you can only get them through a travel agent.

▌ RENTAL CARS

You cannot rent a car in Bermuda. The island has strict laws governing overcrowded roads, so even Bermudians are only allowed one car per household. A popular, albeit possibly somewhat dangerous, alternative is to rent mopeds or scooters (⇨ *See By Moped & Scooter*), which are better for negotiating the island's narrow roads.

▌ VACATION PACKAGES

Packages *are not* guided excursions. Packages combine airfare, accommodations, and perhaps other extras (theater tickets, guided excursions, boat trips, reserved entry to popular museums, transit passes), but they let you do your own thing. During busy periods packages may be your only option, as flights and rooms may be sold out otherwise.

Packages will definitely save you time. They can also save you money, particularly in peak seasons, but—and this is a really big "but"—you should price each part of the package separately to be sure. And be aware that prices advertised on Web sites and in newspapers rarely include service charges or taxes, which can up your costs by hundreds of dollars.

▬TIP➜Some packages and cruises are sold only through travel agents. Don't always assume that you can get the best deal by booking everything yourself.

Each year consumers are stranded or lose their money when packagers—even large ones with excellent reputations—go out of business. How can you protect yourself?

First, always pay with a credit card; if you have a problem, your credit-card company may help you resolve it. Second, buy trip insurance that covers default. Third, choose a company that belongs to the United States Tour Operators Association, whose members must set aside funds to cover defaults. Finally, choose a company that also participates in the Tour Operator Program of the American Society of Travel Agents (ASTA), which will act as mediator in any disputes.

You can also check on the tour operator's reputation among travelers by posting an inquiry on one of the Fodors.com forums.

Organizations American Society of Travel Agents (*ASTA*) ☎ *703/739–2782 or 800/965–2782* ⊕ *www.astanet.com*). **United States Tour Operators Association** (*USTOA* ☎ *212/599–6599* ⊕ *www. ustoa.com*). ▬TIP➜**Local tourism boards can provide information about lesser-known and smallniche operators that sell packages to only a few destinations.**

TRANSPORTATION

▌ BY AIR

Flying time to Bermuda from most east coast cities is about 2 hours; from Atlanta, 2¾ hours; from Toronto, 3 hours; and 7 hours from London Gatwick.

Most flights arrive around noon, making for particularly long waits to get through immigration; however, British Airways flights and one American Airlines flight from New York arrive in the evening.

Flights to Bermuda are occasionally delayed or canceled due to high winds or crosswinds, particularly in late summer and fall. Before you leave home for the airport, you should always call to confirm whether or not there are Bermuda-bound delays.

Bermuda-bound travelers are rarely bumped, even during the island's busiest summer season. Instead, when overbooking occurs, some airlines switch to a larger aircraft.

Have your passport or government-issued photo ID handy. Bermuda is rather scrupulous about ID, and you'll be asked to show your passport when checking in and again when boarding.

At many airports outside Bermuda, travelers with only carry-on luggage can bypass the airline's front desk and check in at the gate. But in Bermuda, everyone checks in at the airline's front desk. U.S. customs has a desk here, too, so you won't have to clear customs at home when you land. Passengers returning to Britain or Canada will need to clear customs and immigration on arrival.

Airlines & Airports Airline and Airport Links.com (⊕www.airlineandairportlinks.com) has links to many of the world's airlines and airports.

Airline Security Issues Transportation Security Administration (⊕www.tsa.gov) has answers for almost every question that might come up.

AIRPORTS

Bermuda's gateway is L. F. Wade Airport (BDA), formerly Bermuda International Airport, on the East End of the island. It's approximately 9 mi from Hamilton (30-minute cab ride), 13 mi from Southampton (40-minute cab ride) and 17 mi from Somerset (50 minutes by cab). The town of St. George's is about a 15-minute cab ride from the airport.

Airport Information L. F. Wade Airport (BDA) (☎441/293–1640 ⊕www.bermudaairport.com).

GROUND TRANSPORTATION

Taxis, readily available outside the arrivals gate, are the usual and most convenient way to leave the airport. The approximate fare (not including tip) to

Hamilton is $25; to St. George's, $15; to south-shore hotels, $35; and to Sandys (Somerset), $50. A surcharge of $1 is added for each piece of luggage stored in the trunk or on the roof. Fares are 25% higher between midnight and 6 AM and all day on Sunday and public holidays. Fifteen percent is an acceptable tip.

Bermuda Hosts Ltd. provides transportation to hotels and guesthouses aboard air-conditioned six- to 25-seat vans and buses. Reservations are recommended. Prices are $25 per person to Hamilton or $30 per person to Southampton, so for most people a taxi is the wisest option.

Contacts Bermuda Hosts Ltd. (☎441/293–1334). **The Bermuda Industrial Union Taxi Co-op** (☎441/292–4476). **Bermuda Taxi Radio Cabs** (☎441/295–4141). **BTA Dispatching Ltd.** (☎441/296–2121 ⊕www.taxibermuda.com). **First Step Taxi Service** (wheelchair accessible) (☎441/293–0301 or 441/735–7151).

FLIGHTS

Nonstop service to Bermuda is available year-round on major airlines from Atlanta, Boston, Newark (NJ), New York City, Washington, D.C., Baltimore, Philadelphia, Toronto, and London, and seasonally from Miami, Charlotte, Orlando, Detroit, and Halifax. Travelers from Australia and New Zealand must fly to Bermuda via London, New York, or Toronto.

Fares from New York City may be found for under $300 on some of the budget airlines but the average price is closer to $500 and can be as high as $800 in peak season, whereas fares from Toronto are typically about $600. Fares from Gatwick vary from $700 in low season to $1,200 in high season on British Airways, or can be as low as $500 on the twice-weekly low-cost airline Zoom. Flight regularity and price is subject to rapid change and airlines recommend that travelers check their Web sites for up-to-the-minute information.

Airline Contacts Air Canada (☎888/247–2262 ⊕www.aircanada.com). **American Airlines** (☎800/433–7300 ⊕www.aa.com). **Continental Airlines** (☎800/523–3273 for U.S. and Mexico reservations, 800/231–0856 for international reservations ⊕www.continental.com). **Delta Airlines** (☎800/221–1212 for U.S. reservations, 800/241–4141 for international reservations ⊕www.delta.com). **jetBlue** (☎800/538–2583 ⊕www.jetblue.com). **USAirways** (☎800/428–4322 for U.S. and Canada reservations, 800/622–1015 for international reservations ⊕www.usairways.com).

❚ BY BOAT

The Bermuda Ministry of Transport maintains excellent, frequent, and on-time ferry service from Hamilton to Paget and Warwick (the pink line), Somerset and the Dockyard in the West End (the blue line), Rockaway in Southampton (the green line), and, weekdays in summer only, the Dockyard and St. George's (the orange line).

A one-way adult fare to Paget or Warwick is $2.50; to Somerset, the Dockyard, or St. George's, $4. The last departures are at 9:45 PM from mid-April through mid-November, 9 PM from mid-November through mid-April. Sunday ferry service is limited and ends around 7 PM. You can bring a bicycle on board free of charge, but you'll pay $4 extra to take a motor scooter to Somerset or the Dockyard, and scooters are not allowed on the smaller Paget and Warwick ferries. Neither bikes nor scooters are allowed on ferries to St. George's. Discounted one-, two-, three-, four-, and seven-day passes are available for use on both ferries and buses. They cost $12, $20, $28, $35, and $45 respectively. Monthly passes are also offered at $55. The helpful ferry operators can answer questions about routes and schedules and can even help get your bike on board. Schedules are published in the phone book, posted at each landing, and are also available at the Ferry Terminal, Central Bus Terminal, Visitors Service Bureaus, and most hotels.

▐ BY BUS

Bermuda's pink and blue buses travel the island from east to west. To find a bus stop outside Hamilton, look for either a stone shelter or a pink or blue pole. For buses heading to Hamilton, the pole is pink; for those traveling away from Hamilton, the pole is blue. Remember to wait on the proper side of the road. Driving in Bermuda is on the left. Bus drivers will not make change, so purchase tickets or discounted tokens or carry plenty of coins.

In addition to public buses, private minibuses serve St. George's. The minibus fare depends upon the destination, but you won't pay more than $5. Minibuses, which you can flag down, drop you wherever you want to go in this parish. They operate daily from about 7:30 AM to 9 PM. Smoking is not permitted on buses.

Bermuda is divided into 14 bus zones, each about 2 mi long. Within the first three zones, the rate is $3 (coins only). For longer distances, the fare is $4.50. If you plan to travel by public transportation often, buy a booklet of tickets (15 14-zone tickets for $30, or 15 three-zone tickets for $20). You can also buy a few tokens, which, unlike tickets, are sold individually. In addition to tickets and tokens, there are one-, two-, three-, four-, and seven-day adult passes ($12, $20, $28, $35, and $45 respectively). Monthly passes are also available for $55 each. All bus passes are good for ferry service and are available at the central bus terminal. Tickets and passes are also sold at the Visitor Information Centres in Hamilton, post offices, and at many hotels and guesthouses. Passes are accepted on both buses and ferries.

Hamilton buses arrive and depart from the Central Bus Terminal. An office here is open weekdays from 7:15 to 5:30, Saturday from 8:15 to 5:30, and Sunday and holidays from 9:15 to 4:45; it's the only place to buy money-saving tokens.

Buses run about every 15 minutes, except on Sunday, when they usually come every half hour or hour, depending on the route. Bus schedules, which also contain ferry timetables, are available at the bus terminal in Hamilton and at many hotels. The timetable also offers an itinerary for a do-it-yourself, one-day sightseeing tour by bus and ferry. Upon request, the driver will be happy to tell you when you've reached your stop. Be sure to greet the bus driver when boarding—it's considered rude in Bermuda to ask a bus driver a question, such as the fare or details on your destination, without first greeting him or her.

Bus Information Public Transport Bermuda (☎441/292-3851 ⊕www.bermudabuses.com). **St. George's Minibus Service** (☎441/297-8199).

▌ BY MOPED & SCOOTER

Because car rentals are not allowed in Bermuda, you might decide to get around by moped or scooter. Bermudians routinely use the words "moped" and "scooter" interchangeably, even though they're different. You must pedal to start a moped, and it carries only one person. A scooter,

on the other hand, which starts when you put the key in the ignition, is more powerful and holds one or two passengers.

Think twice before renting a moped, as accidents occur frequently and are occasionally fatal. The best ways to avoid mishaps are to drive defensively, obey the speed limit, remember to stay on the left-hand side of the road—especially at traffic circles—and avoid riding in the rain and at night.

Helmets are required by law. Mopeds and scooters can be rented from cycle liveries by the hour, the day, or the week. Liveries will show first-time riders how to operate the vehicles. Rates vary, so it's worth calling several liveries to see what they charge. Single-seat scooter rentals cost from $35 to $53 per day or from $136 to $181 per week. Some liveries tack a mandatory $20 insurance-and-repair charge on top of the bill, whereas others include the cost of insurance, breakdown service, pickup and delivery, and a tank of gas in the quoted price. A $20 deposit may also be charged for the lock, key, and helmet. You must be at least 16 and have a valid driver's license to rent. Major hotels have their own cycle liveries, and all hotels and most guesthouses will make rental arrangements.

GASOLINE
Gas for cycles runs from $3 to $4 per liter, but you can cover a great deal of ground on the full tank that comes with the wheels.

Gas stations will accept major credit cards. It's customary to tip attendants—a couple of dollars is adequate.

PARKING

On-street parking bays for scooters are plentiful and easy to spot. What's even better is they're free!

ROAD CONDITIONS

Roads are narrow, winding, and full of blind curves. Whether driving cars or scooters, Bermudians tend to be quite cautious around less-experienced visiting riders, but crowded city streets make accidents all the more common. Local rush hours are weekdays, from 7:30 AM to 9 AM and from 4 PM to 5:30 PM. Roads are often bumpy, and they may be slippery under a morning mist or rainfall. Street lamps are few and far between outside of the cities, so be especially careful driving at night.

ROADSIDE EMERGENCIES

The number for Bermuda's emergency services is 911. Scooters are often stolen, so to be safe you should always carry the number of your hire company with you.

RULES OF THE ROAD

The speed limit is 35 kph (22 mph), except in the World Heritage Site of St. George's, where it is a mere 25 kph (about 15 mph). The limits, however, are not very well enforced, and the actual driving speed in Bermuda hovers around 50 kph (30 mph). Police seldom target tourists for parking offenses or other driving infractions. Drunk driving is a serious problem in Bermuda, despite stiff penalties. The blood-alcohol limit is 0.08. The courts will impose a $1,000 fine for a driving-while-intoxicated infraction, and also take the driver off the road for about one year. Despite much discussion, there's currently no law against using a mobile phone even while driving a scooter.

Rental Companies Elbow Beach Cycles Ltd. (☎441/236–9237). **Oleander Cycles** (✉Paget ☎441/236–5235 ✉Hamilton ☎441/295–0919 ✉Southampton ☎441/234–0629 ✉Dockyard, Sandys ☎441/234–2764). **Smatt's Cycle Livery Ltd.** (☎441/295–1180). **Wheels Cycles** (☎441/292–2245). **World Distributors Ltd.** (☎441/295–2329).

❚ BY TAXI

Taxis are the fastest and easiest way to get around the island—and also the most costly. Four-seater taxis charge $5.35 for the first mile and $2 for each subsequent mile. Between midnight and 6 AM, and on Sunday and holidays, a 25% surcharge is added to the fare. There's a $1 charge for each piece of luggage stored in the trunk or on the roof. Taxi drivers accept only American or Bermudian cash, but not bills larger than $50, and they expect a 15% tip. You can phone for taxi pickup, but you may wait while the cab navigates Bermuda's heavy traffic. Don't hesitate to hail a taxi on the street.

For a personalized taxi tour of the island, the minimum duration is three hours, at $30 per hour for one to four people and $42 an hour for five or six, excluding tip. **The Bermuda Industrial Union Taxi Co-op** (☎*441/292–4476*). **Bermuda Taxi Radio Cabs** (☎*441/295–4141*).**BTA Dispatching Ltd.** (☎*441/296–2121* ⊕*www.taxibermuda.com*).**First Step Taxi Service** (wheelchair accessible) (☎*441/293–0301 or 441/735–7151*).

■TIP→Taxi Travel. When you take a taxi, ask for the driver's personal card so you can call them back later. Most drivers carry them, and it's a good way to avoid any lengthy waits, particularly late at night when there can be an excess of revelers waiting for what seems to be far less taxis.

ON THE GROUND

▌ COMMUNICATIONS

INTERNET

You should have no trouble bringing a laptop through customs into Bermuda, though you may have to open and turn it on for inspection by security officers. It's a good idea to bring proof of purchase with you so you will not run into any difficulty bringing the computer back to the States, especially if it's a new machine.

Most hotels charge connection fees each time a laptop is hooked up to the Internet ($3 to $10), with additional charges (10¢ to 30¢ per minute) during the connection. The Fairmont Southampton has a fully equipped business center where guests can use hotel computers for Internet access (connection charges still apply).

If you do not have an Internet connection at your hotel, there are a few places around the island where you can log on. But it will cost you—$12 an hour is an average rate.

Contacts Cybercafes (⊕*www. cybercafes.com*) lists more than 4,000 Internet cafés worldwide. **Coconut Rock** (☎*441/292–1043*). **Logic** (☎*441/294–8888*). **Silk Thai Cuisine** (☎*441/295–0449*). **Twice Told Tales** (☎*441/296–1995*).

PHONES

The good news is you can now make a direct-dial telephone call from virtually any point on earth. The bad news? You can't always do so cheaply. Calling from a hotel is almost always the most expensive option; hotels usually add huge surcharges to all calls, particularly international ones. In some countries you can phone from call centers or even the post office. And then there are mobile phones (⇨*See Mobile Phones below*), which are sometimes more prevalent—particularly in the developing world—than landlines; as expensive as mobile phone calls can be, they are still usually a much cheaper option than calling from your hotel.

Destination-specific international calling cards from North Rock Communications in Hamilton offer the cheapest way of calling. You can use them on any phones, including public pay phones and mobile phones. You can also get standard international cards from pharmacies, some supermarkets, and many gas stations, which will also get you a better rate than calling directly from the hotel.

The country code for Bermuda is 441. When dialing a Bermuda number from the United States or Canada, simply dial 1 + 441 + local number. You do not need to dial the international access code (011).

CALLING WITHIN BERMUDA
Telephone service in Bermuda is organized and efficient, though service may be interrupted during storms.

When in Bermuda, call 411 for local phone numbers. To reach directory assistance from outside the country, call 441/555–1212.

To make a local call, simply dial the seven-digit number.

You can find pay phones similar to those in the United States on the streets of Hamilton, St. George's, and Somerset as well as at ferry landings, some bus stops, and public beaches. Deposit 50¢ (U.S. or Bermudian) before you dial. Most hotels charge from 20¢ to $1 for local calls.

CALLING OUTSIDE BERMUDA
The country code for the United States is 1.

Most hotels impose a surcharge for long-distance calls, even those made collect or with a phone card or credit card. Many toll-free 800 or 888 numbers in the United States aren't honored in Bermuda. Consider buying a prepaid local phone card rather than using your own calling card. In many small guesthouses and apartments the phone in your room is a private line from which you can make only collect, credit-card, or local calls. Some small hotels have a telephone room or kiosk where you can make long-distance calls.

You can find specially marked AT&T USADirect phones at the airport, the cruise-ship dock in Hamilton, and King's Square and Ordnance Island in St. George's. You can also make international calls with a calling card from the main post office. You can make prepaid international calls from the Cable & Wireless Office, which also has international telex, cable, and fax services Monday through Saturday from 9 to 5.

To call the United States, Canada, and most Caribbean countries, simply dial 1 (or 0 if you need an operator's assistance), then the area code and the number. For all other countries, dial 011 (or 0 for an operator), the country code, the area code, and the number. Using an operator for an overseas call is more expensive than dialing direct. For calls to the United States, rates are highest from 8 AM to 6 PM and discounted from 6 PM to 8 AM and on weekends.

Access Codes **AT&T USADirect** (☎ *800/872–2881*). **MCI Call USA** (☎ *800/888–8000 or 800/888–8888*). **Sprint Express** (☎ *800/623–0877*).

International Calls **Main post office** (☎ *441/295–5151*). **Cable & Wireless Office** (☎ *441/297–7000*)

CALLING CARDS
Buy a prepaid phone card for long-distance calls. They can be used with any touch-tone phone in Bermuda, although they can only be used for calls outside Bermuda. Rates are often significantly lower than dialing direct, but the down side is that some hotels will charge you for mak-

ing the call to your card's 800 number. Phone cards are available at pharmacies, shops, gas stations, and restaurants. The phone companies Cable & Wireless, TeleBermuda, and Logic Communications sell prepaid calling cards in denominations of $5 to $50. The cards can be used around the world as well as in Bermuda.

Phone-Card Companies Cable & Wireless (☎441/297–7022). **Logic Communications** (☎441/296–9600). **North Rock Communications Ltd.** (☎441/540–2700). **TeleBermuda** (☎441/296–9000).

MOBILE PHONES

If you have a multiband phone (some countries use different frequencies than what's used in the United States) and your service provider uses the world-standard GSM network (as do T-Mobile, Cingular, and Verizon), you can probably use your phone abroad. Roaming fees can be steep, however: 99¢ a minute is considered reasonable. And overseas you normally pay the toll charges for incoming calls. It's almost always cheaper to send a text message than to make a call, since text messages have a very low set fee (often less than 5¢).

If you just want to make local calls, consider buying a new SIM card (note that your provider may have to unlock your phone for you to use a different SIM card) and a prepaid service plan in the destination. You'll then have a local number and can make local calls at local rates. If your trip is extensive, you could also simply buy a new cell phone in your destination, as the initial cost will be offset over time.

■TIP➜ **If you travel internationally frequently, save one of your old mobile phones or buy a cheap one on the Internet; ask your cell phone company to unlock it for you, and take it with you as a travel phone, buying a new SIM card with pay-as-you-go service in each destination.**

Most travelers can use their own cell phones in Bermuda, though you should check with your provider to be sure. Cell phone rentals are available from stores in Hamilton, some of which will even deliver the phone to you. A typical charge is $2 a day for the rental while local calls will cost 60¢ a minute. Incoming international calls will also cost 60¢ a minute, but outgoing international calls will cost $1.10 a minute.

Contacts Cellular Abroad (☎800/287–5072 ⊕www.cellular abroad.com) rents and sells GMS phones and sells SIM cards that work in many countries. **Mobal** (☎888/888–9162 ⊕www.mobal rental.com) rents mobiles and sells GSM phones (starting at $49) that will operate in 140 countries. Per-call rates vary throughout the world. **Planet Fone** (☎888/988–4777 ⊕www.planetfone.com) rents cell phones, but the per-minute rates are expensive.

Rentals BermudaCellRentals.com (☎441/232–2355). **Internet Lane** (☎441/296–9972).

CUSTOMS & DUTIES

You're always allowed to bring goods of a certain value back home without having to pay any duty or import tax. But there's a limit on the amount of tobacco and liquor you can bring back duty-free, and some countries have separate limits for perfumes; for exact figures, check with your customs department. The values of so-called "duty-free" goods are included in these amounts. When you shop abroad, save all your receipts, as customs inspectors may ask to see them as well as the items you purchased. If the total value of your goods is more than the duty-free limit, you'll have to pay a tax (most often a flat percentage) on the value of everything beyond that limit.

On entering Bermuda, you can bring in duty-free up to 50 cigars, 200 cigarettes, and 1 pound of tobacco; 1 liter of wine and 1 liter of spirits; and other goods with a total maximum value of $30. To import plants, fruits, vegetables, or pets, you must get an import permit in advance from the Department of Environmental Protection. Merchandise and sales materials for use at conventions must be cleared with the hotel concerned before you arrive. Be prepared for a bit of a wait, as the Customs Office has a reputation for being very thorough. If there are a lot of passengers this process can add an hour or so if you're unlucky. It goes without saying, but you should definitely not bring in any drugs such as marijuana, as drug checks are very thorough and the penalties are harsh.

Information in Bermuda Department of Environmental Protection (☎441/236–4201 ⊕ www.animals. gov.bm).

U.S. Information U.S. Customs and Border Protection (⊕ www.cbp.gov).

ELECTRICITY

The local electrical current is the same as in the United States and Canada: 110 volt, 60 cycle AC. All appliances that can be used in North America can be used in Bermuda without adapters. Winter storms bring occasional power outages.

EMERGENCIES

Police, ambulance, and fire services are all at 911. Pharmacies usually open around 8 AM, some stay open until 9 PM. People's Pharmacy in Hamilton is open from 10 AM to 2 PM on Sunday.

Doctors & Dentists Government Health Clinic (☎441/236–0224 🖷441/278–4900).

Foreign Consulates American Consulate (✉ Crown Hill, 16 Middle Rd., Devonshire ☎441/295–1342 ⊕ http://hamilton.usconsulate.gov).

General Emergency Contacts Air/Sea Rescue (☎441/297–1010 ⊕ www.rccbermuda.bm). Police, fire, ambulance (☎911).

Hospitals & Clinics King Edward VII Memorial Hospital (☎441/236–2345 🖷441/236–3691).

▌ HEALTH

Sunburn and sunstroke are legitimate concerns if you're traveling to Bermuda in summer. On hot, sunny days, wear a hat, a beach cover-up, and lots of sunblock. These are essential for a day on a boat or at the beach. Be sure to take the same kind of precautions on overcast summer days—some of the worst cases of sunburn happen on cloudy afternoons when sunblock seems unnecessary. Drink plenty of water and, above all, limit the amount of time you spend in the sun until you become acclimated.

The Portuguese man-of-war occasionally visits Bermuda's waters, so be alert when swimming, especially in summer or whenever the water is particularly warm. This creature is recognizable by a purple, balloonlike float sack of perhaps 8 inches in diameter, below which dangle 20- to 60-inch tentacles armed with powerful stinging cells. Contact with the stinging cells causes immediate and severe pain. Seek medical attention immediately: a serious sting can send a person into shock. In the meantime—or if getting to a doctor will take a while—treat the affected area liberally with vinegar. Ammonia is also an effective antidote to the sting. Although usually encountered in the water, Portuguese men-of-war may also wash up on shore. If you spot one on the sand, steer clear, as the sting is just as dangerous out of the water.

More recently, divers have encountered the highly poisonous lionfish, which is not a native of the waters. Swimmers will be extremely unlikely to come into contact with one, while divers should just exercise caution around the creatures, which are not aggressive unless provoked.

▌ HOURS OF OPERATION

Most branches of the Bank of Bermuda are open weekdays from 9 to 4:30 and Saturday from 11 to 1. All branches of the Bank of Butterfield are open Monday through Thursday from 9 to 3:30 and Friday from 9 to 4:30. Bermuda Commercial Bank (at 43 Victoria Street in Hamilton) operates Monday through Thursday from 9:30 to 3 and Friday from 9:30 to 4:30. Capital G Bank (at 25 Reid Street in Hamilton) is open weekdays from 8:30 to 4:30 and Saturday from 8:30 to 3:30.

Many gas stations are open daily from 7 AM to 9 PM, and a few stay open until midnight. The island's only 24-hour gas station is Esso City Auto Market in Hamilton, near the Bank of Butterfield, off Par-La-Ville Road.

Hours vary greatly, but museums are generally open Monday through Saturday from 9 or 9:30 to 4:30 or 5. Some close on Saturday. Check with individual museums for exact hours.

Pharmacies are open Monday through Saturday from 8 AM to 6

or 8 PM, and sometimes Sunday from around 11 to 6 PM.

Most stores are open Monday through Saturday from around 9 until 5 or 6. Some Hamilton stores keep evening hours when cruise ships are in port. Dockyard shops are generally open Monday through Saturday from 10 to 5, Sunday from 11 to 5. The Bermuda government recently made it legal for all stores to open on Sunday, although most shops have yet to take advantage of the change. Those that are open—mainly grocery stores and pharmacies—have abbreviated hours.

HOLIDAYS

On Sunday and national public holidays, all shops, businesses, and many restaurants in Bermuda close. Buses and ferries run on limited schedules. Most entertainment venues, sights, and sports outfitters remain open. When holidays fall on a Saturday, government and commercial offices close the following Monday, but restaurants and shops remain open.

Bermuda celebrates a two-day public holiday for Emancipation Day/Somers Day and Cup Match in late July, when the whole island comes to a standstill for the annual cricket match between the East and West ends of Bermuda. National public holidays are New Year's Day, Good Friday, Bermuda Day (late May), Queen's Birthday (mid-June), Labour Day (early September), Remembrance Day (early November), Christmas, and Boxing Day (December 26).

▌ MAIL

Mail services in Bermuda can be erratic, so the following should be taken with a pinch of salt. However, generally allow seven to 10 days for mail from Bermuda to reach the United States, Canada, or the United Kingdom, and about two weeks to arrive in Australia or New Zealand.

Airmail postcards and letters for the first 10 grams to the United States and Canada cost 70¢. Postcards to the United Kingdom cost 80¢, letters 85¢ for the first 10 grams. Postcards to Australia and New Zealand cost 90¢, letters 95¢ for the first 10 grams.

If you want to receive mail but have no address in Bermuda, you can have mail sent care of General Delivery, General Post Office, Hamilton HM GD, Bermuda.

Main Branches International Data Express (☎441/297-7802). **Parcel Post** (☎441/297-7875).

SHIPPING PACKAGES

Through Parcel Post at Bermuda's post office, you can send packages via either International Data Express (which takes two to four business days to the United States and Canada and three to seven days to the United Kingdom, Australia, and New Zealand) or Air Parcel Post (which takes seven to 10 business days to the United States, Canada, and the United Kingdom, or two weeks to Australia and New Zealand).

For the first 500 grams, International Data Express rates are $25 to the United States and Canada, $30 to the United Kingdom, and $38 to Australia or New Zealand. Air Parcel Post rates run $7.65 for the first 500 grams to the United States, $9.10 to Canada, $11.95 to the United Kingdom, and $14.95 to Australia or New Zealand.

Most of Bermuda's largest stores offer shipping of purchases. Some may ask you either to buy insurance or to sign a waiver absolving them of any responsibility for potential loss or damage.

Overnight courier service is available to or from the continental United States through several companies. Service between Bermuda and Canada takes one or two business days, depending on the part of Canada; between Bermuda and the United Kingdom, generally two business days; and between Bermuda and Australia or New Zealand, usually three.

In Bermuda, rates include pickup from anywhere on the island. Prices for a document up to the first pound range from $26 to $37 to the United States, from $30 to $38 to Canada, and from $35 to $50 to the United Kingdom, Australia, or New Zealand. For the fastest delivery, your pickup request must be made before about 10 AM. Note that pickups (and drop-off locations) are limited on Saturday, and there's no service on Sunday. Packages sent to Bermuda may take a day longer than documents.

Express Services DHL Worldwide Express (☎441/295-3300). **Federal Express** (☎441/295-3854). **International Bonded Couriers** (☎441/295-2467). **Mailboxes Unlimited Ltd.** (☎441/292-6563). **Sprint International Express** (☎441/296-7866). **United Parcel Service** (☎441/295-2467).

∎ MONEY

The Bermudian dollar is on par with the U.S. dollar, and the two currencies are used interchangeably. (Other non-Bermudian currency must be converted.) You can use American money anywhere, but change is often given in Bermudian currency. Try to avoid accumulating large amounts of local money, which is difficult to exchange for U.S. dollars in Bermuda and expensive to exchange in the United States. ATMs are plentiful as are the amount of venues that will accept credit cards, even for small items.

Since Bermuda imports everything from cars to cardigans, prices are high. At an upscale restaurant, for example, you're bound to pay as much for a meal as you would in New York, London, or Paris: on average, $60 to $80 per person, $120 with drinks and wine. There are other options, of course; the island is full of coffee shops, where you can eat hamburgers and french fries with locals for about $9.

The same meal at a restaurant costs about $15.

Prices throughout this guide are given for adults. Substantially reduced fees are almost always available for children, students, and senior citizens.

■TIP→ Banks never have every foreign currency on hand, and it may take as long as a week to order. If you're planning to exchange funds before leaving home, don't wait until the last minute.

ATMS & BANKS

Your own bank will probably charge a fee for using ATMs abroad; the foreign bank you use may also charge a fee. Nevertheless, you'll usually get a better rate of exchange at an ATM than you will at a currency-exchange office or even when changing money in a bank. And extracting funds as you need them is a safer option than carrying around a large amount of cash.

■TIP→ PIN numbers with more than four digits are not recognized at ATMs in many countries. If yours has five or more, remember to change it before you leave.

ATMs are found all over Bermuda, in shops, arcades, supermarkets, the airport, and two of the island's banks. Both the Bank of Bermuda—a branch of HSBC— and the Bank of Butterfield are affiliated with the Cirrus and Plus networks. Note that both banks' ATMs only accept personal identification numbers (PIN) with four digits. Typical withdrawal amounts are multi-ples of 20 up to 100. Cash point robberies are a rarity in Bermuda, but if you're concerned, Reid Street and Front Street—which have the most banks—are Hamilton's busiest, and hence safest places to withdraw cash.

CREDIT CARDS

Throughout this guide, the following abbreviations are used: **AE**, American Express; **D**, Discover; **DC**, Diners Club; **MC**, MasterCard; and **V**, Visa.

It's a good idea to inform your credit-card company before you travel, especially if you're going abroad and don't travel internationally very often. Otherwise, the credit-card company might put a hold on your card owing to unusual activity—not a good thing halfway through your trip. Record all your credit-card numbers—as well as the phone numbers to call if your cards are lost or stolen—in a safe place, so you're prepared should something go wrong. Both MasterCard and Visa have general numbers you can call (collect if you're abroad) if your card is lost, but you're better off calling the number of your issuing bank, since MasterCard and Visa usually just transfer you to your bank; your bank's number is usually printed on your card.

If you plan to use your credit card for cash advances, you'll need to apply for a PIN at least two weeks before your trip. Although it's usually cheaper (and safer) to use a credit card abroad for large purchases (so you can cancel payments or be reimbursed if there's a problem), note that some credit-card companies *and* the banks that issue them add substantial percentages to all foreign transactions, whether they're in a foreign currency or not. Check on these fees before leaving home, so there won't be any surprises when you get the bill.

Most Bermudian shops and restaurants accept credit and debit cards. Some hotels insist on cash or traveler's checks, so check in advance whether your hotel takes credit cards. The most widely accepted cards are MasterCard, Visa, and American Express.

Reporting Lost Cards American Express (☎800/992–3404 *in U.S.,* 336/393–1111 collect from abroad ⊕*www.americanexpress.com*). **Diners Club** (☎800/234–6377 *in U.S.,* 303/799–1504 collect from abroad ⊕*www.dinersclub.com*). **Discover** (☎800/347–2683 *in U.S.,* 801/902–3100 collect from abroad ⊕*www.discovercard.com*). **MasterCard** (☎800/622–7747 *in U.S.,* 636/722–7111 collect from abroad ⊕*www.mastercard.com*). **Visa** (☎800/847–2911 *in U.S.,* 410/581–9994 collect from abroad ⊕*www.visa.com*).

CURRENCY & EXCHANGE

The local currency is the Bermudian dollar, which is on par with the American dollar. Both are accepted throughout the island. Bermudian dollar notes all feature the Queen's head and are smaller than their U.S. counterparts. It's worth being careful as both the $10 and the $20 notes

are similar in color (light blue) and could be easily mistaken for one another.

If you need to exchange Canadian dollars, British pounds, or other currencies, for the most favorable rates change money through banks. Although ATM transaction fees may be higher abroad than at home, ATM rates are excellent because they're based on wholesale rates offered only by major banks. You won't do as well at exchange booths in airports or rail and bus stations, in hotels, in restaurants, or in stores. To avoid lines at airport exchange booths, get a bit of local currency before you leave home.

▌ SAFETY

Crime, especially against tourists, is extremely low in Bermuda. Purse snatching is the most common crime tourists should watch out for. While rare, more serious incidents do happen occasionally, so you should guard against being overly complacent. Don't leave unattended valuables on the beach while going for a swim. Exercise commonsense precautions with wallets, purses, cameras, and other valuables. If you're driving a moped, always travel with your purse or bag concealed inside the seat. Always lock your moped or pedal bike, and store valuables in your room or hotel safe. Although an ocean breeze through a screen door is wonderful, close and lock your hotel room's glass patio door while you're sleeping or out of your room. The "back-of-town" area, in particular Court Street, has a bad reputation historically, though the government has made a number of efforts to clean the area up. However, if you do want to go to a venue there (such as the Fodor's Choice Hubie's Bar) it's worth taking a taxi, just to be on the safe side.

▌ TAXES

Hotels add a 7.25% government tax to the bill, and most add a 10% service charge or a per-diem dollar equivalent in lieu of tips. Other extra charges sometimes include a 5% "energy surcharge" (at small guesthouses) and a 15% service charge (at most restaurants).

A $25 airport-departure tax and a $4.25 airport-security fee are built into the price of your ticket, as is a $4 passenger facility charge, whereas cruise lines collect $60 in advance for each passenger, again, normally included in the price of the ticket.

▌ TIME

Bermuda is in the Atlantic time zone. Bermuda observes daylight saving time (from the second Sunday in March to the first Sunday in November), so it's always one hour ahead of U.S. eastern standard time. Thus, for instance, when it's 5 PM in Bermuda, it's 4 PM in New York, 3 PM in Chicago, and 1 PM in Los Angeles. London is four hours, and Sydney 14 hours, ahead of Bermuda.

▌ TIPPING

Tipping in Bermuda is fairly similar to tipping in the United States. A service charge of 10% (or an equivalent per-diem amount), which covers everything from baggage handling to maid service, is added to your hotel bill, though people often still tip a few extra dollars. Most restaurants tack on a 15% service charge; if not, a 15% tip is customary (more for exceptional service).

INDEX